Burden of the Badge
A Year in the Life of a Street Cop

By

Michael S. East

© 2003 by Michael S. East. All rights reserved.

No part of this book may be reproduced, stored in a retrieval system, or transmitted by any means, electronic, mechanical, photocopying, recording, or otherwise, without written permission from the author.

ISBN: 1-4107-4698-4 (e-book)
ISBN: 1-4107-4697-6 (Paperback)
ISBN: 1-4107-4696-8 (Hardcover)

This book is printed on acid free paper.

1stBooks - rev. 05/05/03

Acknowledgements

With special thanks to my mother, Jean, who has more courage than I will ever know, to my father, Donald, who has taught me much more than even he realizes, and to my wife, Deanna, whose patience and understanding know no limits. Finally, thank you to all of the men and women in uniform—police and military—who put fear aside and patrol dark streets and unfriendly countries so our families may sleep safely at night.

Burden of the Badge
A Year in the Life of a Street Cop

A bitter cold evening in February 1997 may have been the first time I realized the startling seriousness of police work. In a fraction of a second that took an eternity to pass, on a call so routine it nearly cost a life, I was confronted with the life-and-death reality of law enforcement. Nearly three full years after pinning on a badge for the first time and becoming a member of the Saginaw Police Department, I learned the split-second decisions made during the course of a cop's career can never be re-lived. It is a lesson I may never forget.

The frigid temperatures of that night were accompanied by a full moon, which hung quietly in the clear evening sky. My shift had been very slow thus far and the graveyard silence of that night was a welcome relief from the normally hectic, call-after-call pace of the 3 p.m.-to-11p.m. patrol shift.

Saginaw, Michigan, much like Detroit, Flint and numerous other old industrial towns, has been dying a slow Rust Belt death for years. In this town where the auto industry once reigned, gangs, drugs and violence are now as much a part of everyday life as the assembly line used to be. With a current population of about 62,500, Saginaw has lost more than one third of its residents since 1970. Prosperity has been replaced by empty lots and abandoned buildings, many of which stand as constant reminders of the better days of the past. It is against this backdrop that I continue to shape my career as a police officer.

In 1997 I had recently taken a position as a Field Training Officer (FTO), a job which requires extensive training of new police recruits. Despite my relative inexperience at that time, I quickly grabbed the FTO opportunity, prompted, quite honestly, by the extra income the position offered. The recruit I was training on this night was Dennis Bunch, a short, stocky guy in his mid-twenties with thinning hair and a friendly demeanor. Dennis appeared to me then to look more like an accountant than a police officer. I look back now and realize he was one of the best recruits I ever trained. Dennis left the Saginaw Police Department after little more than two years to accept a position with a larger police department closer to his hometown. While we only now talk about once a year, the events of that evening several years ago will forever provide a common thread between us.

The night was slower than usual. But when we were dispatched to a residence on the city's Eastside, I let out a sigh of frustration at the stupidity of the call. Central Dispatch advised us an elderly man had called because he was concerned for the welfare of his grandson. The grandson had telephoned him earlier and said he was at a friend's house and some guys had come over and threatened the boy and his friends with guns. Apparently, nobody had been hurt, but the grandfather still wanted us to check and see that his grandson was okay.

Because grandpa was unsure of the exact address from which his grandson called, we checked several different residences, accompanied by another two-man training car that was dispatched as our backup. Each time we checked a house, we were unable to locate the grandson. Eventually, as grandpa would remember another possible location and relay it to Central Dispatch, we would be sent to another residence. It was at the fourth house that we finally located the grandson.

Driving South through a neighborhood comprised of little more than shoebox-like houses and snow-covered abandoned cars, we pulled up curbside, headlights extinguished, about 25 yards from a small white, one-story home. I recognized the house as one where I had been on prior occasions for gang-related activity. Several teenagers standing outside the front door of the residence - having spotted our police cars - immediately ran inside the home, slamming the door behind them.

Unsure of what was happening, but keeping in mind the call involved weapons, Dennis and I quickly made our way through the foot-deep snow to the rear of the house, while the other FTO and his recruit officer approached the front door. We had been at the rear of the house for no more than 15 seconds when the two officers on the other side of the residence beat on the front door and announced: "Police! Open the Door!"

Immediately, the back door of the house creaked opened. Light from the home's interior spilled into the back yard, casting a large, cartoon-shaped likeness of a doorway onto the snowy yard. When a teenage boy walked out of the door onto a small cement-slab porch, the first thing I saw was the black handgun clutched in his right hand, which he quickly turned toward me. By the time my mind registered "Gun!" I was staring down the barrel of what appeared to be a 9mm handgun, not much different from the one I was now swinging from my side toward the kid in an attempt to get off the first shot.

The teen was no more than seven feet away and, as I subconsciously awaited the muzzle flash from his gun and the excruciating pain that would surely follow, I simultaneously screamed: "Drop the gun! Drop that fucking gun! Drop that fucking gun!" Unknowingly, I had also sought cover, backing up two feet, partially hiding my body behind the corner of the house. It was during these split seconds, which passed like hours, that my mind registered the confusion on the boy's face.

While my brain was already screaming the question: "Why haven't you killed this kid yet?" it was also telling me - very clearly - that the kid was not going to shoot. The unsteadiness in his hand and the confusion in his eyes told me the kid was simply not going to pull the trigger. He quickly threw his gun to the ground as if it were burning his hands. Holstering my own weapon as I reached for the kid and took him to the ground, I was soon joined by Dennis, who had sought cover behind a tree and had also nearly shot the kid while repeating my commands. As we handcuffed the teen, all I could manage was to repeatedly yell: "What the fuck are you thinking? What the fuck are you thinking?" His response came as nothing more than a confused stare as we pulled him, now handcuffed, from the snow.

As Dennis took the teen to our patrol car, I retrieved the handgun that he had thrown into the snow near my feet. I was shocked—and, for some reason, infuriated - to find it was a pellet gun.

Heading to the patrol car, pellet gun in hand, I opened the back door to confront the teen face-to-face and I was immediately struck with how innocent this kid looked. Taking the gun out of the picture had changed his appearance dramatically. "What the hell were you thinking pointing a gun at the police?" I demanded.

His reply came low and sincere: "I didn't know you was the police. Some dudes had come over before and they had pulled some guns on us. I thought you was them."

"So you thought you would go after them with a pellet gun?" I replied. "Are you that stupid? You are lucky it was the police 'cause those motherfuckers would have blown your head off. I should have blown your head off. Do you realize you almost got killed tonight?"

In the same calm, sincere, what-do-you-mean tone of voice, he cocked his head like a dog responding to a high-pitched whistle and said simply: "No."

Eventually the teen was lodged at the Saginaw County Jail for felonious assault on a police officer. An hour or so of debriefing between Dennis and myself followed with the discussion mainly involving the call and how it was handled. While Dennis received nearly perfect scores for the day on the evaluation of how he handled the call, he had his own reasons for not shooting the gun-wielding teen.

"Shit, you're the FTO. I was just waiting to see what you would do. I was just trying to get my ass behind that tree," he replied with a nervous laugh when asked why he had not shot the kid. When we parted ways at shift's end, the "what ifs" were still playing in my mind.

The next morning I was awakened by a telephone call from Jerry Schneider, the weekend duty detective, wanting to ask me about the previous night's events. I recognized Jerry as a guy of more than 20 years on the job and I knew him by face and name only. Conversely, to Jerry I was undoubtedly just one of the 26 recruits who had been hired in May of 1994—another faceless, nameless young cop with a lot of cop road left to travel.

"My main question is," Jerry asked, "why didn't you kill this guy?"

I scrolled through my explanation of how I thought the gun was real and I spent a lifetime of seconds awaiting the pain from the first shot when I encountered the teen. However, I told the detective, I quickly saw in the kid's eyes and the nervous way he held the gun, that he was not going to pull the trigger. Jerry's response was more kind than I had anticipated.

"Well, the only person who knows why you didn't shoot this kid is you. No matter what anybody says, you are the one who had to decide whether or not to shoot this kid. Don't listen to anyone else," Jerry responded, anticipating the second-guessing I would undoubtedly receive from co-workers. "With what I'm going to tell you I think you'll be glad you didn't shoot him. I just got back from the jail from interviewing the kid. He is 17 years old and has never had a recorded contact with the police. He has never been a witness, a victim, a suspect or a reporter of a crime with our department. I also spoke to his mother and she tells me her son is has the mentality of a middle-school kid. He still doesn't know why he's in trouble. I think you would have felt pretty bad if you had killed this kid. Don't beat yourself up over this. You did what you thought was the right thing to do."

Weeks later when we went to a pre-trial hearing on the case, Jerry and myself met with the teen and his mother. A plea bargain had been worked out with the assistant prosecutor, but Jerry refused to agree to the deal without my approval. He also wanted me to meet the kid's mother before deciding on the plea arrangement.

Standing in the courthouse hallway, the woman immediately struck me as a kind-looking person. Slight of build with tired eyes, she spoke appreciatively of the detective's work on her son's case. Her son, meanwhile, stood silently, staring at the floor. We talked briefly and I agreed to the plea bargain. The mother thanked me, not for having the restrain to have not killed her son weeks earlier, but for agreeing to the deal which would keep him out of jail. With that she turned and walked away, her son staring at me in a manner which could best be described as confused. I have not seen him since.

Looking back on the events of that evening, it remains one of the proudest—and most disappointing—days of my career. It was a day when all my training failed me miserably because *I* failed to take a young man's life. Had my instincts been wrong, my hesitation could have cost my own life, yet by the grace of God, everyone lived to learn something.

That day's incident appeared in no newspapers; it's only a good story, it would seem, when the cop kills the bad guy because then there's room for debate. I received no awards or recognition for my actions that day, save for a verbal pat on the back from a detective who in his days had seen much worse, and who was now nearing the end of his own long career. My only other acknowledgement came in the form of locker room ridicule from a sergeant and a few co-workers, who told me I was wrong for not killing the teen.

So goes the life of a cop.

It was on this night that in 1997 that I decided to write a book about the everyday experiences of a police officer: the highs and lows, the exciting and the mundane, of the lives we touch and of the lives we see lost. It is a job where hope and faith strike and odd balance with death and despair, and living to see retirement requires both physical and psychological resiliency. It is a job I love, and a job I often love to hate.

This book is written with the humility of a police officer who knows he has not seen and done it all. None of us has. I have had many challenging experiences. However, many police officers have done many more brave and daring things than I will ever know. Yet every man and woman who puts on the uniform is, in one form or another, a hero in my eyes.

The following account of nearly a full year in my career as a police officer is a day-by-day, call-by-call account of a year in my on-the-job life. From the incredibly boring re-occurring calls for breaking and entering alarms and loud music, to the unpredictable human nature that often leads to violence and murder—it's all part of the daily grind of being a cop.

Sunday, January 27

Roll call is sparse on this mild Sunday afternoon. With only nine second-shift officers scheduled, I am hoping for a quiet day. Any major crimes will throw the shift into catch-up mode and pile up calls for service, which the midnight shift still will be mopping up eight hours from now.

Two years ago, there would have been 15, 20 or, on a good day, as many as 25 officers working second shift. That was before the city of Saginaw, a past-its-prime, former auto industry boomtown, found itself in a financial free fall, unable to sustain costs of basic city services. With a thin wallet and a thick stack of bills, two consecutive years of police and fire department layoffs followed.

Prior to the layoffs, it was hard to drive four blocks without seeing another cop. This was a satisfying feeling—to know help was only seconds away. Now Saginaw County Central Dispatch regularly asks for cars to respond to crimes in progress. Too often the response is a deafening silence. There simply is no one available.

As a child growing up in the seventies, I got hooked on the police shows of the era. The shows were not as messy as real life. Cops never got pink-slipped. Back then the bad guy didn't get away and the cases were neatly solved by day's end. In reality, however, the bad guy often does get away and an eight-hour shift is never wrapped up neatly with a bow on top. Often a day on the street consists of nothing more than gathering witness statements, photographing dead bodies or battered faces, and turning it all over to detectives for follow-up investigation. That investigation may take days, if not weeks. The loose ends from one day's work sometimes stay untied forever.

Roll call lasts about 15 minutes and is conducted by a sergeant, today's highest-ranking supervisor. It is a chance for officers to get updated on new information. Today, two officer safety issues are passed on via the supervisor.

The first memo details how some street gangs have been using tennis balls as explosive devices. By gutting the insides of the ball, filling it with pellets and gunpowder, or another type of explosive material, they have created a sort of urban hand grenade. These grenades will explode when thrown against a hard surface, sending pellets, with a shotgun effect, hurling outward to injure those unlucky enough to be in the area.

The second memo involves a recent rash of flashlight bombs being left at crime scenes to injure or kill responding police and rescue personnel. The thought being, after dealing with the scene, a cop or medical response person would see the flashlight lying on the ground and pick it up to return it to its owner. The flashlights have been rigged with either a timer or a motion-sensitive mercury switch, causing them to explode. The memo concludes that more than 20 of these flashlights have already been located and at least one police officer has been killed handling them.

Roll call ends on this note. Time to go to work. Have a nice day.

4:46 p.m.—Breaking and Entering in Progress

After cleaning up a few calls that the day shift was unable to attend to, I am dispatched to an anonymous report of two males breaking into a house. Another officer is sent as backup, which is protocol for in-progress calls.

The caller says a couple men forced their way into the front door of a residence and left with two bags of items. There is a good description of the suspects and they supposedly walked into a store two blocks away.

Within minutes I locate both subjects at the counter inside the store. Their description matches perfectly and I order both men outside to my car. They give the usual back talk, but eventually come outside after a brief verbal altercation. Most suspects like to play the initial power struggle game, just to see who has the stronger will.

Outside the store, a road sergeant arrives to assist. He walks one man to his patrol car and we check both for weapons. My guy argues, saying I'm disrespecting him. After a minute he finally takes a seat in my patrol car so we can return to the alleged crime scene.

Meanwhile, the other man is found to be carrying a small amount of marijuana. He is handcuffed and placed into the sergeant's car. We return both men to the scene. The man in my car insists he did not break into the house. He says the homeowner, who is visiting a neighbor, told he and his friend to go to her house, get two bags of returnable bottles, and redeem them for cash at the store.

Shortly after we arrive, the homeowner returns and verifies the story. She had indeed sent the men to her home to get some returnable bottles. I explain the neighbor's call of the men breaking into her home. She laughs and says her front door sticks sometimes and that must be why the men had to force the door open. She politely thanks us for responding. I release the man in my back seat after verifying his identity. He has been largely uncooperative. However, I give him a brief, well-rehearsed talk about my job and about me looking out for my safety. We part on good terms with a handshake and a "take it easy, man." Usually these situations do not end cordially. But this guy is a little more tolerant than most and accepts my explanation as an apology. That's okay with me. Anytime you can make one less enemy on the street it is a good thing.

Meanwhile, my sergeant isn't having the same luck. His subject is 52 years old, although his years on the street have left him weathered and looking closer to 70. He is halfway to a mid-afternoon drunk. Sitting in the patrol car, alcohol and his temper have gotten the better of him, his non-stop yelling muffled only by the closed windows of the vehicle.

We arrive at the county jail within 15 minutes to lodge the man on a charge of possession of marijuana, giving him a second check for weapons as a jail intake officer looks on. The intake area smells of body odor, weak air freshener, and the strong, alcoholic breath of our suspect. The man now directs his attention toward me.

"You white-ass, honky motherfucker! I'm gonna get your badge!" he screams, slurring slightly and spitting as he yells. I ignore the man as I am just not in the mood for debate.

There are two things fairly certain in police work. First, all suspects turn into bad asses once they walk into a jail. Out of necessity, they put on a good show so the other inmates think they're tough. This is a basic animalistic survival skill and, while it is annoying, I understand the purpose. This usually means the arresting officer is a "punk," a "bitch," or some kind of "motherfucker." Race usually is made to be the main issue, especially if your skin color does not match that of your suspect. Second, the bad guys always want your badge, which some days, quite frankly, I would be happy to give them. I have many times departed the Saginaw County Jail a "white-ass, honky, motherfucker" who is about to lose his badge.

6:56 p.m.—Assault in Progress

Central Dispatch advises of a call from a hysterical woman, stating someone has been hurt. The caller gives no further information, just a general location where help is needed. I don't know if I am responding to a shooting, a stabbing, or a domestic assault. Too often cops are forced to respond to calls for assistance where the complainant is too hysterical or too uncooperative to communicate exactly what is happening. Responding to these unknown situations immediately compounds the stress of the call.

About a block from where the caller said help is needed, I nearly run over a woman and two children running down the middle of a darkened street. The woman is crying hysterically. When I get out to find out what's wrong, she says she has to go and tries to run away. I grab her arm and ask her who needs help as she keeps repeating: "My sister got jumped. My sister got jumped."

As she tries to run away a second time, I grab her again to get more information. Eventually, she says her sister got beat up by a boyfriend. She says her sister is okay and left in a truck with a friend. She also says the suspect has left. She says she has to go.

Another officer has located the scene a block away. People at the house confirm the suspect and victim both left and the victim is not injured. Without either person present, there is nothing left to do. An ambulance and fire department rescue vehicle are already in the area. They are now instructed to clear. Two other officers and myself clear the scene as well. In total, three police officers, two firemen and two ambulance paramedics are all tied up for about 20 minutes because no one would take the time to explain what was happening. These are the tax dollars I see wasted every day.

The rest of the night is relatively quiet and I am able to end my shift on time with few calls holding for the midnight shift to clean up.

Monday, January 28

It's another mild January day with temperatures around 50 degrees. My vacation starts tomorrow and I am hoping for an uneventful day.

3:20 p.m.—911 Hang-up Call

One of the most annoying dispatch calls is the "911 Hang-up" call. Someone dials "911"and hangs up when a dispatcher answers. Usually, it turns out to be small children playing on the telephone. Central Dispatch tries to alleviate the need for police response by calling the residence back and confirming everything is okay. Invariably, however, they get no answer or whoever does answer the phone simply hangs up again. That is the case on this call.

Arriving at the house, the other responding officer knocks twice on the front door and gets no answer. We move quietly to the rear of the house. At the back door, I knock again and a young female comes to the door. She is carrying an infant child. She stares at me for a minute and says in an irritated voice: "Is there a problem?" Equally annoyed, I respond: "You tell me. Is there? Someone called 911 from here and hung up the phone. Is everything okay." She retorts with a snotty: "Yeah." We clear another call that needed no response.

The day ends with nothing more exciting - or annoying - than my first call of the day.

Wednesday, February 6

3:10 p.m.—Prisoner Transport

Another officer and I are sent to a local hospital to pick up a prisoner and transport him to the Saginaw County Jail. The prisoner has been hospitalized since his arrest last month and has an outstanding warrant for cocaine possession. He is being discharged from the hospital today.

At the hospital we locate the man sitting in his room with several family members. Surprisingly, he knows we are coming and he is quietly awaiting our arrival. He could easily have left with relatives, and hospital personnel probably would not have tried to detain him. However, he wants to clear up the charges.

The nurse gives me medical instructions for the suspect's tracheotomy, which I tell her I will pass along to the jail nursing staff. The suspect, a slightly built male in his 30s, hugs his family before we leave. He mumbles a few grainy words through the tube in his throat, but they tell him not to try to speak. His brother hugs him and says they will be at the jail to post bail shortly. We cart the suspect to the first floor via wheelchair and he is at the county jail within 15 minutes. His medical condition keeps him from talking during the ride. The silence is refreshing.

4:40 p.m.—Suspicious Vehicle

Responding to a call from church members reporting a suspicious vehicle in the area, I arrive shortly after another officer, who advises me of a vehicle stuck in the snow behind an abandoned house across the street. We locate the vehicle, which is axle deep in snow and mud. The two occupants—a male and female in their forties - say they were driving behind the house to "talk," which likely means they are there to smoke drugs or have sex. Probably, they are there to do both.

While my backup officer speaks to the male, I talk to the female. Dressed in army fatigues ands a heavy jacket, she's talking a mile a minute and her eyes are darting all over the neighborhood. She giggles often and it's clear she's already smoked whatever crack cocaine she had. I search her pockets with her consent and locate a crack pipe.

After placing her under arrest, I put her into my patrol car and call for a female officer to conduct a more thorough search. The suspect and I small talk while waiting for the female officer to arrive. She's unusually courteous for a crack-smoking prostitute. A computer check of the woman helps me determine she has an outstanding warrant for operating a vehicle under the influence of liquor (drunk driving). She gives me a sheepish smile when I tell her of the warrant. "I was gonna tell you about that," she says.

The male subject leaves after we find he is not wanted. He departs looking for friends to help get his car unstuck.

Meanwhile, a female officer - a usually cheery girl in her twenties—arrives and immediately gives me a "thanks-a-lot, jerk" smile as she gets out of her vehicle. Female police officers get to experience more than most women on a typical day. This day is no different. One downfall of being a female cop is conducting same-sex searches on prisoners, when necessary. Usually they are prostitutes and drug addicts. The task is not one to be envied.

Putting on a pair of rubber gloves, the officer asks the fatigue-clad woman if she has any sharp objects. She continues to small talk while pulling an assortment of lighters, half-smoked cigarettes and wadded-up toilet paper from the suspect's pockets. I reach out with an envelope to hold the woman's belongings and the officer drops in a pair of reading glasses and some ink pens. Finally, from one pocket, she pulls a pair of soiled panties and plops them in the envelope as well.

"Oh, girl, you wasn't supposed to pull them out. Them's my extras," says the woman, legitimately embarrassed. We shrug it off with a laugh as the search concludes. I am amazed the woman is embarrassed at the sight of her own dirty panties. She surprisingly has some modesty left.

The female officer finishes her search and offers another mock smile. The short drive to jail is uneventful and the small talk with the still-embarrassed crack addict is polite. She doesn't call me a "white-ass, honky, motherfucker" even once. We part on good terms at the jail and she leaves for her cell with a smile, knowing she'll at least get a meal or two.

10:07 p.m.—Domestic Assault

The shift has been slow. But less than an hour before quitting time, I am dispatched to a domestic assault.

The small, cracker box house I pull up to looks like the others in this poverty stricken neighborhood. The house is quiet and I enter before my backup arrives.

Inside, a woman is arguing with her intoxicated boyfriend - a large, boisterous man in his twenties. I keep my distance while talking to them and awaiting a second officer. I shouldn't have come inside alone in the first place.

My backup—a younger officer with imposing physical features - arrives about a minute later. I am relieved to see him walk in. He takes the boyfriend into the next room to talk, while I continue speaking to the female caller. She says the suspect threw a vase at her and assaulted her. Meanwhile, the intoxicated suspect continues to rant, yelling nonstop at the woman. We take him into custody for domestic assault with a weapon.

On the way to jail, he asks five times why he's been arrested. I tell him repeatedly, knowing the answer is not sinking into his booze-soaked brain. Still, I continue answering because it keeps his mind occupied and keeps him from yelling a lot.

At the jail, he starts the usual tough-guy routine during a weapons search. "I did six years in prison," he spouts off. "A year in the county ain't nothin'." He makes this statement the same way a prospective employee speaks of his education and experience during a job interview. Ironically, in a way this is his resume, which is a sad statement about the man's life.

I finish the paperwork on the case and get home an hour late.

Thursday, February 7

It's another unseasonably warm February day as we prepare to check into service. Logging onto my in-car computer, I see there are 15 calls for service pending. Six of the calls are in-progress, meaning they will be given a high priority. It's a bad start to the day.

3:25 p.m. - Cutting

This is already my third dispatch call in the 10 minutes since checking into service, having been disregarded from the previous two calls by the first-responding officer. Arriving at scene, I locate a man bleeding from the head. He said he had been walking around the corner from his house, when another male approached him and began an argument. The other officer on scene begins questioning the victim while awaiting medical personnel.

"Who assaulted you?" asks the officer.

"I don't know," comes a quick, annoyed reply.

"What did he look like?" the officer continues.

"I don't know," the man answers again, as a trail of blood runs down the side of his neck.

"What was he wearing? How old is he?" the officer continues, obviously frustrated.

For the third time "I don't know" is the only response.

Two friends of the victim are nearby. I ask if they know who assaulted the man. They do not. Soon, these two are upset that the police "are not doing anything" for their friend, even though no one can offer the slightest idea about the suspect's identity. I don't engage them in debate, as it will be pointless. They continue to complain about "the police," a generalization I hear daily, as I continue to ignore them.

Finally, the ambulance arrives and the victim gets in to be treated. The other officer and I walk around the corner and locate a bloodstain on the sidewalk in front of a residence. Stepping onto the porch, we are met at the front door by a woman, who says there was a fight in front of her house. She says the suspect is gone. Not surprisingly, she doesn't know the man's name, what he was wearing, or where he was going when he left. From the woman's tone, we are obviously not her choice for most popular public servants.

I clear from the call as the first-arriving officer leaves to write his report. There are still 15 calls for service holding.

4:30 p.m.—Drug Activity

After clearing up a few low priority calls, I am sent to a report of persons dealing drugs on a street corner. Like many of these calls, the suspects are described only as young black males wearing all black clothing. The call is also nearly three hours old. The dope peddlers are long gone by the time I arrive to check the area.

5:40 p.m.—Armed Robbery

Central Dispatch sends a call that a man has pulled a gun on two teenagers. The caller does not know either the suspect or the victims, and the victims have not called to complain. Another patrol car checking the area eventually finds the victims, who say a man had indeed pulled a gun on them and robbed them of cash.

I meet with the caller, who tells me she watched as a man in his twenties or thirties pulled a gun on the two teens and chased them. She also says the "victims" sell drugs in the area and the gunman was chasing them because they had not returned some drugs they were supposed to sell for him. Both of the teenage victims later deny this.

An officer takes the teens to police headquarters so a relative can pick them up. At the station one of the juveniles tells me the story of how he was robbed. He also shows me about $150 in his sock that the suspect never found. He says it is money his "mama" gave him. Later, awaiting the arrival of relatives, a detective walks past and asks why the teens are in custody. He informs us he recently had a case against one of the boys for possession of marijuana. Later in the day both juveniles are released to relatives. I am sure I will see both of them again before long.

9:47 p.m.—Man with a Knife

We locate the venue, an upstairs apartment in a half-burned-out, two-story house. The caller is outside. She is a female in her thirties and she says her boyfriend pulled a knife on her. She says he's still inside and she wants him out. She is obviously drunk as she follows us up an inside stairwell. At the top of the stairs, she is babbling and cannot get the key in the lock to let us inside. After several tries, she says her boyfriend must have changed the locks and she hands the keys to the other officer at scene, who opens the door on the first try.

Because of the alleged weapon involved, I ask the woman to wait at the bottom of the stairs while we check inside. However, she decides it's time to take matters into her own hands and responds by grabbing my gun and trying to pull it from the holster. "Gimme that gun," she slurs. She is too frail and intoxicated to make a serious try for the weapon and I quickly bat her arm away. I yell for her to get to the bottom of the stairs or she's going to jail. The distraction could easily have cost the life of anyone there. While we turned our attention toward the victim's drunken attempt to disarm me, her boyfriend could have emerged from inside and made a fillet of any of us. Fortunately, we find the man has left the residence prior to our arrival. I am frustrated by the drunken woman's actions, but the shift ends safely. I can't ask for more than that.

Friday, February 8

1:30 p.m.—Court Appearance

It's my off day, but as often happens, I am under subpoena to appear in court on a previous crime. This is my fifth court appearance on the same case - a year-and-a-half-old home invasion, involving three women entering the house of another lady and stealing her stereo to settle an old debt.

The incident is still fresh in my mind as I review the case report. Arriving at the venue that day, I began interviewing witnesses. As we talked, one witness pointed out the front window of the home and said: "That's them! There go the girls right there that broke in!" At a stop light in front of the house, the three suspects, driving two separate cars - one a stolen vehicle - had driven back by the scene and got caught at the red light. The three offered no resistance when I confronted them and they were easily apprehended.

In court on this day, however, things are not going as well. For the second time, the main witness has refused to show up in court. I am told she falsely reported moving to Mississippi to avoid testifying. Even after detectives determined she was still living in Saginaw, she successfully avoided being served a subpoena for the trial. Without the primary witness, the Assistant Prosecutor handling the case has no option but to dismiss. He says we may re-issue charges against this suspect in the future. I know better. The prosecutor's office is as overworked as the police department. There is not enough time to re-issue charges on a nearly two-year-old case with an uncooperative witness. For my benefit he feigns dismay as we talk of the dismissal. I don't give him the same courtesy, returning an I-don't-really-care shrug of the shoulders. I concluded years ago that cops and prosecutors are able to do only so much to stop crime. If citizens won't do their part, so be it. I am sure, however, the uncooperative witness some day will lament the shortcomings of the criminal justice system when she eventually becomes a victim.

After an hour-long appearance I leave court and have the rest of the afternoon away from work, detectives, prosecutors and bad guys.

Sunday, February 10

3:17 p.m.—Domestic Assault

Another officer and I arrive at the scene of a domestic assault in time to see a male running from the house as we turn the corner a block away. The female victim, running out of the house as well, points at the male, indicating he is the problem. The man has a sizeable head start and darts between two houses to the East. Circling the block, I expect to find him coming out on the other side. When I clear the next corner, however, he is not there. He's obviously no stranger to running from the police.

I come back around the block to see if he has doubled back, but he has not. He's likely somewhere in the middle of the block, hiding in a maze of the rickety fences, burned out garages and way-past-their-prime abandoned homes, which dot the neighborhood. The wind has picked up and snow is starting to fall as I get out of my patrol car. Meeting up with the other responding officer, we are surprised to not find the suspect's footprints in the freshly fallen snow. We check two abandoned houses, three garages and a doghouse, but the man is nowhere to be found. Possibly, he has escaped to our East, resuming his flight after we began checking inside buildings. Since there we no officers available to watch that side of the block, his eventual escape would have gone undetected.

Returning to speak with the victim, she advises the suspect - her live-in boyfriend - assaulted her prior to our arrival. She says he has assaulted her in the past. She has assaulted him as well, the woman adds. Today, the fight was on when she took away his house keys. I give her a case report number for the domestic assault complaint. She says she does not want him back in her house. I leave knowing this cycle of assaults will likely continue.

5:53 p.m.—Stolen Vehicle

An elderly man is reporting his grandson took his vehicle without permission. Actually, the man tells me, the vehicle belongs to the funeral home he owns. I write him a report and tell him we'll try to get the vehicle back. The vehicle information goes on the patrolman's daily log.

6:37 p.m.—Non-Injury Vehicle Accident

It is still snowing and, as usual on snowy nights, Interstate 675, a few miles of which runs through the city limits, is the sight of numerous car accidents. I respond to a one-vehicle accident and the driver tells me she lost control entering an on-ramp. She is not injured, but her vehicle will need a few thousand dollars in repairs. A tow truck arrives to remove the wreckage. The entire call, including the report, is finished within about an hour. The rest of the night is pleasantly uneventful.

Monday, February 11

3:30 p.m.—Juvenile Assault

A mother reports her daughter is the victim of an assault by another child. She invites me into her living room to talk. The house smells of dirty clothes and body odor. Several kids run around yelling as I gather information.

The stench of dirty houses bothered me for the first few months on the job, but after a while it's like background music in an elevator—you know it's there but you don't give it much attention. Many of the people I see daily live in poverty and have done so all their lives. Cleanliness isn't the highest priority when survival is a day-to-day issue. I give the caller a case report number and retreat to the fresh, cold afternoon air.

5:03 p.m.—Juvenile Assault

A teenage girl says her eight-year-old nephew was assaulted by an 18-year-old drug dealer a couple of blocks from home. She says the drug dealer picks on neighborhood kids all the time. After talking to the victim I check the area for the suspect. He is supposed to hang around one of several neighborhoods in this Northeast section of Saginaw.

The area I check covers dozens of blocks South of one of the few remaining auto plants in the city, and provides a depressing view of days gone by. The landscape is dominated by vacant fields where houses once stood and vacant houses where fields will soon be. There are few residents left in this section of town. The ones that remain are either drug dealers, drug addicts, or people too poor or too stubborn to distance themselves from this desolate landscape.

Driving some of the streets while looking for the suspect, I pass vacant blocks where the Daniel's Heights Housing Project once stood. It was here, during my first month on the job that a now-retired sergeant took a Polaroid photo of me during a drug apprehension. "Here," he said that day, "send it to your mom." And I did send it to my mom, thinking of that photo as proof that I was helping make Saginaw a better place. The housing projects are long gone now, having been demolished a couple years later. The Polaroid photo has also long since disappeared. That is probably for the best. Most days, I would have a hard time convincing even myself that I have helped make Saginaw a better place.

My search for the assault suspect is futile, but I continue to drive and remember.

Two blocks away I pass another abandoned house. Years earlier I responded here for a report of a shooting. I arrived that day to find a teenage boy, his head exploded from a gunshot wound, lying near death on the front porch. Several witnesses screamed details of a drive-by shooting. A bright colored car; maybe it was orange. It was driving Northbound. No, maybe it was Southbound. Some said the driver did the shooting. Others said the passenger was the gunman.

The witness accounts quickly told the story of an entire neighborhood lying. The real story, which surfaced about an hour later, was that the boy had been killed by an accidental gunshot wound to the head, inflicted by a young friend showing off a handgun. I later heard the boy who did the shooting had been given the gun as a present by relatives. I spent about six hours guarding the crime scene that day, eventually helping locate the weapon used. We had to search this long because nobody would tell where it was. The gun was finally located inside the house, where someone hid it as a young man lay bleeding to death on the front porch.

The memory of that day comes rushing back in an instant while passing the house. It's not necessarily sad; just another memory of another life wasted. Touring the city of Saginaw eight hours a day, five days a week, every cop passes spots where they witnessed horrible things. On slow shifts, my memory is stirred several times daily by the sights of days gone by, while driving past other places that will most certainly provide future unkind memories. The memory of a porch splattered with blood and brain matter is vivid on this day. Within the hour it will be washed away by a fresh vision of needless death.

6:04 p.m. - Shooting

While sitting at the police station talking to the desk officer, I hear the radio come to life with the dispatch call of a possible shooting. The venue is a small building which houses college-level classes for a Mid-Michigan university. The dispatcher indicates students hearing shots fired in the hallway. Three cars—one more than usual for an in-progress call—are sent to the scene. However, at least 10 patrol cars, myself included, actually respond.

About halfway through the three-mile trip to the venue, a sergeant and two patrol officers call on scene. The sergeant, his voice noticeably shaken, advises to have responding medical units step up their response. This is never a good sign. When a second officer calls for someone to break out the crime scene tape, I know it will probably be a homicide. Arriving on scene about a minute later, another officer says the victim is probably not going to live, having suffered at least two gunshot wounds to the head, from what he could gather.

The confusion following a major crime is magnified in this case, as there are more than two dozen witnesses to the crime. Students and professors from two classes were unfortunate enough to see and hear the victim get shot by an ex-boyfriend.

The suspect has fled prior to police arrival. Some officers are busy roping off the crime scene, while others are gathering suspect information and trying to calm witnesses. I assisted directing medical personnel through the crime scene to the victim, while listening to my portable radio for more information on the suspect. Seconds later, an officer grabs me and asks for help interviewing witnesses. There is a room full of hysterical students, he says, and he needs helping calming them, gathering information and conducting quick interviews. Detectives have already been called to the scene, and it should expedite processing witnesses if we can gather this information for investigators.

Inside the classroom, there is much crying, hugging and general disbelief over the shooting, as we begin the task of gathering information. The witnesses react better to this process than expected. Some continue to cry as I ask them their name, date of birth and other seemingly trivial information. I try to offer some emotional support, but it is awkward. This process of gathering witness statements appears callous to most. They would rather go home and be with their family and friends after what surely is the biggest shock of many of their lives. I can't blame them, but we trudge on, quietly asking the same questions of each, and getting the same story from most: A guy walked into the room and said he was looking for someone. He left and checked a second classroom, but returned to find the victim inside the room he had first checked. He asks to speak with her and she walks outside the classroom with him. Within seconds, shots are fired.

After a while, we have everyone identified and we know how to contact each. But, we inform them they cannot leave until detectives arrive and say it's okay to go. "How long do we have to stay?" asks a male student, disgustedly. It is obvious he wants to leave, maybe to go home to his family or maybe to the nearest tavern to begin washing away the evening's events. Looking at the many people in the room, it's obvious they have many other places they would rather be.

"Hopefully, not too long," I reply. It is the only answer I can offer the man.

I know the process will probably take hours, but I thought it best to let the detectives explain this. They will ultimately release the witnesses when the time comes. Meanwhile, I learn the suspect has already turned himself in at the police department. He had driven there directly after the incident and calmly explained to the desk officer that he had just killed someone.

After a while several of the witnesses ask to use the bathroom. Trying to protect the integrity of the crime scene, I am instructed to take them, one at a time, outside the classroom through an emergency exit, then through the parking lot and back inside a back door to the bathroom. This helps us keep the crime scene from being contaminated. But, through a doorway near the bathroom, each witness can see the large blood stain covering the carpet. About six inches away lies the victim's blood-splattered student identification card on a neck strap. They each give the stain a long stare, but ask no questions. I am glad for this.

I engage in small talk with each witness en route to the bathroom breaks. Everyone seems to have calmed. The local news media is outside, taking pictures of us as we walk, which makes many of the witnesses uncomfortable. I find it somehow humorous: "Homicide witnesses use bathroom! Story at eleven!"

Returning each person to their classroom after an all-too-short vacation from reality, I thank them for being patient. Most respond with a weak smile. Oddly enough, during this meager five minutes together, I feel I connect with each of these people. Just walking and offering a word of encouragement or understanding, I get the chance to ease the pain, however slightly, of people going through one of the worst times of their lives. I have always felt police work offers some great rewards. It's ironic now that one of those rewards is the often-absent human compassion I was able to find while providing bathroom break escorts at a homicide scene.

A short time later, I am told I can leave and resume patrol duties. I would like to speak to each of the witnesses I have met before departing the scene, but I can't. They are busy recounting the evening's events to the detectives who have recently arrived. They will be dealing with this incident for a long time to come. I leave feeling I have provided some comfort, however brief, with those I have just met and probably will never see again.

9:30 p.m. - Vehicle Pursuit

Three-and-a-half hours after a woman lost her life, I sit down to recount the stories of those who witnessed her last minutes on Earth. But before I can get the first words of my report typed, an officer calls for assistance. He is chasing a stolen vehicle about 10 blocks from the police station. Responding to the call, I hear him yell that the suspects have bailed out of the vehicle and he is chasing them on foot. Seconds later, he informs Central Dispatch he has two people at gunpoint. Another officer arrives to help take the two into custody. I head toward the officer's patrol vehicle, which is in the middle of the road, engine running, siren still blaring, screaming to the neighborhood that someone's misbehaving again.

The suspect vehicle is also still running, sitting up on the curb, where it appears to have struck a signpost. The front seats are reclined back way too far for the driver to be able to effectively control the vehicle. There is rap music booming from a tape player in the dashboard. After securing the vehicle, I complete an impound form and give it to the initial officer as he arrives with two juvenile suspects. They are in their early teens, but glare with the cold, uncaring eyes which cops too often see.

I want to show them the body of the woman murdered earlier in the day. I want to show them they are wasting their lives. I want to show them there are good people who have died not wanting to, while they voluntarily throw their own lives away. But, I know this would not change them. I return their cold stares while briefly talking with other officers. I return to the police station disgusted and I finish my report. I am home in time to watch the 11 o'clock news, where the lead story tells of a college student who was shot and killed today.

Tuesday, February 12

3:15 p.m.—Breaking and Entering Alarm

The day is cold and gloomy with a misty rain as I pull onto a B&E alarm at a small three-bedroom home. The home, which was built by a non-profit group, is a couple of years old and stands in stark contrast to the aging homes surrounding it. The non-profit association began years ago constructing modest homes in Saginaw for people of modest incomes who have shown they are responsible enough to be homeowners. The homes are usually built in clusters in dying neighborhoods and give a nice boost of appearance, as well as hope, to otherwise failing neighborhoods. Wisely, the homes are equipped with alarm systems.

The front door falls open when I check it and I ask Central Dispatch to stop all on-air radio traffic until my back-up officer arrives and we can check the home's interior. The other officer arrives within seconds. With guns drawn, we check the residence in a thorough, although too-rushed-for-safety manner. Checking open doors on B&E alarms has become so common that most officers don't perform the task safely enough. We were all warned repeatedly in our respective police training academies that complacency is what often kills cops. Those warnings often fall by the wayside as the seemingly endless days of a career slowly fall from the calendar.

The homeowner, having been contacted by her alarm company, arrives as we are leaving. She says her son must have left the door ajar when he left for work. She thanks us, saying she'll talk to her son, and we part ways.

4:12 p.m.—Purse Snatching

A woman who appears to be in her late-forties answers the door at the residence and invites me in to hear the details of her purse being stolen. The interior of the two-story home is the picture of hopelessness. Aging, yellow shades are drawn to the windowsill, a position they appear to have held for years. The room is dimly lit and is consumed by the stifling heat and dusty odor of the past-its-prime furnace, which I sense is seeing the last of many winters in the home's basement.

There are two beds in the living room. In the center of the room is a portable, metal-framed, bathroom chair. The plastic, bucket-shaped receptacle hanging below the seat is obviously not empty as the smell of urine fights for control of the room.

The woman says a young boy who used to live in her neighborhood came to her door about 20 minutes ago. He said he wanted to re-pay money his family borrowed when they were neighbors. He told the woman to get her purse and he would give her the cash. When she returned to the door with the purse, the boy grabbed it and disappeared down the street. Not knowing the boy's name or where he now lived, there is little follow-up. I had checked the neighborhood for the boy prior to arriving. He was nowhere to be found and was now probably enjoying the fruits of a day's work.

6:15 p.m.—Family Trouble

A stocky younger white male meets me outside the residence when I arrive. He says he used to live there until he and his girlfriend broke up. He says he wants to get the remainder of his clothes from the house, but his ex-girlfriend will not let him. And a phone—he wants his phone back. That's all he needs. Oh, and his tires - he left two car tires in the basement and he wants those also. I tell him I'll ask, but I cannot make the woman give him the items.

The woman who answers the door looks worn out. There are several kids clinging to her and running around the interior of a home that is much cleaner than I expected. She says the man's clothes were ruined when her basement flooded and she threw them out. She says the tires are gone also. She tells me the man is "a crackhead" and she kicked him out because she didn't want him around her children. Before I leave the house, I check the male for warrants using my hand-held radio. He has none. As I'm leaving she hands me a telephone to return to him.

Outside, I return the cheap plastic phone to the man and explain the plight of his other belongings. He is not happy, but he thanks me and leaves.

6:42 p.m. - Breaking and Entering Alarm

The homeowner returns at the same time as another officer and myself. We check the house and determine it to be a false alarm.

7:00 p.m.—Assault

Responding to an assault, I arrive within about two minutes of the dispatch call. The victim already advised the suspects had left, so no back-up officer is sent.

The venue is a two-story wood-framed home, sitting across the road from the bottom of an embankment leading up to the expressway. The roar of traffic on Interstate 675 is loud and constant. Calling the home dumpy would be understating the truth. The exterior is a mix of chipped paint and warped boards. Inside, the house is quite dirty. Old, crusty food sits on the table. The victim yells her way through the story of being assaulted. Two children constantly interrupt. A headache sets in as I leave to write the assault report.

Walking down the front steps, the thought hits me that this has to be the worst possible place to be poor and hopeless - sitting a stone's throw from the expressway. Every day people leading better lives pass by at 70 miles an hour. Some people, like the woman I just left, are stuck watching, their broken down lives keeping them forever on the shoulder of life's highway. The quickest route out of town stares them in the face, day after day, but they don't have the motivation—or a car, for that matter—to get on it and make a run for a better life.

8:30 p.m.—Warrant Suspect/Man with Gun

Nearly simultaneously, two priority calls go out. First, several officers working a basketball game at a local high school call for assistance. There has been a fight and one subject pulled a gun. They are now chasing him. Nearly every available patrol officer, myself included, heads toward the high school to assist.

Moments later, however, a plain-clothes officer on the other end of town radios that he just had a warrant suspect run from him. He is on foot alone, trying to locate the suspect. Sensing the second officer will be in need of help more than the four officers working at the high school, I turn around and start toward the North side of town.

As I drive, the officers chasing the gunman advise they are okay and they have the suspect in custody. A moment later, the second officer advises his suspect is also in custody. I make it to neither scene and I am of no help to either situation.

9:35 p.m. - Disorderly Adult

For what seems like the twentieth time in the past six months, the call goes out for a man begging for money at a local party store. The man is mentally challenged and we have tried everything to keep him away from the store, including pleading with family to keep him away. When that didn't work, he was issued citations for trespassing. When that didn't work, he was jailed for trespassing. Yet, he returns daily. Every time he returns, the store's owner calls to complain. Every time the store's owner calls to complain, we have to spend valuable time responding. Many times he is gone by the time we arrive, which is the case tonight.

9:40 p.m.—Threats

A man who was evicted from his apartment makes threats to shoot his former landlord's wife and blow up her car. I stand by as another officer deals with the caller.

10:10 p.m.—Cutting

A female reports being cut in the face by her boyfriend. I respond with two other officers. At the venue, we find the victim, who sustained a minor cut on her face from a butcher knife. We are unable to locate the suspect, who has fled the scene on foot. It is nearly quitting time and the two other officers at scene handle all the paperwork so I do not have to work overtime.

Wednesday, February 13

Training Day

Ironically, just two days after responding to a woman being shot to death outside of her classroom at an educational facility, I attend a nine-hour "Active Shooter Training" class. The training deals with responding to in-progress shootings in the workplace, shopping malls, restaurants and other crowded venues. The class mainly focuses on school shootings. Throughout the day, these places are morbidly referred to as "target-rich environments," meaning there are plenty of people around to shoot. It's a chillingly accurate description.

Due in part to the well-publicized school shootings of recent years, law enforcement has been forced to change its response to active shooter situations. It is no longer acceptable for first responding officers to secure a perimeter and wait for the SWAT team to arrive. The objective now is for the officers to organize, enter the facility, locate the shooter, or shooters, and end the situation. Our trainers use politically correct terms during this exercise, but everyone is aware that "neutralizing the problem" really means "killing the bad guy." Even in the midst of today's violent world, the trainers are still forced to sugar coat reality.

The training concludes with four-hours of practical work, during which teams of officers enter an elementary school and ferret out the shooters who have already killed several students. A half dozen or so role players have volunteered to assume the roles of shooters, dead and wounded students and, in some cases, hostages. Background noise of screaming kids, gunshots and riot-like sounds is pumped into the hallways via large speakers to give the training more reality.

The course changes and gets tougher each time through. By my team's third run, I am surprised by the intensity. Even knowing everything is simulated there is a sense of anxiety and caution. Several times we locate dead or dying student in the hallway. As instructed, we leave them for search-and-rescue teams, which are to follow. This goes against all our prior law enforcement training, but our job is to "neutralize the problem." We tell one student pleading for help to stay still and wait for assistance. Eventually, we locate and kill the mock gunman.

The final run of the day involves a larger team of officers. Inside the building we encounter two gunmen, a couple of dead students, and a large homemade bomb. We are faced with two gun battles and, eventually, a hostage situation. I am shot twice in a hallway ambush with no where to run for cover. It is a helpless feeling. I wonder how much more real an actual hallway gunfight would have been. I hope to never find out.

The day ends with the rescue of the hostage by my remaining team members and the apprehension of a final gunman. All things considered, it was good training and a day well spent.

Saturday, February 16

I am scheduled for desk duty every Saturday this month, answering telephones, taking walk-in complaints and assisting road officers via the desk radio. Many officers don't like this duty. While often boring, I find it to be a nice one-day break from working the road. My day produces nothing more stressful than irritating telephone calls and a jammed copying machine.

Sunday, February 17

3:12 p.m.—Family Trouble

The call is given as a family trouble with a lot of background noise and arguing over the phone line. Driving slowly down the street looking for the correct address, I find the house. Directly across the street there is a stripped car in the driveway of a boarded up, one-story structure. The abandoned house has been spray-painted with graffiti. Garbage litters most other yards. Music booms from a car a few houses away.

Everything appears quiet, however, at the house where I am responding. My backup also arrives. A teenage girl answers the door and says she is the sister of the caller. She says everything is okay and her sister's boyfriend has left. I ask to speak to the caller to confirm this and we are invited in.

"She in bed," says the sister, who then turns facing down a hallway. "Come out here! The police wanna talk to you," she shouts to her sibling. The girl sits down and watches television, now ignoring the two cops in her living room.

A minute later I ask where her sister is. She responds that she's probably still in bed. "You can go back there. It's on the left," she says.

Walking down the narrow hallway, we find the caller slowly getting up out of bed. She looks at us with weary eyes as she plops her feet on the floor.

"We just need to know if you're okay," I tell her.

"Yeah. I'm okay. He gone," she replies. She says she was not assaulted and she does not need the police.

We leave, passing the sister in the living room. She says nothing. Walking out the front door, I am again facing the boarded-up house and stripped down car. This is the first sight that greets these two girls when they walk out their front door every day. Music still booms from a few houses down the road. Several people out in the street stare at the cops walking to their cars. Depression looms heavy in the air.

4:25 p.m.—Family Trouble

A mother-son confrontation has turned bad. Mom tells us her adult son grabbed her arms and shoved her into a corner. The whole family is yelling and they are upset at the son. After confirming the story with family members, the son is arrested for domestic violence. As soon as he is handcuffed, however, mom decides she doesn't want him to go to jail. She wants him to go to an uncle's house instead. The family suddenly is divided. However, knowing a domestic assault occurred, we must take the son to jail. Nobody is happy with the decision and by the time we leave with the son we are everyone's enemy.

5:20 p.m.—Breaking and Entering Alarm

We check the venue, which is a city school. The building appears secure and we clear the call in relatively quick fashion.

5:40 p.m.—Disorderly Adult

A local party store calls to complain about an adult harassing customers in the parking lot. The adult is there when I arrive. He complies when I tell him to leave the property.

6:50 p.m.—Breaking and Entering Alarm

This is one if many alarms that come in today. We check the building and clear the call in about 10 minutes. I leave from the alarm and park with two other officers near a local zoo. We take a few minutes to catch up on daily reports. One of the officers points to the woods to our East and recalls finding a homicide victim there a few years ago. After being shot by an acquaintance during a dispute over a girl, the victim's body was dumped in the woods. After being arrested for the killing, I am told, the suspect later recounted how he had gone to the woods several times and turned the victim's body over so it would decay evenly. He also said he cut the victim open with a knife so small animals would assist the decaying process by feeding off the victim's insides. I recall the crime for only a few minutes and we then turn the conversation to less gruesome topics.

9:00 p.m.—Family Trouble

The call for two teenage brothers fighting turns into nothing more than a brief family counseling session at their mother's request. No one has been hurt. No report is taken.

9:53 p.m.—Disorderly Juveniles

Several juveniles are trying to break into cars in the parking lot of a small hotel. By the time we arrive, they are gone, having been scared off by the night clerk. They were only entering unlocked vehicles and it looks like their take for the night's work was less than a dollar. It's a poor neighborhood. You don't make much money stealing from cars around here.

Monday, February 18

It's about 30 degrees outside and the sun is shining as Central Dispatch sends me to relieve a day-shift car, guarding the area of a possible homicide.

The scene is a large, fenced field behind an aging, but still operational, foundry on the city's North side. Amidst piles of dirt and scrap metal that gets moved from place to place out here for whatever future use they may have, a security guard has found the body of an elderly man. The man had been missing for weeks. His description has been relayed to officers in roll call every day since shortly after his disappearance. It won't be repeated tomorrow.

Saginaw Police Department detectives at the scene tell me they're unsure if it's a homicide. They're waiting, as I now will, for the Michigan State Police (MSP) crime lab to arrive and process the scene for possible evidence. Two MSP crime lab technicians arrive at the location a short time later. Additionally, there are four detectives, several plant security officers, and myself at the scene. We keep the security officers out of the crime scene, but they have offered to guard the perimeter, keeping unauthorized people from entering the field via several in-roads.

As afternoon settles into evening, the setting sun turns the air bitterly cold. MSP personnel take their final photographs of the scene. We now await an ambulance, which is on the way to take the man's body to the morgue for an autopsy. Looking to the West with the hulking, old auto plant silhouetted against the setting sun and the old man's body in the foreground, lying in the frozen dirt, somebody remarks: "If this isn't a postcard for Saginaw, I don't know what is." I let out a slight laugh. Based on my experiences, if I were to design a postcard of Saginaw, this would surely be it.

I clear the call at about 8 p.m. It's my only call of the day.

Tuesday, February 19

3:22 p.m.—Runaway Report

The caller, a mother of seven, states her youngest son has run away from home. Her son is 15 years old and likes to get drunk and smoke marijuana, she says. The boy ran away because she does not approve of his lifestyle. After gathering pertinent information, I give her a case report number and tell her we'll notify her if we locate the boy. This is her youngest child, she adds as I am leaving, and she is glad it is her last.

3:30 p.m.—Attempt Breaking and Entering

I recognize the combined house-store structure as I pull on scene. I have been here before. The old woman living here is one of those colorful, upbeat people who can immediately brighten up the darkest day.

The woman slowly rounds the corner of the building as I park my patrol car. She is an elderly black female, who I guess to be 4'10" and 95 pounds. She is carrying a shovel that almost dwarfs her and she smiles when she greets me. She tells me how some neighborhood kids tried to recently break through her steel-barred storm door. The door houses her mail slot and her mail gets delivered between that door and her front door. They were after a check, she says. She invites me in too see the damage and we walk around back and enter through the store's rear entrance because her keys are inside the house.

The store is cold and almost barren. There are 20 or so items scattered about on various shelves. The floor is partially torn up and she explains she is having work done and will be closed for a while. A door behind the counter leads to her residence. As we enter, she grabs the red-handled shaft of a broken snow shovel and uses it as a cane. The shovel portion has been removed and the shaft is wrapped in black electrical tape. With the extra support she walks briskly for a woman who is surely in her eighties. She shows me the front door and I tell her I'll try to keep a close eye on the place. She doesn't know the kids who tried to break in, but says they live down the street somewhere.

We walk back through the store and she tells me she's been running the place for about 20 years. She reminisces with me about one night a few months ago when she was in her home and heard voices in the store. After listening at the door for a moment she realized someone had broken in.

"I came out and said: 'Nigga, get outta here or I'll shoot you. I got a forty-five'," she says, referring to the gun she keeps for protection.

"That forty-five will talk!" she says to me, as she lets out a laugh that warms the room. She continues on, telling me of an attempted robbery years back. A man came in and, thinking the frail-looking woman was an easy target, swung a knife at her during a robbery. She responded by pulling out her handgun.

"I shot him right in the foot. I called ya'll," she says, "When you got here, I just told you: 'follow the blood and you'll find him.' You caught him alright." She laughs again.

After a few moments I leave with a handshake. I am less than half the woman's age, but I don't have nearly her enthusiasm on most days. I am embarrassed at the thought. She is still smiling as I pull away in my patrol car.

5:30 p.m.—Disorderly Adults

Driving through one of the North-side drug hot spots, two men are sitting on the steps of an abandoned house, drinking a pint of liquor. They give me an "Oh-shit" look as I pull up. I've dealt with both before and they are pretty harmless when they're semi-sober. I check both for weapons and drugs, and gather identification to check them for warrants.

"I gotta be honest with you, sir," one of the men says as I check his pockets. "I don't do no drugs. I'm just an alcoholic. Honest"

Both men are cooperative. One has an outstanding warrant, but it's been issued by the Grand Rapids Police Department and we are outside of their pick-up range for his offense, meaning the warrant isn't serious enough that they will make the trip to come and get him. I do not issue citations, but tell both they have to leave the area. As they depart, one of them wants to shake my hand. I politely decline and just nod my head. While both are courteous, it is obvious bathing is not high on their to-do list.

9:30 p.m.—Assist with OUIL Traffic Stop

Another officer is dispatched reference a cellular telephone caller following a possible drunken driver. I respond to the area to assist. By the time the initial officer pulls over the suspect vehicle, it has already driven up onto the curb several times and narrowly missed causing an accident. The first officer has determined the driver is not intoxicated, but diabetic. He calls for an ambulance and I clear the scene within five minutes.

9:40 p.m.—Runaway Report

A father calls about his son running away from home. The boy has only been gone about 10 minutes, the father advises. We normally do not take runway reports unless the person has been gone for a longer period of time, I tell the man. He understands and says he'll call back later if his son does not return. The son returns within 20 minutes of my departure.

Wednesday, February 20

3:40 p.m.—Disorderly Juvenile Report

It's cold and rainy as I respond to the first call of the day. The complainant owns a flower/gift shop. She says several nine-year-old kids have been coming into the store, saying they're going to fall on her front walk and file a lawsuit against her. She's upset and demands a report. I explain a report will not prevent a lawsuit, but I will write it for her anyway.

The shop she runs is neat, clean and well stocked. Across the main street from her shop is a warehouse with several loading docks for large trucks. Across the side street a small barbershop still welcomes customers. A large reception hall sits near the barbershop. This tiny oasis of business, plopped down right in the middle of a residential area, seems to be holding its own. With weeds growing through the pavement and graffiti adorning its walls, the only eyesore is a shuttered building next to the barbershop, bearing the name *Hideout Bar*. I wonder how many criminals actually did hide out there during the bar's heyday.

Heading back to the police station to write this report, I pass a huge, vacant church about 10 blocks from the flower shop. Some of its windows are covered with warped boards. Some stand open to the winter elements. The structure dominates a city block, awaiting its only possible future—a wrecking ball. A hand-painted sign hangs above the front door, proclaiming "God's Property." Even God, it seems, has fallen on hard times in Saginaw.

6:05 p.m.—911 Hang-up Call

The caller, a female in her forties, states she was arguing with her husband, but everything is okay now. She says she is leaving for the night. She is drunk, as she has been every time I have seen her in the past eight years. She says she does not need the police now. I gladly leave.

The bad weather has kept things quiet. My shift ends with nothing to distinguish it from any other eight-hour day.

Sunday, February 24

3:10 p.m.—Disorderly Adult

The caller is the owner of a small grocery store nestled in the middle of one of Saginaw's busiest drug neighborhoods. It's a grocery store in name only. The inside is one modest-sized room with bare, warped wooden floorboards. Wooden shelves hold a small variety of goods for sale. Coolers run along the back wall of the store, holding the business's most popular item - beer.

A short time ago, a man who had been previously banned from the premises pushed his way in against the store owner's protests. When the owner told him to leave, he responded by saying he would come in whenever he wants. The owner points to a house down the street where several young men are fixing a car. He says the man went to that house. He says the man has recently been released from prison and has been harassing everyone in the neighborhood. I leave to have a talk with the trespasser.

Down the block, the group of five men, all in their early twenties, look at me with indifference as I pull up to the house. A couple of them wander away, a normal reaction in this neighborhood when the police come calling. I ask to speak to the man who caused the problem in the store.

"He gone," says a chubby, twenty-something male. When I ask where he went, the silent answer comes in a blank stare and a shoulder shrug. The guy knows talking to cops is a dangerous pastime in this neighborhood. There are more eyes watching than those of the few young men still milling about in the yard. I don't press the issue.

I think back to a conversation I had with the store's owner a few months ago. He said he was tired of dealing with all the problems of this neighborhood. He's going to close the store for good soon, he said. He used to have competition from another store about two blocks away, but that place closed down a couple years ago. Now, ironically, his biggest competition is from the customers he serves. He's tired of the problems. Soon, this store will also join the legion of discarded buildings littering the area.

3:33 p.m.—Disorderly Adult

Walking up a sidewalk to the house, I am met by the caller, a nearly crying female in her early twenties. Her boyfriend's mother keeps coming over and wanting to fight her, she says. She has come over four times today. She's crazy. She just moved to Saginaw from Detroit. She'll fight anybody, anytime for any reason, the woman says.

The crazy woman apparently doesn't like her son dating this young lady. She walked up the road, heading North and she is wearing army fatigues. Checking the area, I am not able to locate the suspect.

4:44 p.m.—Drug Activity

A report of drug activity on a traditionally active street corner turns up nothing. Turning the corner onto the street, no one is out. The three drug-dealer vehicles described by the caller are also gone. Checking the screen on my in-car computer, I see the call came in more than half an hour ago, which explains why all the bad guys are now absent.

4:50 p.m. - Larceny

A stocky, lightly bearded man greets me at the sidewalk when I arrive. He tells me this is his great aunt's house. She is 98 years old and she runs a "candy store" out of the house. Every neighborhood in Eastside Saginaw seems to have one of these - certain houses where kids can buy candy, pop, or - in the summer - frozen ice in a small cup. There are no signs on the houses and you can't find them in the yellow pages, but every kid knows where they are.

The man is obviously angry, but holds his temper well as he tells of a group of neighborhood kids who came to the house earlier in the day. They asked for different treats and, as the caller's great aunt went to retrieve the items, the kids scrambled about the house stealing what they could. They took a cellular telephone and a video game player with several games, the latter items belonging to a younger child who was visiting at the time. The man points out a house where the culprits can be found and I go there to check it out.

The house I head to is small and dirt covers much of the paint on the home's exterior. There is garbage on the porch. A middle-aged woman answers the door, dressed in shorts and a t-shirt. She's not overly friendly, but she's not hostile. She tells me her kids have been in the house all day and they didn't go to the "candy house" today. She says she'll call around the neighborhood and find out what she can. She says she'll go to the "candy house" and tell them if she finds out anything. I leave knowing the stolen property will probably never be found.

6:00 p.m. - Suspicious Situation

A complaint comes in reporting five dogs are standing around near a fence. The caller says they don't appear hurt, but it is suspicious that they're all gathered together. Years ago I lost the ability to be surprised by the stupidity of some of the calls that come in. Driving to the call, I cannot shake the thought of the once popular paintings of dogs involved in various human activities, like playing cards and shooting pool. I have visions of a pack of dogs gathered around, smoking cigarettes, shoulder holsters slung over fur, planning to rob a party store. I check the area and find no dogs.

6:30 p.m.—Premises Check

With no calls holding, I drive to the top of a five-story parking structure in the downtown area to check the premises. I often drive up here if I'm not busy and watch the sun set over the city's West side. Standing five stories above the downtown Saginaw streets, the city looks serene. The day is unseasonably warm and traffic noise provides the only background to a glowing orange sunset.

Driving back down the ramp I see it is still littered with beer bottles from a sold-out concert two days ago at the Saginaw County Events Center. The Events Center is directly across the street, but it looks like much of the partying happened in the parking ramp. There is a small fortune in returnable bottles and cans within eyesight.

A block from the ramp, I find an elderly man with two plastic bags full of bottles, ambling his way down the sidewalk. When I pull alongside him, he stares at me with distrustful eyes. I ask if he's collecting bottles and he says he is. I tell him he could easily make ten bucks gathering the bottles in the parking ramp, but he'll need a bigger bag. He pulls a black garbage bag from the pocket of his tattered blue coat and he starts to walk toward the structure. He stops suddenly and turns back toward me. "You ain't gonna come up there and arrest me for going in there are you," he asks. I assure him I am not setting him up as I drive away.

Fifteen minutes pass and, with no calls going out, I drive up the parking ramp to check the bottle collector's progress. He's only on the third floor and his bag is nearly full. I head to the top floor and start throwing empties into the back seat of my patrol car. Driving down the ramp with about $3 worth of empty beer and pop bottles, I meet him back on the third level. Between the loads we've both collected, we have a new problem: he now has so many empties he can't carry them all. I tell him to throw his garbage bag in the trunk and I'll drop him at the nearest store. We've got to hurry, though, because I might get a call at any time. His untrusting stare returns as he gets into the back seat. He immediately tells me his name and date of birth. "Check me," he says. "I ain't got no warrants."

We make it to the store within two minutes. I don't bother checking him for warrants.

"I ain't never going to say nothing bad about no police," he says, loading his empties into a shopping cart.

"Even cops can be alright now and then," I reply.

He walks away without answering, but he is smiling a semi-toothless grin as he leaves.

7:00 p.m.—Follow-up Investigation

The caller says she is the mother of the girl who had her video game player stolen from the "candy house" earlier in the day. She says people in the neighborhood told her an address where some boys had her child's game player. She says she walked by and saw some kids through an upstairs window. They were playing video games. She thinks her daughter's game player is in that house.

A thin middle-aged woman opens the door at the house when I go to check the caller's story. I explain about the theft. She is helpful and walks me into her living room and points out the television set. She says it's obvious she has no video game player. I tell her I would like to check upstairs because that is where the caller said the game player is supposed to be. She says she has a television upstairs as well, but there is no video game player upstairs. I cannot check the upstairs, she says, because someone is asleep up there. I don't need to check anyway because there is nothing up there, she continues. I push the issue a bit, telling the woman if I check upstairs then I can at least let the victim's mother know she was wrong and the video game player is not here. She refuses, getting more defensive, and I leave empty handed.

Monday, February 25

3:20 p.m.—Disorderly Adult

Another call comes in from a local party store complaining of a disorderly adult begging for money. The suspect, as usual, is gone when I arrive.

3:23 p.m.—Men with Guns

An anonymous caller reports three males carrying rifles in a field next to a community center. I head to the call along with several other officers. We are informed before we arrive that two of the men have placed the rifles under their coats and are walking down the street. A moment later, the caller advises the two are back in the field, have left the guns there, and they have now gone inside the community center.

Arriving officers watch from various corners of the community center. Within a couple minutes, three adult teenagers come out a North-side door. Two of them match the caller's description and they are taken into custody. The guns are located in the field. Two are pellet guns and another is a small caliber rifle. The two teens we detained are identified and released. The witness is uncooperative. There is not enough evidence for a charge to jail either.

4:03 p.m.—Domestic Assault

After contacting the female victim, I am told her live-in boyfriend pushed her into a wall and choked her with his forearm, prompting the victim's daughter to call 911 for help. The suspect has since left and I take information for the domestic assault case. While the victim shows no sign of injuries from the struggle, having a credible witness—the daughter - helps substantiate the case. I write a report and a domestic assault investigator will follow up on the case tomorrow.

4:15 p.m.—Breaking and Entering Alarm

Because there are no other officers available, I stop and assist on a B&E alarm on the way to write my previous domestic complaint. The home is found to be secure.

4:25 p.m. - Follow-up to Domestic Complaint

Before I can reach headquarters, Central Dispatch advises the suspect from my previous domestic assault has returned. The caller says she locked him out of the house and he's now taking items from the garage.

I am the second officer to arrive and the initial officer is already talking to the suspect, a stocky man in his forties. His booming voice displays his agitation. The suspect's father and son are there also. He's telling the other officer why he's taking items, but avoids questions of the earlier alleged assault. I ask if he choked his girlfriend earlier. He states he did not.

As we place the man into a patrol car, his son wants to know why. When I tell him his father is being arrested for domestic assault, his irritation becomes obvious. He looks to be about nineteen or twenty years old and owns the quick temper of many guys his age. He's mad because his father is the only one of the couple being arrested. He wants his father's girlfriend arrested as well. When I inform him there was a witness to the assault, he demands to know who the witness is. That is not his concern, I explain. This does not sit well.

"That's why I don't like you cops!" he yells. "Ya'll some flippy motherfuckers!"

Going a step farther than I should, I tell him it's nothing personal against his father. But, because there is a witness, his father is being arrested. He says I just want to take someone to jail. "My paycheck is no larger or smaller whether I take him to jail or not," I explain.

"Man, I don't give a fuck about your paycheck! I probably make as much money as you. My paycheck is probably the same as yours or bigger!" he screams.

I walk away. He missed the point and there is no winning this argument. We leave for the county jail with an unhappy father in handcuffs and an equally pissed-off son in the driveway. A few days from now, the father will come to police headquarters and accuse me of stealing money from him during this arrest.

6:46 p.m.—Disorderly Adults

A call goes out for disorderly adults - not an uncommon occurrence for a street corner in this drug-infested neighborhood. By the time we are able to respond, the street corner is empty. Strong winds and fairly heavy snowfall combine to calm the city as the police radio goes virtually dead for a couple of hours after this call.

10:15 p.m.—Breaking and Entering Alarm

I am sent to a B&E alarm of a school and I'm still about two miles away from the alarm call when another officer says he needs assistance. He has spotted an apparently mentally ill man walking down the middle of a busy street, swinging his fists at passing cars. The officer has already placed the man in his back seat, but now the guy is trying to kick out the patrol car windows. I am only four blocks away and divert from the alarm call to assist.

There are two patrol vehicles in the middle turn lane of this five-lane road when I arrive and I can hear the man kicking at the windows of one of them. We position ourselves to take him out of the car and do so as two more officers arrive. The man is well-built and about six feet tall. His hands are already cuffed, but he constantly pulls away while yelling at us and at passing cars. Most of his talk centers around God.

"The Lord's gonna come down here and smash all you motherfuckers 'cause he's back!" the man screams. "I have got the Lord in me. Shoot me! Bust me in the head! The Lord is here! The Lord is here!"

We have long since called for an ambulance and a couple officers are trying to calm the man as we wait. Several cars come to an abrupt stop while passing. Their curiosity nearly causes several accidents and could easily get any one of us hurt. I yell at two drivers to move on and get dirty looks in return. The ambulance arrives within five minutes and transports the man to a hospital for mental evaluation.

Tuesday, February 26

3:20 p.m.—Civil Dispute

Standing outside an auto repair shop, a man in his twenties tells me the shop is keeping his van inside and won't give it back. He says his girlfriend called the repair shop a month ago to come and look at the vehicle and the mechanic just took the vehicle to their shop to be repaired without even asking. Now, more than a month later, the man wants his van back. And he's not going to pay for anything, he says.

The repair shop owner, a man in his seventies with the spunk of a twenty-year-old, gives a different version. The van is registered to the girlfriend. The girlfriend gave them the keys and asked for the van to be taken into the shop and fixed. When they later informed her the van could not be fixed and she would have to come and pick it up, she refused. The van is going nowhere until he gets payment for towing and storage, the older man says.

Standing outside the shop a short time later, we inform the younger customer there is nothing we can do for him. He had better pay for the costs or pursue a civil lawsuit against the repair shop if he wants his van back. Eventually, he decides he will pay.

4:11 p.m.—Missing Person

An elderly woman reports that her adult daughter has been missing for about a day and she's concerned.

I gather the necessary information for a missing person report. The daughter contacts her parents about three hours after I leave and says she's okay.

5:00 p.m.—Prisoner Transport

Another officer and myself are sent to the Bay County Jail to pick up a prisoner who has a felony warrant for cocaine possession. This trip normally takes an hour, but icy roads make this a two-and-a-half hour transport. We are nearly involved in an accident on the way back to Saginaw County when a car spins out in front of ours. No one is hurt and we arrive safely after 7 p.m.

There are at least 10 traffic accidents during the time we are gone, including one near fatality. We are fortunate enough to miss all of them. The rest of the evening is uneventful.

Wednesday, February 27

3:10 p.m.—Drug Activity

I respond to another call for drug activity in a familiar drug area. No one is out when I arrive.

3:41 p.m.—Fight at Residence

An anonymous cellular phone call leads us to a reported fight at a residence. Upon arrival, everything is quiet at the aging, two-story, green house. No one answers the door and after several minutes we leave.

3:55 p.m. - Family Trouble

The caller tells Central Dispatch she is having an argument with her daughter and, unless the police arrive soon, she will kill her daughter. Central Dispatch disregards both responding officers two minutes later when the mother calls back and says the dispute is over.

5:15 p.m.—Family Trouble

When I arrive, an officer is already talking to the caller, a man in his thirties. The officer tells me the man lives here and wants to get some belongings, but his girlfriend is mad and won't let him into the house.

When we contact the woman, she steps onto the front porch and says the man cannot come in. We tell both of them we cannot decide who can and can't enter the house. They both have a legal right to be there because they are both residents of the home. We advise them, however, if things get physical one or both of them likely will go to jail. The man asks her again if he can come inside.

"You can't come in my house," she responds. "You was in here and saw my son and didn't say 'fuck you, motherfucker, or nothin'!" I have no idea what this comment means, but it doesn't sound good. The man is obviously afraid to force the issue. He leaves after the woman gives him a couple of items from the house.

I clear the call and drive north, where my attention turns to a makeshift shrine on side of the road.

The flowers lying next to a telephone poll are in the shape of a heart. They look stiff and brittle, frozen by the bitter February air. I glance at them only for an instant, but it's long enough. Memories of a mild October evening replay in my mind.

It was Halloween—October 31, 2000. The late autumn air smelled of decaying leaves. The streets were active with the buzz of children. Sometime after darkness had fallen I was dispatched to this neighborhood on the city's Eastside for a fairly routine call of shots fired. Soon, though, the call began to take the shape of something more severe. More calls were coming in, Central Dispatch advised. There was a rifle involved. Someone was shooting at a car. A vehicle had crashed into a telephone pole. The car was on fire and there may be people trapped inside.

Arriving at the scene within about 45 seconds of being dispatched, Officer Matthew Ward and myself could see the fire from six blocks away. As we pulled on to the scene, the front end of the car was engulfed in flames from bumper to windshield, a telephone pole protruding from the engine compartment. There was a person slumped down in the driver's seat.

Opening the driver's side door, the only things more intense than the heat were the driver's gunshot wounds and the blood they produced. As Matt and I tried to pull him from the car, I recall waiting for an explosion and wondering if my wife would still love me after I became disfigured by fire this night. By the grace of God, that did not occur. Matt and I extracted the driver, during what seemed like an eternity, and dragged him to a front lawn, streaking blood along the pavement. The relief of being away from the burning car lasted for only a second.

"There's another one in here!" Matt shouted after going to check the vehicle's back seat.

Returning to the burning car, we began pulling a second man from the rear seat. A Saginaw Fire Department Inspector, who had been on fire prevention patrol in the area, ran past with an extinguisher and started to work on the engine compartment. Sirens screamed from blocks away. The man in the back seat was modestly built, but seemed to weigh a ton. He too had been shot. There was a pistol lying on the floorboard near his feet. Two more police cars screamed up the road. A fire truck followed and several more emergency vehicles descended upon the intersection from various directions.

Red and blue lights shattered the darkness as we finally freed the second man and dragged him away from the car. Wailing sirens filled the air. Then came a muzzled explosion. I turned quickly and, through the smoke, could no longer see the fire department inspector. For a brief second, I thought about how to tell his wife he had been killed. Then he was visible again. He would later tell me how the tires on the car had blown out from the heat while he tried to extinguish the engine fire. He joked about needing to change his underwear.

By now, Halloween was a distant memory for this neighborhood. Tonight, the scary stuff was no longer pretend; the blood and screams were for real. Fire engines, ambulances and police cars clogged the street. People - some carrying fire hoses and some toting medical bags - rushed to do their jobs as a young man breathed his last breath and died on a stranger's front lawn. The other man survived, although I have never been told, nor have I inquired, of his injuries or the extent of his recovery.

After being hired together in May of 1994, Officer Matthew Ward and I have remained the closest of friends. We never discussed this incident at length after it occurred. This night, however, remains one of the most vivid memories of my career, as I am certain it is permanently engrained in Matt's mind also.

9:21 p.m.—Armed Robbery

A young male has just robbed a local drug store at gunpoint. He fled on foot from the business after removing the entire cash drawer from the register. His description is distinct and several officers, myself included, arrive within two minutes. The surrounding area is nothing more than several businesses—most of them permanently closed—and a railroad yard. I know we have a good chance of catching the robber.

A couple minutes later—less than five minutes after the robbery occurred—an officer sees a car pulling out from behind a building near the train yard. The driver tries to act casual as he passes the officer, but seconds later the chase is on. By the time I get close I am a distant third car in the pursuit. I break off and take a route paralleling the suspect in hopes of containing him should he change directions. The chase goes less than a mile, however, as the suspect drives his car down some railroad tracks and blows out his tires. By the time I arrive, three officers are taking him into custody. He is resisting as best he can, lying face down in the snow, but he is handcuffed quickly.

The gun, the cash drawer, and several items of clothing the suspect had been wearing during the robbery are all in the trunk of the car. Prior to leaving for jail, the suspect makes a brief unsolicited comment to an officer at scene: "I'm fucked!"

My shift ends after this call. The loot is recovered, the bad guy is going to jail and no one was hurt. I wish every shift ended this way.

Sunday, March 3

3:20 p.m.—Breaking and Entering Alarm

The day is snowy and cold and my enthusiasm is non-existent. By the time I arrive at the alarm, the first arriving officer has already determined the building is secure.

3:25 p.m. - Assault Report

The man sitting in the lobby of a local hospital relates the details of being assaulted by his sister's boyfriend. He's in his late teens and he doesn't show signs of serious injury. I give him the case number and advise him how to follow up with the complaint. Like many police agencies, our department is too under-staffed to investigate most misdemeanor criminal offenses. The victim usually has to do some of the legwork, with the assistance of the prosecutor's office. The report takes about half an hour to write. Simply by talking to the victim I know he will not pursue charges and this is a waste of my time.

6:58 p.m.—Breaking and Entering Alarm

Checking the house for signs of forced entry I am greeted at the front door by a younger couple from Grand Rapids, Michigan. They are watching the house for a relative who is in the hospital. They were not sure how to use the alarm and they apologize. The man thanks us for responding so promptly and says he feels better about his elderly relative living in a city where the police respond to alarms so quickly. I thank him for the compliment, but caution that our quick response was due to the weather and low volume of calls. At times, these alarms can go unanswered for hours.

9:06 p.m.—Disorderly Adult

Security personnel refuse a man entry to a low-income housing facility and he becomes threatening and disorderly. By the time I arrive, he has departed on his bicycle and is nowhere to be found.

9:11 p.m.—Stolen Vehicle Recovery

A woman calls the police department's front desk and says she has found her stolen vehicle. Actually, she says, the vehicle wasn't exactly stolen. Her husband loaned the vehicle to an acquaintance a few days ago and the acquaintance never brought it back. As a courtesy, two officers are sent to stand by with the woman while she tries to get the keys from the man who failed to return the car.

When the woman knocks on the door at an Eastside residence, no one answers. I ask her the name of the man to whom the vehicle was loaned. She says she only knows him by a nickname. Moments later, a large, fit-looking man opens the inside door.

"That's him! That's him right there!" the woman screams.

The man looks at me warily, waiting for me to rush the door, but I don't move. The woman looks at me, waiting for me to rush the man. Still, I don't move.

"Ma'am, I can't do anything about this. Your husband loaned him the car; it wasn't stolen. Ask him for your keys," I tell the woman.

She asks for her keys and the man says he doesn't have them. He says someone around the corner has them. He closes the door.

I tell the woman I will call a tow truck to take her vehicle home. I also tell her it probably wasn't smart for her husband to loan the family car to a man he only knew by a street name. She isn't listening.

I radio for the tow truck, but less than a minute later an obese woman waddles her way down the street, yelling that she has the keys. The caller takes her car keys from a woman she has never met, starts the car and drives off without protest or question.

Disgusted, but not surprised, I remain eternally amazed by the manner in which some people choose to live their lives.

Monday, March 4

3:20 p.m.—Malicious Destruction of Property (MDOP)

It is sunny with a wild, bitterly cold wind. Standing at the counter of a convenience store I am gathering information from the clerk, who had her vehicle damaged overnight. The store is overstocked and untidy, with items clogging the aisles. I can see by the store's design that it used to carry the moniker of a well-known national chain. The current owners even adopted the same colors and a similar name. There are several other similar stores scattered across the city. I'm not sure when the popular chain store pulled the plug on its name, but I would guess it has been 20 or 30 years since crime and urban decay drove them from this part of the city.

A young man enters the store as I am waiting for a case number to be assigned for my report. Carrying several quarts of beer to the counter, he barely looks 17—well under the legal age for purchasing alcohol in Michigan. He makes the purchase and walks outside, where he gets into a truck with a young man of similar age. As they drive out of the parking lot onto East Genesee Avenue, I enter their license plate into my in-car computer. The vehicle's owner is only 19, but more importantly, he has warrants for his arrest from another jurisdiction. The physical description of the vehicle's owner also matches that of the driver.

By the time I catch up to the old, blue pickup and pull it over, we are downtown. When I approach the vehicle, the driver says he owns the truck. When I ask if he knows about his warrants, he says he does. I handcuff him and place him into my patrol car.

Returning to the truck, I ask the passenger his age and he indicates he is 23 years old. When I ask for identification, he has none. I ask if he has any warrants for his arrest and he replies honestly: "I'm not sure - probably." I put him in the back seat of my car next to his brother and a check shows six warrants for his arrest all out of Bay County, which borders Saginaw County to the North.

During a subsequent search of the truck I locate a marijuana pipe behind the passenger seat which the passenger admits is his. "Could you not keep that, sir," he asks. "My dad kinda passed that down to me. It's been in the family." At least he's honest.

With help from the desk officer, I am informed the Bay City Police Department will meet me at a spot halfway between our jurisdictions and they will take custody of the older brother. The driver has better luck. After several messages, the police department that issued his warrants fails to respond. After half an hour, I release him and tell him how to take care of the warrants. Twenty minutes later I meet officers from the Bay City Police Department and they take custody of my prisoner. Two hours of report writing follows.

6:47 p.m.—Family Trouble

The suspect of a domestic assault has departed by the time I arrive and I disregard a backup unit, which is en route to assist me. The female caller is calm as she greets me at the door.

"He's at it again," she says as if I am a close friend. "You been here before. I remember you from when you was in training."

"I don' think so, ma'am. I went through training eight years ago," I reply.

"Yup. That's about how long he's been doing this. I remember you," she says. Her memory is obviously much better than my own.

Ten minutes later, I hand the woman a case report number and advise her to call if her live-in boyfriend comes back. She thanks me. Walking down the snowy driveway, I wonder if I'll still be coming back here eight years from now.

9:21 p.m.—Family Trouble

A woman is yelling at me from her front porch. For safety reasons, I have parked three houses away and I am walking down a dark sidewalk to her house. Her yelling ruins any hope of a silent approach to the residence.

Her 17-year-old son is in the basement, she says. He assaulted the woman's daughter and then made threats to kill the whole family. He also said he is going to shoot the police when we arrive. The woman tells me he has shut off power to the house from the circuit box in the basement.

When I enter the living room, there are at least six other people—adults and children—in the room. It is dark and people continually pass through the room as if nothing is happening. I feel very vulnerable as I keep an eye down the back hallway where I am told the basement stairs are. Rap music booms through the kitchen and down the hallway, rising up from the suspect's basement lair. I advise Central Dispatch we'll need a couple more officers here. When the first back-up officer arrives, we discuss the situation and walk toward the back of the house.

Suddenly the power returns on the main floor. The back stairwell and basement remain dark, however. I walk halfway down the stairs to a landing and yell around the corner for the teen to come upstairs and talk. He turns the music up louder. Several more officers arrive. Several more times I yell for him to come upstairs. Finally, the music turns off.

"Come on down and talk then," he yells angrily.

"You come up and show us you don't have any guns. I'm not walking down there when you've been making threats to shoot people," I respond.

"Man, I ain't got no guns. Come on down and see," he replies, sarcastically.

Peering from the top of the stairs into the darkness, I can envision this pissed off teenager, crouching with a handgun in the darkness, ready to unleash a rage of bullets upon the first person he sees. The house is cold and dirty. The stench in the house rivals that of a hundred sweaty, unwashed armpits. I am overcome with a rare and powerful thought: This is not where I want to die. I wonder if these sights, sounds and smells are the same as other officers have experienced before being shot to death.

Pushing the thoughts aside, I return to the conversation at hand. Hoping to avoid having to enter the basement, my response is loud and forceful: "You come up and talk to us or we send down the dog. It's your choice!"

One of our K-9 officers is here with his German Shepherd - a large-headed beast named Mohawk. We would rather not send the dog into the basement either, but it may become necessary, instead of sending an officer down first.

Unexpectedly, the young man emerges weaponless and is arrested after we hear his version of the incident. No guns are found in the basement. He is lodged on a domestic assault charge. It is a neat ending to what I thought was going to be a very messy situation.

Wednesday March 6

3:50 p.m.—Felonious Assault

A car accident leads to one man pulling a gun and threatening the man at fault. I arrive moments later to assist officers who have located the suspect vehicle. It turns out the gun in question is a pellet gun. The victim is not very cooperative, either. The gun is seized, but nobody goes to jail due to the victim's lack of cooperation.

5:20 p.m.—Breaking and Entering Alarm

A B&E alarm at the downtown bus station proves to be false. This is at least the third time the alarm has been tripped this week.

5:25 p.m.—Suspicious Persons

By the time this call goes out, it is already more than an hour old. The subject of the call is gone.

5:37 p.m.—Breaking and Entering Alarm

An employee is still in the building when we arrive. He is having trouble with the alarm system and set it off accidentally.

6:30 p.m.—Fight

Three or four persons are fighting in the parking of a neighborhood store. I arrive within two minutes and find a large man near the front door of the store. He appears to be about 6'4" and maybe 260 pounds. I ask what's going on as I walk toward him.

"Three of 'em jumped me," he says, smiling. "I took care of 'em. I'm tight."

He refuses assistance and wants no report. His resolution is swifter and more efficient than anything I can offer, and I depart knowing justice was served.

8:00 p.m.—Breaking and Entering Report

An unknown suspect broke into a home and stole a video game player. I take the report and my night ends quietly.

Thursday, March 7

3:30 p.m.—Family Trouble

The trouble is over before the police arrive. A middle-aged man informs me the woman he called about has left the residence and he no longer needs police assistance.

4:11 p.m.—Check the Well Being

A man calls from North Carolina and says he hasn't been able to reach his father via telephone for four days. His father is a cancer patient and he would like the police to check the man's well being.

The address where I am dispatched is decrepit, and the powder blue paint on the house's exterior is peeling badly. It is the worst looking house on an otherwise well-kept block. The storm door to an enclosed front porch is half covered with plywood and creaks as I open it to enter.

After two loud knocks on the door, I am relieved to hear an old man's voice from inside the house. I hoped the man was not deceased. I can never get used to spending hours inside a house, ripe with the stench of days-old rotting flesh, waiting for the medical examiner to arrive. Fortunately, the man living here was not only alive, but quite lively as well.

I inform the man why I am here and he invites me inside. The front hallway and living room are dark and smell of years of stale, non-circulating air. Crates and boxes are stacked as high as my chin on several tables. Appliances, large and small, sit throughout the room. An old washer blocks off one corner of the room. The old man says he will call his son. As I turn to leave, thinking our conversation is over, he begins complaining that he is a military veteran and he gets little or no money from the federal government.

"I hope all them motherfuckers in Afghanistan get killed; All our soldiers. I hope they all die," he says. "Shit, the government don't give me nothin'. I hope they all die."

I depart without debate, reminding him to call his son.

5:36 p.m.—Breaking and Entering Alarm

Responding to yet another alarm at a local bus station, I find the building is secure and depart within minutes.

6:47 p.m.—Suspicious Vehicles

The complainant has called for police response several times during the past week, reporting everything from suspicious people and vehicles to shots fired near her home. She appears to have mental problems, but we still must respond to her calls. Today, she says there are two cars full of drug dealers in front of her house. There are no cars in the street when I arrive and she will not answer her door to talk with me. The remainder of the evening is pleasantly uneventful.

Friday, March 8

It's the last of seven straight working days and I'm anxious to get it finished. After roll call, a sergeant advises I have been assigned a brand new patrol vehicle for the remainder of the year. The car is still a few weeks from being ready, however. I'll have to make due with a spare vehicle until then, I am told. My car this day has 95,173 hard police miles on it and handles worse than I expect.

3:10 p.m.—Prisoner Transport

Minutes after loading equipment into my vehicle, I am sent back to police headquarters to transport a teenager to the juvenile detention center. He was caught earlier in the day in a stolen car. He's not concerned about his fate today, smiling during the entire 15-minute ride. At the juvenile detention center, he is greeted by staff, who ask him why he's back. It's not his first stay here and he knows most of the staff by first name.

4:15 p.m.—Lost Child

A thirty-something mother is crying when I enter the office of a newly remodeled elementary school. She and a teacher's aid relate the story of how the woman's young son walked out of school at the end of the day, refusing to take the bus home. The mother tells me her son has a mental disability. He also doesn't know his way home, which is more than two miles from the school.

Several other officers are pulled from less pressing assignments and we begin a patterned search of the area. A short time later, a couple of cellular phone calls report the child is walking through neighborhoods Southwest of the school, looking confused. Eventually, a Saginaw County Sheriff Deputy on a traffic stop sees the child walking past. He picks up the child and the search is over.

When I take custody of the boy from the deputy, the child is crying. He's not scared, but he knows he's in trouble. We talk about safety and why he needs to ride the bus home. He sniffles quietly and nods his head. At the school his mother is a mixture of relief and anger. She cries as she holds the boy. Not thirty seconds later, the school's principal - a distinguished-looking, middle-aged woman - talks to the boy in a soothing tone. She tells the boy of the important role he plays, not only in his family, but also in life. She tells him about making the right decisions. She tells him why he must be careful for the benefit of everyone. I leave the school, the principal's speech still in mind, feeling more hopeful than I did an hour ago. The principal, whom I met for the only time this day, left me with a lasting memory of caring and compassion. Sadly, this woman would pass away from illness by year's end.

5:17 p.m.—Landlord/Tenant Dispute

The tenant has been evicted from a small business space downtown and the caretaker of the property won't let him back in to retrieve belongings. The dispute has turned verbally hostile. When we explain to the young tenant the matter is civil and there is nothing we can do for him, he becomes disrespectful.

"Man, I don't even know why you are here. The police don't do nothing," he exclaims.

I launch into an explanation of the limits of what the police can do in this situation. He doesn't listen. Like many people, I envision this young man probably believes the police, in general, have too much power. Now, however, he would like me to overstep the limitations of my job to suit his current needs.

He drives off angrily, realizing he will not get his way on this day.

6:15 p.m. - Assist with Warrant Arrest

Checking another officer's traffic stop, he asks me to stand by for a few minutes. The driver of the vehicle he has pulled over has no identification and might be lying about his name. Eventually, he finds out the real name of the driver, who indeed has several outstanding warrants for his arrest. A female passenger has also lied about the suspect's name. She is given a ticket rather than a trip to jail. She takes the suspect's car home while the suspect heads to the county jail.

8:00 p.m.—Shots Fired

A neighbor complains someone keeps coming out of the house across the street from her and firing a gun into the air. I recognize the house as one where I've been sent in the past. The home's occupants do not like the police. There are people inside but no one will answer the door. I tell Central Dispatch I'll give the area attention tonight. No further problems are reported.

9:20 p.m.—Shots Fired

Another report of shots fired, this time in a different area, produces nothing. Several other officers assist checking the neighborhood, but we find no one with a gun and no dead bodies on the ground.

9:33 p.m.—911 hang up Call

The house is dark when I arrive. There is not a sound from inside the residence. No one answers the door. With no indication of a problem, the call is cleared. My night ends shortly thereafter.

Tuesday, March 12

My mood turns glum before roll call even begins. The rumors again are spreading—the city, which had projected a budget deficit of more than one million dollars for the upcoming fiscal year, is expected to announce the actual deficit may be four times that amount. This undoubtedly means reduced city services and layoffs. Some people I work with today will probably not be here by summer's end. With every pink slip delivered the safety of the remaining officers, myself included, becomes a larger issue.

Saginaw is one of many auto industry boomtowns left to rot by the industry which brought it to life. City streets have become graveyards of boarded up houses and overgrown lots. A once prosperous business district is now dotted with empty spaces where buildings once stood. The few remaining buildings stand like scattered teeth in the rotting mouth of a street bum. Some that remain are infected with abandonment and will soon fall from the landscape. Some days the gritty feel of this town it heaps on my mind a sense of hopelessness that lingers long after the workday is done. The rank taste of despair is strong today.

3:55 p.m.—Breaking and Entering Alarm

The small house is secure upon my arrival and the call is cleared within minutes.

4:54 p.m.—911 Hang-up Call

We arrive to investigate the call at an old home, which has been divided into apartments. After knocking on an upstairs, interior door for two minutes with no luck, I turn to leave. As I turn, a thin woman in her thirties walks up the stairway. She babbles on, saying that someone called for the police from her apartment, but that person has since left. It is not even time for dinner and the woman is drunk and nearly incoherent.

5:59 p.m.—Panic Alarm

The alarm turns out to be false and the call is quickly cleared.

6:38 p.m.—Disorderly Adult

A young girl calls from the pay telephone at a party store asking for the police. She tells me a man drove past her a while ago and gave her the finger. I talk to her for about five minutes, knowing there is nothing I can do.

7:26 p.m.—Assault in Progress

The anonymous report originates from a chicken-and-rib, take-out restaurant. A man is assaulting a woman in the parking lot. I locate them both walking two blocks North of the venue. They are arguing, but both insist no assault occurred and they don't need the police. I recognize the woman as a long-time prostitute and drug addict. Today she appears to be just drunk. The two walk off together after I check both for warrants.

7:55 p.m.—Disorderly Adult

A security officer at the apartment building for low-income tenants leads us to the elevator and uses a security key to get us upstairs. At the fourth floor, there is no answer at the apartment where we were dispatched. Everything is quiet and we depart without being able to locate the complainant.

9:05 p.m.—Breaking and Entering Alarm

I pull onto the alarm call and locate a woman from the bank's cleaning crew in her car outside the building. She says the alarm is malfunctioning and she's trying to get a supervisor to come and help her set it properly. I leave after verifying her story.

9:30 p.m.—Drug Activity

Driving past a house to check out a report of drug activity, everything is quiet. There is no one in the street and no one hanging out at the house.

10:00 p.m.—Family Trouble

The couple we contact is in the process of divorcing. They are yelling at each other. Their four-year-old daughter is crying as her father holds her. Both want to talk about the other person's shortcomings. Neither appears to be without fault. After 15 minutes, the man says he has to go to work for the night and there will be no further problems. The woman agrees. Driving to the police station to end the night, I wonder how couples come to that point. I hope to never learn the answer firsthand.

Wednesday, March 13

4:01 p.m.—Threats Report

The woman sitting at a cheap desk in the office of the apartment building is nice. She appears to be in her late forties. Her tone is level as she relates how a former tenant moved out, breaking his lease. Today he came back for his security deposit and, when he was told he would not get it back, he threatened to start "kicking ass." The report is a formality in case the threats are carried out. The woman is not scared. It's obvious she's been through this before.

4:50 p.m.—Fight

The caller says there is a large group fighting in the street. When I arrive there are teenagers running away between various houses. Several teenage girls run up to my car and start yelling about someone getting jumped. I soon learn the fight started between two former friends over some borrowed clothes that were not returned.

A block from where the fight started, I am told the suspect is inside a brown two-story house in the middle of the block. The house stands out as the eyesore of the neighborhood. The rest of the houses in this predominantly working-class neighborhood are small, but well kept.

Several people, adults and teens, stand in the front yard of the suspect's house. When I ask to speak to the suspect, a thin, haggard-looking woman yells for her to come out of the house. A young girl in her mid-teens opens the door and walks down the wooden stairs toward me. An overwhelming smell of body odor escapes out the front door and follows the girl into the front yard. She tells me her version of the story as if she's on the stage of a trashy daytime talk show. Her butchering of the English language and her over-animated body language are too annoying to be considered funny. I advise both sides of the dispute how to follow up on the case report that will be filed. I have worked primarily the Eastside of Saginaw for the past three years and have not been to this West-side neighborhood in over a year. I am now glad this neighborhood is not near my patrol area.

7:30 p.m.—Suspicious Vehicles

The call for two suspicious vehicles is 34 minutes old before there are officers available to investigate. Not surprisingly, the vehicles are gone before we arrive.

7:49 p.m.—Domestic Assault

The female victim says her baby's father struck her in the face with a beer bottle during a dispute. The fight occurred at a mutual friend's house with six witnesses present. The suspect is gone, but the witnesses, I am told, will be cooperative. When I ask what happened, all six persons state they didn't see a thing. The victim is livid over the silence of her friends. I give the victim her case number and she leaves after cursing her friends for not helping. Friendship, apparently, only goes so far.

8:40 p.m.—Family Trouble

An anonymous call of a family trouble on a street corner turns up nothing. There is no one on the street for blocks and there is no sign of a problem.

8:45 p.m.—Loud Music Complaint

A report of loud music from a residence is unfounded. All is quiet.

9:15 p.m.—Assault

An assault call turns out to be minor and is handled by other officers at the scene.

Thursday, March 21

By the time my shift starts I have already worked four hours of overtime. The four-hour traffic detail was funded by a State of Michigan grant, focusing on traffic violations. With overtime nearly non-existent at our department due to budget concerns, I jumped at the chance for the extra pay. It was also a good opportunity to practice traffic stop skills. These days, I rarely have the time or motivation to initiate traffic stops during a normal work shift. The four extra hours helped me get back into the practice of concentrating on the safety issues involved with these situations.

3:20 p.m.—Breaking and Entering Report

A large man with bear-like hands greets me at the front door of a small house where junk is piled high in the front yard. He invites me in and walks me around the house, pointing out where someone smashed in a window to gain entry. The house belongs to his brother, he says. He's been watching the house since his brother went into a retirement home. This is the second break in since his brother left the house three weeks ago.

We talk for a short while. The man says he will probably just board up the house. He tells me he's originally from Alabama and they don't have as many problems in Alabama because when you go to jail in Alabama, they work you so hard you don't want to go back. Michigan jails, he says, are like country clubs: televisions, good meals, exercise rooms. Going back to jail in Michigan is like a vacation, he says. I tell him I thoroughly agree and we part with a handshake.

4:42 p.m.—Breaking and Entering Report

As soon as I finish writing a report for the man from Alabama, Central Dispatch sends me to another report. This breaking and entering is about a mile away from the previous one, but the circumstances are very different.

The thirty-something man in front of the house is livid. He's the landlord and recently had to evict a tenant for not paying rent. After lengthy court proceedings, the tenant was finally evicted a couple of days ago. Today, the man returned to find the home destroyed. Every wall inside the house has been broken through, probably with a sledgehammer. Kitchen cabinets are destroyed. Carpeting is ruined. The words "Fuck You" and "Bitch" are spray painted on the walls in black paint. I photograph the damage and give him a case report number before departing. His insurance claim will be substantial.

7:55 p.m.—Breaking and Entering Alarm

The building is secure and the alarm is cleared within minutes of being dispatched.

8:00 p.m.—Assist Family Independence Agency

I meet with two workers of a state governmental agency, which oversees the well being of children and needy families. The workers relate to me the story of possible sexual abuse of a child at a residence. There is rumor of a child pornography problem at the house as well. Upon our arrival at the home there is no one there. Since we do not have a search warrant, we advise the workers to call us back when they want to check the residence again.

9:41 p.m.—Suspicious Person

I watch a white female in her thirties walk aimlessly through downtown. She approaches two males in a parked car, but they drive away when they see my patrol car. She is not one of the usual downtown prostitutes. A couple of blocks later, I call her to my car to identify her.

"I'm going home," she says as she continues to walk away. "I'm sick of getting shit on in life."

I order her to my car a second time. This time she puts up no fight and gives me her identification. She goes through the usual story that she's not a prostitute. She's just "waiting for friend" to pick her up. She has no warrants and I let her go with a warning that she'll go to jail if I see her conducting anymore business downtown.

"See ya, baby. Have a good night," she says, walking away with a smile. With the weather warming, I know I'll see her often during the summer.

Friday, March 22

3:10 p.m.—Mental Pickup

It's cold and snowing lightly as the day begins. The shift commander directs me to my first assignment of the day after roll call. Handing me a mental pick-up order, he sends another officer and myself to a local rescue mission to pick up a mentally ill woman, who allegedly has not been taking her medication. For the woman's safety, a mental health worker asked a judge for a legal order to have the woman taken to a mental health facility for evaluation.

At the rescue mission, I speak with the front desk attendant. She calls the woman's room and asks her to come to the front desk. The worker, a pleasant woman with gray hair, says the female is not very stable and may fight being taken into custody. We wait in the lobby of the old, yet well-maintained building. Several homeless residents pass by and shy away from making eye contact. An air of desperation permeates the building. A man in his twenties walks past, reading The Bible. He offers a sheepish smile.

Our wait lasts only minutes as the subject of our petition walks around the corner and stops abruptly at the sight of our uniforms. She gives us an "I-give-up" grin and sets down her purse. We explain why we are there and place her into handcuffs. She offers no resistance and chats freely during the twenty-minute ride to the mental health facility. She says she hasn't been taking her medication and she has been irritable lately because of this. She also says she has been living on the streets for 19 years. Her weathered face reflects every day, I think to myself. Within an hour and a half she has been dropped off and all the paperwork for the transport is completed.

5:37 p.m.—Disorderly Adults

The call for disorderly persons is on the city's North end. Before I can make it to the call, the primary officer has pulled on at the house. He disregards me over the radio, telling Central Dispatch the caller said she no longer wants the police.

8:15 p.m. - Check the Well Being of a Citizen

A woman calls from another state and says she has left her husband. She just talked to him on the telephone, however, and is concerned that he is okay. He sounded strange during their phone conversation, she says. At the woman's former residence, I find the house mostly dark. There is no answer at the door and no sign of trouble. The desk officer informs the caller of this via telephone and the call is cleared.

Tuesday, March 26

3:18 p.m.—Breaking and Entering Alarm

The primary officer calls on scene and disregards me before I can respond to the alarm.

3:35 p.m.—Check Citizen Complaint

Following the direction of a memo from the chief's office, I drive by a home on the Eastside of the city to check for the smell of dog shit. A resident has complained to the chief's office and said his neighbor is letting dog waste accumulate in his yard and it smells badly. In between in-progress calls I drive paste the residence and smell nothing foul. This is something that was not covered in the police academy.

3:37 p.m.—Vehicle Inspection

Completing one of the more mundane tasks of the job, I fill out a vehicle inspection form for a citizen so he can get a car re-titled. The process takes less than five minutes.

3:45 p.m.—Family trouble

The dispute is so ridiculous it is humorous. A boyfriend and girlfriend are arguing because she gave him $5 for gas to drive her to some stores. After a few stops, the boyfriend protests the gas she bought is almost gone and he's not taking her anywhere else. When they get to his home, she refuses to get out of the car, insisting he take her to more stores. With no other option, he calls the police to remove her from his car. After 15 minutes of debate and the threat of her being taken to jail, she finally agrees to get out of the car—but only after her boyfriend drives her to her own home.

4:18 p.m.—Vehicle Inspection

The female caller wants to chat, but I complete the required paperwork and leave with barely a word. It's busy and there is little time to shoot the breeze.

5:25 p.m.—Disorderly Person

The woman who called is an alcoholic. She constantly calls Central Dispatch when she is drunk and today is just another foggy day in her miserable life. She says her chest hurts and she needs medical help. Because of her violent behavior, ambulance personnel will not respond to her residence without police assistance. By the time I arrive, there are two firefighters from the fire department's rescue squad, two paramedics and another police office at the venue.

Inside the small apartment, boxes and garbage clutter nearly every square foot. Old food sits out on the table. A fireman takes a 22-ounce can of beer from the woman and pours it down the drain. Within minutes she is taken to a local hospital at her request. Within an hour she will probably check herself out of the hospital like she always does. This process is repeated dozens of times each year.

6:30 p.m.—Transport

I am told to transport a young woman to the rescue mission. She's in town from out of state. She says she is a heroin addict. We've had several complaints involving her in the past 24 hours. She also has made complaints that officers are not helping her enough when she calls for a variety of stupid reasons.

The woman is jittery and looks like she hasn't slept in days. She tries making small talk during the short drive, but I do not respond. I have no use for a heroin addict, who calls the police for mundane issues, complains about how she is talked to, and then begs the cops for a ride when she has no place to stay. I drop her off at the rescue mission without a word.

6:54 p.m. - Fight

The streets are empty as I pull on to a call of several subjects fighting in the street. I check the neighborhood for a few minutes, but there is nobody out.

7:09 p.m.—Suspicious Situation

I have been to this house about a half dozen times in the past two months. The female caller continually complains of drug dealers around her house. Today, she says drug dealers are getting into the crawl space beneath her home. She says they stay down there for hours, drinking beer, talking and shaking the foundation of the home. She says they have shaken the home so much, her toilet is coming loose from the floor. While talking to her, I look about the house. It is clean. It is well heated. There's plenty of food. The caller, while a little nutty and certainly paranoid, is taking care of herself well. I tell her I'll keep an eye on her house for her. She smiles and thanks me.

7:30 p.m.—Disorderly Adults

Investigating a report of two panhandlers at a local grocery store, I find they are gone. The caller does not want to be seen by police. I clear the call quickly.

8:20 p.m.—Relieve Desk Officer

I am called in to police headquarters to work the front desk for the remainder of the night because the desk officer has to leave work early. During the remainder of the evening, I take four telephone calls from the intoxicated woman I dealt with earlier in the day. She is back home and she is drinking again. She says she has the body of a deceased Saginaw County Sheriff Deputy in a casket in her bedroom. She is clearly crazy. She is crying and mostly incoherent. By the end of the night, she has called Central Dispatch again and police and medical personnel are again sent to her home to check her well being.

Wednesday, March 27

3:15 p.m.—Stolen Vehicle Report

It's a warm, sunny day and the calls for service are piling up quickly, my first of which is from a man who reports his vehicle was stolen from a downtown street earlier in the day. He left it parked with the keys in it for a few hours, he says. I take the information for the report, but quickly get re-routed to a more pressing call.

3:30 p.m.—Shots Fired

Several neighbors are reporting some male subjects just kicked in the front door of a residence and there are shots being fired inside. I am heading to police headquarters to write a stolen vehicle report, but divert to assist on this call.

I am the third officer at scene. There are bullet holes in the front window of the home. The front door is lying open, having been kicked in. A shell casing is on the floor. There is, however, no blood. No one is inside the residence. Outside, about a dozen neighbors are milling about. Some watch us. Others pay no attention whatsoever. None of them seem overly concerned. Several other officers have now arrived so I clear the call and start back to write the stolen vehicle report.

3:38 p.m.—Attempt Breaking and Entering

Before I get a half a mile from the previous scene, Central Dispatch is looking for officers to assist on an attempted breaking and entering on the city's West side. I volunteer to assist a sergeant, who is the only other available person to take the call.

At the venue, I speak to the caller. He's a large man in his early twenties. He says he was showering and heard his dog going crazy. When he got out of the shower, he heard someone trying to kick in the front door of his home. He came out another door onto the front porch and startled a younger male, kicking at the front door. After punching the suspect in the head five times, he chased him for a few blocks but couldn't catch him.

With the assistance of a Michigan State Police unit, which was nearby, we have already checked the area for the suspect with no success. I take the information for another report and advise the victim there will be a detective assigned for follow-up investigation.

5:45 p.m.—Family Trouble

The combatants are gone by the time we arrive and no report is wanted.

6:37 p.m.—Suspicious Vehicle

An anonymous caller reports a suspicious vehicle parked in the road. She thinks the vehicle is stolen. A check of the vehicle shows it is not.

6:47 p.m.—Armed Robbery Report

The victim says he was shooting dice in a street game. He was winning big, but the other players apparently weren't happy about his luck. Before the game ended, one man shoved the victim to the ground, another stuck a gun to his head and they jumped in the vehicle of a third man, leaving with $4,000 of the victim's winnings. I write a report for him, knowing it will probably go nowhere.

7:40 p.m.—MDOP Report

The man parked alongside Interstate 675 with his hazard lights on says someone threw a rock off an overpass and smashed his windshield. The suspects are long gone by the time I arrive and I gather information so he can file a report for an insurance claim.

10:02 p.m.—Fight

A report of a fight in progress results in nothing. No one is located when officers arrive. I am disregarded from the call before I can get there.

Thursday, March 28

3:20 p.m.—Disorderly Persons

Checking into service, most of the calls for service are old and this one has been holding for a while. The day shift usually gets backed up on calls in the early afternoon, leaving a list of "clean up" calls for second- shift officers to mop up. The disorderly persons on this call are long gone by the time I arrive.

3:35 p.m.—Disorderly Juveniles

My second call of the day is also almost an hour old. The caller says several juveniles were seen entering an abandoned house. The caller thinks they may be doing drugs in the house. Another officer and myself arrive at the house at the same time. The structure has no front door or windows. It sits on the corner of a neighborhood of small, but mostly well-kept houses. Nearly every block in the city, however, seems to have one or two of these abandoned homes. We check the house and it is empty.

3:40 p.m.—Loud Music Complaint

A block from the previous call, I can hear music booming from four houses away. Two speakers sit on the front porch of a small red house. A heavy-set girl in her twenties walks out to my car as I pull up. She's smiling.

"Is it too loud?" she asks, already knowing the answer.

I respond with a laugh: "You know it's too loud. The neighbors are bitching about it. If you could turn it down so I don't have to write any tickets and you don't have to pay any tickets, that would be cool."

She agrees and turns down the music. Our brief encounter is surprisingly pleasant. Too often people blow up over something as simple as being asked to turn down their music. Hers is a welcome response.

3:45 p.m.—Possible Domestic Disturbance

A man and a woman are seen arguing in the parking lot of a business on the city's North end. The lot is empty by the time I arrive. Checking the call screen on my computer a second time, I realize why the subjects are gone—the call has been holding for 75 minutes.

4:31 p.m.—Family Trouble

A chunky younger woman holding a child is screaming at the top of her lungs outside the residence when I arrive. The primary officer is already on scene. He's standing about five feet from the woman, letting her vent. Her boyfriend stands by the curb with a smile on his face. He calmly listens as she berates him in front of us.

"He's a fat, dope-sellin' motherfucker - straight up!" she screams. "Check him. Check his record. He runs from ya'll all the time."

"Yeah, I run from the cops," the man replies calmly. "So what?"

I don't like him and I don't like her, but that's beside the point. There's nothing for us to do here, but get one of them to leave. Several relatives of the two are also in the yard. Eventually, the woman leaves, but not quietly.

6:00 p.m.—Drug Activity

A report of two men selling drugs in front of a vacant house produces nothing. They have since moved on. The experienced drug peddlers don't stay planted in one spot for too long.

6:10 p.m.—Non-Injury Auto Accident

A heavy-set man in his fifties is leaning against the rear bumper of his car when I arrive. He offers a friendly "hello" and explains that he was backing out of his driveway when a car pulled into his driveway and struck his vehicle. The female driver of the second vehicle offers the same story, but clearly, she thinks the man is at fault.

"I'm just pullin' in here to turn around and that man backs up and hits my car!" she exclaims. "He just backs right up and hits me."

I explain he has the right of way in his own driveway and he doesn't have to yield to other traffic until he is entering the roadway. She does not understand. She does not want to understand. The man tries to explain it to her again. I try to explain it to her again. Her frustration grows with every word. I quit explaining and take down the information for the report, which I agree to write because her vehicle was still halfway in the road at the time of the accident. Technically, this could probably be considered a private property accident, for which no report should be taken. But she is insists on documentation, so I write the report mostly to pacify the woman.

"Contact your insurance company with this case number if you file a claim," I tell her. "Maybe they'll see things differently." She leaves without a word.

The day ends much quieter than it started. I receive no more dispatch calls during the shift and spend the rest of the evening patrolling the city.

Friday, March 29

3:45 p.m. - Breaking and Entering Alarm

It's rainy and cold and by the time I reach my first call it's pouring. A relative in town from Washington has accidentally set off the alarm, but the homeowner will be there in a minute to turn it off. I identify him as we stand on the front porch. I comment on the weather. He says this is nothing compared to the rain they get in Seattle.

4:00 p.m.—Suspicious Situation

The young woman I speak with relates several stories of strange people following her home in different cars. She says another man has been knocking on her back door. She says one of the people following her is an admitted killer. Her thoughts are scattered and her speech incoherent at times. She is clearly mentally ill. Several persons inside the home glance my way from time to time with obvious indifference. I listen for a few minutes and tell her I'll keep an eye on her house as best I can. This makes her happy.

6:21 p.m.—Suspicious Situation

An anonymous caller says the front door to a downtown barbershop has been left unlocked and the owner is nowhere to be found. The caller is concerned. When we arrive at the building, the caller is gone. The door is locked and everything appears normal.

7:01 p.m.—Check for Domestic Assault Suspect

Two West-side officers have gone to the hospital for a domestic assault. The suspect and victim are both reported to be at the hospital. When officers arrive, they find the suspect has left on foot. He's supposed to have a gun. Two officers are needed to check a residence for the suspect. I arrive at this home with another officer and find the suspect is not there.

The investigating officers then request we check two local bars where the suspect is known to hang out. We enter the first bar cautiously. I carry my gun near my right thigh, but out of sight. The place goes quiet when we walk in. About twenty people are scattered throughout the bar and all heads turn toward us. None match the suspect description. We check the bathrooms and ask the bartender if she's seen the guy we're looking for. She says she has not. Everyone in the bar seems relieved as we leave. No one is more relieved than I. I don't like going into bars to look for an armed person. There are too many people. There are too many places to hide. There are too many intangibles. It's an ambush waiting to happen.

The second bar is larger, but there are fewer people. We check the building and find our suspect is not here either. There are a couple tables of men and women. Two large men wearing blue baseball hats are leaning on the far end of the bar drinking oversized draft beers. They look like they're about fifty years old and appear to be regulars.

"Who you guys looking for?" says an older, petite waitress standing near the bar.

Needing to break the tension, I reply: "We're looking for two bigger guys in blue baseball hats drinking large mugs of beer."

Before I can finish the sentence, both men simultaneously remove their hats and slowly place them on the bar without breaking their stare at the television on the wall. Everyone in the bar, including me, breaks into laughter. We leave without the suspect, but the laugh was worth the trip.

7:43 p.m.—Breaking and Entering Alarm

The first responding officer determines this is a false alarm and disregards me while I am still en route to the call.

8:00 p.m.—Domestic Assault

A reported domestic assault turns into a property damage report. A man's estranged wife came to his new apartment and threw a brick through the rear window of a vehicle parked outside the apartment. The estranged wife claims she was assaulted during the incident. There are several witnesses for both the man and the woman. Everyone appears to have seen something different. Several are obviously lying. The report will be sent to a detective who will have to determine what charges, if any, will be filed.

10:19 p.m.—Domestic Disturbance

The suspect is gone by the time I arrive. The caller says everything is okay and she does not need the police.

Wednesday, April 3

3:35 p.m.—911 Hang-up Call

Forty-five minutes after Central Dispatch receives the call, I arrive on scene with another officer. Fortunately, there is no emergency. The woman who answers the door explains her child must have been playing on the telephone. She thanks us for responding, not realizing our delayed response probably would have done her no good had she really needed help.

4:00 p.m.—Hold-up Alarm

Responding to hold-up alarms at this downtown plasma donation center has been a weekly occurrence for some time now. Still I approach the building cautiously. A haggard-looking middle-aged man meanders his way down the sidewalk toward the building as I approach. I ask him to stay away from the front of the building. He gives me a confused look, but complies, turning back to walk the other way. Another officer joins me shortly after I enter the lobby. It appears to be business as usual and a girl at the front desk laughs when I tell her of the alarm. She apologizes and says there is a new girl working who must have set it off. She says it won't happen again. Within two hours, however, other officers are dispatched back to the business for the same alarm, which again proves to be false.

4:12 p.m.—Drug Activity

A report of drug dealers peddling their wares on a street corner near a local high school is dispatched. Before I can get within a mile of the venue, the first responding officer advises the bad guys are gone. I disregard the call.

4:30 p.m.—Check for Runaway

An anonymous caller advises Central Dispatch there is a runaway hiding in an Eastside residence. The caller does not know the runaway's name. When I knock on the door, a heavyset woman wearing a bandana on her head opens the door. I inquire about the runaway. The woman looks both ways out the front door to see if anyone is watching our encounter. Without making eye contact, she says there was a young girl at her home earlier in the day she thinks was a runaway. It was a friend of a family member. She told the girl to leave to avoid any trouble. The woman says she'll call if the girl returns. She closes the door while still surveying the neighborhood.

5:35 p.m.—Disorderly Subjects

I repeat a near daily occurrence by telling four young men to move from in front of a local convenience store. The store has become a gathering place for loiterers and drug dealers. The four leave quickly after the warning. They will undoubtedly be back.

5:56 p.m.—Prisoner Transport

Arriving at police headquarters, the desk officer asks me to transport a man to jail. He has a domestic violence warrant and turned himself in moments earlier. Our conversation en route to the jail is friendly. The man is well over six feet tall and is cramped in the back seat of the patrol car. This does not bother him, however, as he mostly complains about his soon-to-be ex-girlfriend, who he says has lied about the domestic assault complaint.

6:36 p.m.—MDOP Report

A small wood-frame structure in the heart of one of Saginaw's numerous drug neighborhood is the target of someone's ire. Several windows in the house have been smashed out. I write a report for the landlord so she can file an insurance claim.

Thursday, April 4

3:40 p.m.—MDOP Report

The report ends up reading as follows: A woman gave her car and some money to a man to have a new engine installed. Now she cannot find the man. A relative of the man tells the victim her car was burned up in a fire. No one knows where the man lives or how to reach him. The woman is now missing the car and her repair money.

4:00 p.m.—Drunk and Disorderly Adult

On the way back to the police station to write the previous report, I stop to assist two officers with an intoxicated subject. The man is leaning on a patrol car outside a check-cashing store. He is nearly too drunk to stand and his mouth foams as he talks.

"Fuck you, you bitch!" he screams at least 10 times at the officers who are speaking to him.

While we wait for an ambulance to arrive, the man weaves together a string of "Fuck you, motherfuckers" and "honky bitches" in a thick-tongued drunken tirade. He momentarily focuses his attention on me. He tries to cover the 20 feet to my patrol car to confront me, but realizes he can't walk that far. He stops to rest on the trunk of another patrol vehicle. When the ambulance arrives, he greets the first paramedic with another "fuck you, bitch!" The man is transported to a local hospital. He will be released after his blood alcohol level drops, only to go back into the streets and sink further into the drunken abyss which is his life.

5:31 p.m.—MDOP report

A brick thrown by unknown persons through a car window leads to another report, which ties me up for nearly an hour.

6:38 p.m.—Breaking and Entering Alarm

The premises I check is secure and the call is cleared quickly.

7:37 p.m.—MDOP Report

The elderly woman I encounter on the front porch is furious, but she's too old to yell much. Her son just left after breaking out two of her windows. She says her son is in his forties and he smokes crack cocaine. He sometimes comes around, but she won't let him in. Today, he took exception when she refused him entry. He broke the windows and left on foot. I check the area, but I am unable to find the man.

9:40 p.m.—Shots Fired

Several people call to report 10 or more gunshots fired in their neighborhood. Another officer arrives in the area shortly after me and we do a sweep of the neighborhood looking for suspicious persons or bullet-riddled bodies. We find neither.

10:02 p.m.—911 Hang-up Call

When I inquire at the front door an elderly woman at first advises she did not call 911. She then says she may have called by mistake while making another call, but everything is okay.

10:10 p.m.—Family Trouble

Several young girls run into the house as I arrive. The complainant is in front of the house in her car. She explains she is there to pick up her son, who was visiting relatives. They are arguing over whether or not her son should attend a relative's funeral. Several people now come out of the house and begin—nearly in unison—yelling their opinions about their family matters. The woman eventually leaves with her son, but not before a half-dozen people have screamed for at least five minutes. This is my last call of the night.

Friday, April 5

It's a typical baseball opening day in Michigan. The temperature hovers in the 30s and snow flurries continue throughout the day. It's the first day of what would become a miserable spring for the local team, the Detroit Tigers. My spring undoubtedly won't be much better.

3:10 p.m.—Drug Activity

Like so many times before, the dealers are gone before the police arrive. I advise Central Dispatch I will give the area attention during my shift, knowing I probably won't have the time to do so.

3:16 p.m.—Neighbor Trouble

The house I am sent to looks like nearly every other house on the block. They are all small, square, two-story structures. A semi-ancient lumber company sits across the street, providing a less-than-scenic view from the front porches in the neighborhood.

The woman who answers the door yells out her complaints to me, even though I am standing less than five feet away. Her disagreements with the neighbors seem trite I think to myself, compared to her other obvious problems. Her clothes are filthy. She is very over weight and obviously poorly educated. The distinct smell of body odor flows past me as we talk. If not for the freshness of the cold early-April air, I would be forced off the porch by the stench. Thankfully, our conversation ends within a few minutes. I pray I don't get called back here during the warm-weather months.

4:15 p.m. - Fight

A reported fight in the parking lot of a local store turns out to be a dispute over a car accident in the parking lot. With the help of another officer, the problem is quickly resolved.

4:43 p.m.—Fight with Weapons

A reported knife fight turns out to be little more than an argument. The caller tells Central Dispatch there are weapons involved to ensure a quick response from the police. I am disregarded en route to the scene.

4:52 p.m.—Attempted Abduction

The shift is less than two hours old and we are already falling way behind on calls. A Michigan State Police unit offers to take this call as I am being dispatched from the far South end of the city. I graciously accept the help from the other police agency and clear to assist on other backlogged calls.

4:53 p.m.—Disorderly Person

The suspect is gone before I arrive at scene. I disregard the backup officer.

5:01 p.m.—Assist Officer

Another officer investigating a shooting asks for assistance trying to find the crime scene. He is at a local hospital with the victim, who drove himself there after being shot in the shoulder. The victim is unsure where the shooting occurred and gives several possible locations. I am unable to locate blood or shell casings at the location where I am dispatched. The victim's story is shaky at best. The scene is not located.

The crime most likely will never be solved. The victim, I am told, couldn't care less.

6:02 p.m.—Family Trouble

The reported troublemaker has left the scene, knowing the police were on the way. The victim does not want to make a report.

6:44 p.m.—Breaking and Entering in Progress

A caller states two young boys on bicycles have ridden behind a neighbor's house and appear to be trying to break in. The caller says the neighbor is out of town. I locate the boys within minutes of the call. The homeowner is gone, but the homeowner's daughter is home. The two young men have come to see her. She states everything is okay.

7:22 p.m.—Disorderly Persons

The disorderly persons are gone and the call is cleared within minutes.

7:30 p.m.—Family Trouble

The suspect has departed. The elderly woman I speak to says the suspect is her son. Tonight, her son began pushing around his sister. The woman tells me her son has been hanging out with the wrong crowd and smoking a lot of marijuana. She says she will have to evict him soon. Before leaving, I advise her how the eviction process works and where to file the paperwork.

9:36 p.m.—Assist Officers

A state police unit has pulled a traffic stop and asks for another car to stop at their location. When I arrive there are about 20 people standing around watching. The fifteen-year-old unlicensed driver of the vehicle is in the back seat of the patrol car. His mother, a front-seat passenger, is drunk.

"These motherfuckers on a Friday night," she screams, standing outside her vehicle. "Ya'll a bunch of motherfuckers!"

The MSP troopers handling the stop are patient with the woman. They hand over to me the brother of the driver. At the time of the traffic stop, he also had become disorderly and started threatening the officers. He's handcuffed as I place him into my car. We talk as the officers deal with the drunken mother. He's cooperative as I identify him and check him for warrants. Eventually, the mother calms down and the crowd of onlookers thins. The underage driver gets a traffic citation. No one goes to jail.

Saturday, April 6

3:40 p.m. - 911 Hang-up Call

I arrive at the venue, a single-family dwelling, shortly after the call is dispatched. The door to the home is unlocked and ajar, but no one answers. I follow another officer into the house to investigate further. The home is only a few years old. It is built on the sight of the former Daniels Heights Housing Project. The home is clean and in good condition - a vast improvement from the dozens of two-story, brick, duplex-style structures that once occupied this land.

There is no one home as we make our way through the house. There are no signs of a struggle. We leave not knowing the reason for the 911 call.

3:56 p.m.—Suspicious Vehicle

The day is cold, but sunny. I have a ride-a-long today, a teenage girl who is pleasant enough, but too young to take seriously when it comes to discussing law enforcement, which, she says, is the profession she is going to enter. Completing an eight-hour ride-a-long is a requirement of a career center she is attending. As I look for a reported suspicious vehicle, she tells me she is not going into uniform police work.

The girl says she'll enter the FBI or CIA instead of being a uniformed cop. She asks matter-of-factly if there are any requirements to become a police officer. I explain the state's pre-requisite written and physical agility tests that must be completed before applying to a police department. I explain the lengthy hiring process: the interview, written tests, background investigation, physical tests and psychological tests. I tell her about the four-month-long, state-mandated police academy and then the four-month-long field training officer program most departments require after an officer is hired. She seems discouraged. I believe she expected she would fill out an application, smile a little and a government agency would whisk her away to a secret agent camp where she would get her gun and a bag full of disguises. Federal law enforcement is tough to get into, I explain. The reality of her chosen profession hits hard. She is fairly quiet the rest of the day.

I never locate the suspicious vehicle.

4:03 p.m.—Family Trouble

A woman explains her live-in boyfriend assaulted her. He then left with their children. She wants him to stop being cruel to her. She is crying and she is mad. When the primary officer gives her a case report number and advises we will try to locate the suspect, she says she doesn't want him arrested. She just wants him to quit abusing her. I leave disgusted.

Michael S. East

4:30 p.m.—Suspicious Person

A man stripping salvageable parts from an abandoned building shows me paperwork giving him permission to do so. The building is being torn down, he says, and the owner told him he could take what he wants. This call had been reported as a possible breaking and entering in progress, but it is legitimate. I've seen many businesses occupy this building during my employment: a non-profit organization, a fireworks store, a church. None have lasted. The demolition will be a welcome change to the neighborhood.

4:50 p.m.—Disorderly Juveniles

A local convenience store calls to report several juveniles throwing rocks at the store windows. It's the second such call at this store within 24 hours. The first arriving officer calls out that he will be speaking to the juveniles. Moments later he asks for assistance. I arrive as the third of six cars to respond. About two dozen people are in the street, most yelling anti-police rhetoric. One teenager sprints toward me from about 150 feet away, fists clenched, wanting to fight. I prepare to take him to the ground, but never get the chance as another teen grabs him by the neck and drags him away to avoid trouble. The crowd disburses after about 10 minutes.

Speaking to the initial officer later at the scene, he relays the story of what occurred. He talked to the store's owner, who told him where to find the kids who were causing the problem. When the officer found them a few doors away he called them to his car to talk. The kids, all younger than 12 years old, began to talk to him when several adults came out of a house, one yelling: "Fuck the police. You ain't gotta talk to them!" The adults kept taunting and, eventually the kids got into the act until several more people spilled into the street and a mini-riot was in the making.

The call ends with a report being taken for the property damage and a mother coming to the scene to claim her teenage son, who is in the back of a patrol car. No arrests are made.

6:59 p.m.—Assist General Public

Patrolling a well-known drug neighborhood I find several kids around five and six years old playing with a refrigerator that has been dumped on the street corner. The door is still on the appliance and they are taking turns climbing inside and shutting the door on each other. I explain the dangers of suffocating inside the refrigerator. Another officer arrives and we remove the door from its hinges and tip the refrigerator on its side, off the roadway. The children are laughing and playful and want to talk about cop stuff. Moments later, a young woman walks out of their house across the street and yells for them to "get away from them police." She offers no hello. She offers no thank you. The kids smile as they run away. That, however, is thanks enough.

7:15 p.m.—Family Trouble

We stand by at a family trouble as a woman packs her things to leave her husband. I don't know the whole story, but they both ask us to stay until she leaves so there will be no physical altercation. She screams at him endlessly while she loads her belongings. Catching bits and pieces of what she is saying, the fight seems to revolve around other women, drugs and irresponsibility. After about 25 minutes she departs and we leave the scene as well.

10:00 p.m.—Possible Breaking and Entering of Vehicle

We are unable to find a suspect or a vehicle being broken into. The call was anonymous and we have no way to follow up.

Tuesday, April 9

3:06 p.m. - Fight

Speaking to the principal of a charter school for socially challenged students, I learn all the combatants have left the scene. The principal would still like me to write a report, however, even though the victim and the suspect have left.

I recall reading in the newspaper last week this school will close after the school year. Enrollment is down, student tests scores are too low, and the university which had provided the school's funding is pulling out. The principal looks distracted as we talk. This school is seeing its final days and the depression is evident among the few staff members still here today. I know the feeling, I think to myself. I hand the principal the case number he requested. He thanks me half-heartedly, but his mind is elsewhere.

3:30 p.m.—Felonious Assault

The victim I meet at a local convenience store is jittery and has trouble maintaining his thought process. He's obviously been smoking crack. He said his "friend" pulled a knife on him. We return to his home a few blocks away and check for the suspect, but she is gone. The man says she is probably on the street somewhere. He is given a case number for a report, which he will no doubt never pursue.

When I reach my patrol car, I check the calls holding on my in-car computer. There are eight calls for service holding; six are in-progress. By 4 p.m. a dozen calls for service cover the computer screen.

4:30 p.m.—Abandoned Vehicle

An hour after responding to the previous assault call, the report has been written and I'm back in the road. The in-progress calls have been cleaned up, leaving a few calls to be checked. I tag an abandoned vehicle and make myself available again.

5:05 p.m.—Family Trouble

Two sisters are arguing. The woman who called owns the home and has let her sister move in. Her sibling, however, is an alcoholic and has been drinking again today. When I explain that I have no legal authority to make her sister move out, the caller screams at me continually. I advise her of the proper way to evict her sister from her house. There is nothing more I can do.

5:38 p.m.—Man with a Gun

There has been trouble brewing in this neighborhood for the past few days. Today appears to be no different. I am the third officer to reach the area, but we locate no one with a gun. The caller states the suspect came to his house with a gun, making threats, but left before the police arrived. The caller says he does not know why the armed man is upset with him. The caller is lying, but we leave without learning the truth.

6:00 p.m.—Check the Well Being of Children

An anonymous caller states several children have been left alone. At the residence there is a 17-year-old watching the other children. I verify the children are okay and that they are properly supervised.

6:20 p.m.—Assist Officers

An officer calls for assistance chasing a suspect in a hit-and-run vehicle accident. The suspect struck another car and drove about 10 more blocks before bailing out of his own vehicle. The ensuing foot chase attracts the response of a half dozen officers. I arrive on scene shortly before the suspect is located hiding in a backyard. While we are attempting to locate this suspect, other calls go out for a knife fight and a man with a gun.

6:45 p.m.—911 Hang-up Call

Checking an upstairs apartment we find everything is okay. As usual, a small child playing on the telephone has prompted our response.

7:20 p.m.—Property Damage Report

A complaint of a vehicle striking a fence in a private driveway leads to a property damage report, which keeps me tied up for less than an hour.

9:20 p.m.—Breaking and Entering Alarm

The alarm location appears to be secure. The call is cleared within minutes.

Wednesday, April 10

3:30 p.m.—Injury Accident

The call comes in as a juvenile struck by a car in front of a local middle school. At this time of day, with school just letting out, I anticipate a messy scene. Fortunately, the pedestrian who was struck suffered only minor scrapes. He's more annoyed at the fuss being made than anything else. I take the information for the accident report while school personnel contact the child's parents.

5:02 p.m.—Prostitute

Driving through downtown, I see a woman sitting on the window ledge of a vacant bar. I continue on and stop back about five minutes later. She is still there. She rolls her eyes as I pull up to the curb and get out of my car.

"You working today?" I ask.

She smiles and responds, while pointing at a man a block away: "I wish. That gay guy over there gets more dates than I do. I'm 51 years old and I got a bad hip. I'm just resting for a minute."

I sit next to her on the window ledge and get her identification. We talk, as I check her for outstanding warrants. She tells me she does not prostitute much anymore, but she used to make decent money working the streets. She's friendly and cooperative. She agrees to leave the area after I find she has no warrants.

5:12 p.m.—Disorderly Adults

Completing a nearly daily task, I clear out some disorderly teens hanging out in front of a neighborhood store. Like flies on road kill, they'll be back later in the day.

5:15 p.m.—Disorderly Person

The subject of the call is gone when officers arrive.

6:15 p.m.—Drug Activity

Drug sales in the neighborhood I am dispatched to are not unusual. This caller, however, says there is a white male selling drugs out of his car in the street. This is a nearly all-black neighborhood and I am curious to see the gutsy guy who has set up shop here. It appears, however, business was not good or he encountered hostile competition. He's gone when we arrive.

6:49 p.m.—Breaking and Entering Alarm

The residential alarm checks out okay. No one is home, but the house is secure.

7:18 p.m.—Prostitute

Passing the same abandoned bar where I spoke to a prostitute earlier in the day, I spot another lady of the evening meandering slowly down the sidewalk.

"Hey, whiteboy. How you doin?" she says, not an ounce of disrespect in her tone. She is smiling and her demeanor immediately makes me laugh. She's heavyset and wearing a multi-colored shirt. A bit too festive for a Saginaw prostitute, I think to myself, but she certainly livens up the block. I warn her to keep moving. She complies and walks away, still smiling.

7:28 p.m.—Drug Activity

There are several males milling about the front of a local store when I arrive, none matching a description given by the complainant. After talking to the other responding officer for a few minutes, we depart the area.

7:46 p.m.—Fight with Weapons

There was a fight, but there were no weapons. The caller again added that information to get the police to respond faster. All the combatants are now gone, however.

7:55 p.m. - Loud Music

A heavyset male in his 20s is sitting on the front porch of a small house when I pull up. His radio is booming, but he agrees to turn it down with a nod of his head. He never speaks a word and looks disinterested when I tell him he'll get a citation if I get called back.

8:02 p.m.—Abandoned Vehicle

A stripped down vehicle sitting by the curb has drawn the attention of a neighbor, who called for the vehicle to be checked out. After determining it is not a stolen car, I tag it for removal at a future date.

Thursday, April 11

It's sunny and 70 degrees as the shift starts. Day shift officers are working on a fresh shooting, which one officer tells me appears to be gang related.

3:12 p.m.—Threats

Responding to a call of subjects threatening to kill a store's owner, I bring up calls pending on my in-car computer. Twelve calls, six of which are in progress, await officers. The call to which I am now responding turns out to be two hours old. The suspects are long gone.

3:30 p.m.—911 Hang-up Call

Another case of children playing on the telephone has drawn us to this residence. We leave the scene with apologies from the homeowner for wasting our time.

3:38 p.m.—MDOP Report

An elderly woman tells me the details of someone driving over her lawn, tearing up about 18 feet of her well-groomed front yard. The 84-year-old woman laughs as she relates stories of her many years living in Saginaw. It's obvious she loves to talk to people. She is very friendly and energetic and is a delight to speak with. I stay about five minutes longer than I should before leaving to write her report. It's a rarity in this job that I get to speak with someone as upbeat as this woman. These are, by far, the best five minutes of my day.

5:40 p.m.—Warrant Arrest

I am sent, with another officer, to a Michigan Department of Corrections probation office in the city. They are holding a subject on a probation violation arrest warrant. They have him in custody. By the time we arrive to transport the suspect to jail, they have been waiting for well over an hour.

While performing a pat down search on the suspect, he declares he has no weapons. As I explain I still must check, one of the probation officers tells of another subject they arrested a while back. He was taken into custody on a warrant. During a search they found crack cocaine and shotgun shells in his pockets—not exactly the right items to carry to a meeting with your probation officer.

7:30 p.m.—Desk Duty

Just more than halfway through the shift I am called in to cover desk duties for the rest of the day.

Friday, April 12

Roll call brings news of two possible shootings, which are supposed to occur during our shift. We are advised to give the respective areas attention when we have time. Not surprisingly, both shootings are said to be gang- and drug-related.

3:22 p.m.—Family Trouble

The house where I am dispatched is all too familiar. It was during my four-month training period nearly eight years ago when I was first dispatched here for two brothers fighting. By the time we arrived, one brother had already stabbed the other a dozen times or more. For me, however, the stabbing took a back seat to the unbelievable number of roaches infesting the home. Standing in the living room interviewing witnesses that night, there were bugs everywhere. Focusing on my note pad, I could see roaches moving on every wall. My skin was crawling for hours that night after departing the house.

Today, I stand on the front porch and when a young girl yells for me to come in, I tell her to come outside to talk to me. She tells me her uncle has been yelling at her. Her uncle, the stabbing victim from years earlier, has just gotten out of prison recently. An adult family member comes outside and assures me everything is okay. The uncle has left for the day and it was just a verbal argument to begin with.

3:35 p.m.—Warrant Arrest

A woman calls and says her child's father is at an address on the city's North side. She says he hasn't paid child support and there is a warrant for his arrest. After confirming the warrant does exist, I check the residence. A relative says the suspect left shortly before I arrived. She says she will tell him to take care of the warrant. I am quite sure he will not.

3:45 p.m.—Parking Complaint

A complaint of a vehicle being parked on the front lawn, which is a violation of city ordinance, proves to be false.

3:50 p.m.—Premises Check

Parking a few doors down from where a drive-by shooting is rumored to occur sometime today, the street is quiet. I recognize the target house as one where we've had problems before. Across the street from the house, two teenage boys and an older woman are working on a driveway. They appear to preparing to pour concrete. They glance at me every few minutes. Finally, I drive over to the woman and explain why I am there. She frowns with concern and thanks me for the information. She says they'll be careful. Maybe they'll knock off work for the day, she says. I tell her that might be a good idea.

4:10 p.m.—Prostitute

Two women having a cigarette outside a downtown shoe store wave me to the curb as I drive past. They tell me a heavy-set woman has been working the corner nearby for an hour or so. She ducked into a bar down the street when I came around the corner. I leave and promise to watch for her from a different location. Within minutes she emerges and starts waving down cars. Pulling up next to her, I find her to be an appalling sight. She is about 60 pounds overweight and wearing tight pants and a sport-bra-style top. Her clothes are stretched to the point of nearly busting their seams.

When I ask her for identification, she reaches inside her tight-fitting top, feeling underneath her breasts for I.D. She does not find it. I tell her to check her pants pockets. When she does, she throws a crack pipe onto the ground from her pocket. After checking her for warrants, I issue her a citation for possession of drug paraphernalia. I release her with a warning to leave the area. She quickly complies.

4:55 p.m.—Officers Need Assistance

Two Michigan State Police troopers call for assistance near a local high school. They are on a traffic stop and they're fighting with a passenger. I am the fifth police car to arrive. The suspect is in custody so I keep watch now over our biggest threat area—the 50 or so people who have crowded around to watch. Some look on quietly. Others scream obscenities at us. We clear the scene after about 10 minutes with one suspect headed to jail.

8:00 p.m.—Prisoner Transport

Another officer and I drive to a pre-designated location between Bay City and Saginaw to take custody of a prisoner from the Bay County Sheriff Department. The suspect has a warrant issued by the Saginaw Police Department for drug possession and soliciting a prostitute. The suspect turns out to be in his mid-twenties. On the way back to Saginaw, he talks about his bad luck. He talks about his passion for smoking pot. Neither the other officer nor myself are interested. Neither of us responds, yet the man drones on and on about all his tough breaks in life. When we leave the Saginaw County Jail, I am happy to be rid of him.

Wednesday, April 17

It is unseasonably warm for early spring with temperatures in the eighties. I worked desk duty the previous night. About an hour after yesterday's shift, a man was gunned down in the middle of the street about two blocks from police headquarters. The annual rash of pre-summer violence appears to be starting early this year.

3:20 p.m.—911 Hang-up Call

A well-dressed woman in her thirties meets me in the front yard when I arrive on scene. She tells me she called 911 when her ex-boyfriend showed up, causing problems. After she called for the police he left, but not before snatching her cellular telephone and its carrying case from her waistband. The woman requests a case report. She says she may seek a personal protection order.

4:30 p.m.—Assist Detectives

Two detectives in an unmarked vehicle ask for a uniformed officer to assist them. While driving through a neighborhood investigating a case, a woman jumped into the back seat of their car and asked what they were doing. When they reply they are "just driving around," she offers to perform oral sex on them. Twenty dollars for two blowjobs, she offered, not yet realizing they were cops.

When I arrive, the thin and worn-looking woman is sitting on the ground in handcuffs. She is crying. She's well known to most Saginaw cops as a prostitute and drug user. She tells me the detectives solicited her. As they gather her information for the case report, I tell the woman she'll probably have a tough time fighting this charge in court. Twenty minutes later I drop her off at the jail and resume patrol duties.

5:05 p.m.—Family Trouble

A young boy calls and says his stepfather is fighting with his mother. When we arrive, the woman answers the door. She is surprised to see us. We inform her of her son's call. She says she was having an argument, but everything is okay. She is upset with her son for calling the police.

5:39 p.m.—Panic Alarm

This is the fourth time I have responded to an alarm at this residence in the past two months. As usual everything is okay. I tell the resident once again to get the alarm checked so we can avoid the false calls. She says she will. I am sure she will not.

5:50 p.m.—Disorderly Adult

The man I speak to relates the events of half an hour ago. He was outside his house when a younger man in his early twenties drove through the neighborhood several times at a high rate of speed, apparently trying to impress some girls who are out in the neighborhood. When the caller finally yelled for the man to slow down, an altercation ensued. The driver threatened to "go get his boys" and come back to do a drive-by shooting. The caller just wanted to let me know. I tell him I'll keep a watch on the area, but I know I probably won't have time to keep this promise.

6:20 p.m.—Assault

Twenty minutes of talking to neighborhood teenagers results in a lengthy juvenile assault report. The parents insist the incident be documented. The problem could have been worked out without police involvement, but the parents are more impatient than their children and refuse deal with each other to resolve the problem.

7:45 p.m.—Assault

The call goes out as several men beating another in the lot of a party store. When I arrive a few old men are standing outside. They say some guys were fighting, but they all left. One guy was bleeding, they tell me.

I check the area and eventually a woman waves me down. The victim is in her house, she says. The man I encounter inside is holding a towel to his face. He doesn't want to talk to me. When he removes the towel, the female homeowner nearly vomits. The skin surrounding his mouth on the right side is torn open about an inch into his cheek. All his front teeth are gone.

"Am I gonna need stitches?" he asks, slurring his words and spitting blood through the opening where his teeth used to be.

"You're gonna need a lot of stitches," I tell him.

"Will these teeth grow back?" he asks, spewing more blood as he talks.

"Not at your age they won't," responds a sergeant, who arrived on scene just a moment ago.

Medical personnel have arrived and they escort the man to the ambulance. I return to the store to look for the man's teeth. In the parking lot, the same old men are still there. I ask if they have seen the guy's teeth.

"They right over here," says a man with a dirty, graying beard. He walks over near a large green trash dumpster and kicks three teeth into a small pile. After putting on rubber gloves, I pick up the teeth - roots still attached - and place them into a plastic envelope. At the hospital, a nurse says they can try to put the teeth back in the victim's mouth. She drops them into a glass of milk and asks the victim to hold them until the doctor can examine him. Another officer has offered to write the report. I clear the call.

9:35 p.m.—Felonious Assault

The combatants have all left by the time we arrive at scene. There is no victim or suspect and, therefore, no report to be taken.

9:57 p.m.—Disorderly Juveniles

The call is for juveniles shooting off fireworks. They are also gone by the time police arrive.

10:09 p.m.—Family Trouble

The altercation is between a mother and son. The mother is an obese woman with a foul mouth. She is sitting on the front porch, yelling at her adult son, who is gathering belongings to move out. As I speak with her, mom lets loose with a continuous barrage of "fuck yous" and "motherfuckers," directed at her son. Eventually, both the mother and son say they don't want us there. They will resolve their problems without the police. I am happy with this request and leave the scene.

Thursday, April 18

The weather remains unusually pleasant for early spring. The morning newspaper carried a front-page story detailing seven shootings, which have occurred in the city within the past 10 days. Even though spring violence is an annual ritual in Saginaw, the local media always react with renewed surprise, as if they're describing some distant relative they just bumped into after a long absence. The sad reality, however, is that warm-weather shootings are as natural in this town as the daily rising of the sun.

3:05 p.m.—Prisoner Transport

Detectives have a suspect in custody after interviewing him about a crime. With enough evidence to lock him up, they ask for two uniformed officers to transport the man to the county jail. When I arrive in the detective division, the suspect is sitting in an interview room. He is not handcuffed and sits at a table with a cocky smirk on his face. The other officer accompanying me handcuffs him and we head for the jail. The suspect is young, but carries himself with the confidence of someone much older.

While leaving the jail about 15 minutes later, the officer who accompanied me on the transport says he has dealt with the suspect often. "He just turned seventeen," the other officer says. "This is his first time in county. He's scared shitless."

Not scared enough to go straight, I think to myself. If anything, county time will make him tougher and stronger. Eventually - if he lives that long - this kid will probably serve time in a state prison. Today, unfortunately, is not where the cycle of incarceration ends for this young man; this is just the next step on what will most likely be a miserable and unproductive life.

3:37 p.m.—Mental Transport

I arrive at a local hospital with the same officer from the previous transport. We are here to pick up a mentally ill person and transport him to a mental health facility. After about half an hour hospital personnel finally locate the patient. He is friendly enough and we talk a bit during the drive. At the end of the trip, we find there is a problem with his paperwork, which leads to another lengthy delay. Finally, the patient is accepted into the mental health unit. We part ways on friendly terms. The call takes more than two hours to complete.

6:05 p.m.—Abandoned Vehicle Impound

I spend about half an hour impounding an abandoned vehicle, which I had tagged for removal a week prior.

6:30 p.m.—Abandoned Vehicle

Another abandoned vehicle sits behind a house, full of garbage. The caller says a former tenant left the car there when he moved. The caller also says he removed a dead dog from the vehicle a few days ago. The car smells of rotting animal flesh. I quickly tag it for removal and write a brief report.

6:55 p.m.—Abandoned Vehicle

The abandoned vehicle trend is getting a little monotonous. The caller at this house, however, has left, having had to wait too long for police response. We will be called back another day.

Friday, April 19

3:10 p.m.—Juvenile Assault

All parties are gone by the time I arrive at scene.

3:26 p.m.—Stolen Vehicle

A woman tells me her brother took her vehicle and pawned it off for drugs. She says she saw the car parked at a drug house about a mile away, but she was too afraid to go ask for it back. I take the information for the stolen car report and check the drug house. No one is at the house. Neither is the car.

5:24 p.m.—Family Trouble

The argument is between an aunt and her niece. The aunt has allowed her niece to live with her, but is now kicking her out because the aunt feels her young relative is "running with the wrong crowd." The two stand in front of the house for a while yelling, but the niece knows she has lost the argument. She says she'll move out. We stay at scene until the niece leaves.

5:58 p.m.—Breaking and Entering Alarm

I arrive on scene well before my back-up unit. A cleaning crew has just entered the building and set off the alarm by accident.

6:26 p.m.—Mentally Ill Person

I am dispatched to police headquarters as the desk officer has advised Central Dispatch there is a disorderly, mentally ill woman needing assistance in the lobby.

I arrive to find the woman standing in front of the police station. She is very large and wearing a multi-colored, two-piece knit skirt and top, neither of which fits very well. Both are nearly see through. She is crying and makes little sense. An ambulance arrives within a minute and she immediately goes with the paramedics. She says she wants to go to the hospital because she is depressed. The ambulance personnel advise us they will take care of her.

7:00 p.m.—Desk Duty

Covering the desk officer's lunch break, I take a couple of mundane walk-in reports at headquarters, which keeps me unavailable to answer calls for some time.

9:48 p.m.—Disorderly Juveniles

According to the caller, several juveniles were in front of her home throwing rocks at passing cars. One man stopped his car and threatened to get a gun. The caller says none of the kids live at her home. They all stay down the street. She doesn't know their names or who they are, though. She is mad because her children were accused. I tell her to keep her kids inside after dark and she shouldn't have a problem.

10:18 p.m.—Breaking and Entering of a Church

The B&E Alarm went off about 10 minutes prior, but there were no officers available to respond. When an alarm company guard arrived at scene, he found a window had been smashed and it looked like entry was made into the building. I arrive first and verify it's a valid breaking and entering. I ask for additional officers to respond to help check the building. Several officers are pulled from other calls to assist.

The church covers nearly an entire city block. Six officers, a sergeant and a K-9 Unit assist checking the building's interior and watching the outside. With dozens of windows and doors, the suspects could easily try to escape as we are checking the interior of the premises. The search takes about 30 minutes. The suspects, it appears, either never entered through the broken window, or exited prior to our arrival. I clear the call and get home about half an hour late.

Saturday, April 20

3:05 p.m.—Attempted Suicide

The dispatch call of a suicidal teenage male armed with a knife greets the afternoon shift officers as we check into service. Despite the volume of calls holding, four officers respond due to the threat of violence. When we arrive we find the young man engaged in an argument with several family members. He is not threatening suicide we are now told. Relatives also tell us he did not have a knife. The mention of a weapon, however, produced the desired results—quick police response. We clear the scene after about 15 minutes as the family assures us everything is under control. I do not expect to, nor do I receive, an apology from the family for the inaccurate information they gave regarding the call.

3:48 p.m.—Disorderly Juveniles

A report of several juveniles bullying another near a playground basketball court provides little by the way of excitement as everyone has left the park prior to police arrival.

3:57 p.m.—Suspicious Situation

We arrive to find two men from a furniture rental company standing in front of a well-known dope house. A tall man in his twenties appears to be the one in charge. He explains this is his third trip to the residence in as many days. Every time he has come out to repossess some furniture items, no one answers the door. Now, he adds, there is a foul smell coming from inside the house. He thinks someone is dead inside.

It's sunny and about sixty degrees. The front door is standing partially open and there is an awful smell rolling down the front steps. My back-up officer enters the home first and we move room to room. The stench is strong, but it's not as thick as the smell of a dead body. There is a large big screen television standing in the living room, surrounded by trash and an assortment of car stereo parts. The electricity and water have been shut off. In the kitchen I can't resist the temptation to open the refrigerator door. A small amount of food sits rotting inside. The refrigerator, I find, is a partial origin of the house's foul odor. Inside the deep door pockets sit several steaks and packages of chicken, rotting in an inch-deep puddle of blood, which has seeped from the clear plastic wrappings. I close the door quickly enough not to see the maggots, which assuredly have taken up residence. In the front of the house, I find a closet full of dog feces off the main bedroom. I leave the building after about five minutes, but the odors are now clinging to my uniform. We inform the caller there is no dead body, although a decaying body may have smelled more pleasant than what we did encounter.

4:27 p.m.—Family Trouble

A boyfriend-girlfriend trouble turns out to be nothing more than a verbal argument. The woman insists we are not needed and says she'll call if she wants assistance. She is not the least bit grateful and speaks to the two other officers and myself with annoying indifference.

5:25 p.m.—Juvenile Assault

The victim—a young teenager, who is obviously no angel - says another kid shot him with a pellet gun. The father of the victim says he does not want to file charges, but asks if we will go to the suspect's house and talk with him.

When we arrive at the suspect's home, there are no adults and about a half-dozen kids hanging around. They're all younger than 15, but they try to act much older, mouthing off as we talk to the suspect, who is equally as indignant. He yells, saying he didn't do anything, which gets his friends going even more. Seconds later, his mother pulls into the driveway. He starts to tell her the cops-are hassling-me story. She tells him to shut up. She's had previous problems with him. Mom sends her son's friends home and apologizes. After explaining why we're there, mom says she'll handle the problem. Her son is crying as we leave.

9:40 p.m.—Unknown Trouble

I arrive at the house a few minutes after the primary officer and medical personnel. There is a teenage girl lying motionless on the floor. Her grandparents are there and they say she likes to fake being hurt to get attention. When a fire rescue worker puts smelling salts underneath her nose, she pulls away and opens her eyes. She closes them again and pretends to fall back down, but she is just playing games. Ambulance personnel advise us the girl is okay and they don't need the police. The grandparents thank us for coming and apologize for being a bother.

10:00 p.m.—Shooting

A reported shooting sends six police cars, an ambulance and a fire rescue truck scrambling to a residential neighborhood, where we find the call to be nothing more than a hoax.

Wednesday, April 24

The day starts with news of two more shootings the previous night, continuing a rash of recent violence in the city.

3:15 p.m.—Breaking and Entering Alarm

The alarm turns out to be accidentally set off by the homeowner.

3:20 p.m.—Family Trouble

A man and woman, each about twenty years old, are arguing in the front yard when I arrive with a back-up officer. It's a typical fight. She wants him to move out, but he won't go. She is mad at the police for not making him leave. The tattered house they are fighting over is not worth the argument. A fence in the yard is falling down. Fast food wrappers and paper blow in the breeze among spent shotgun shells, which litter the dirt patches in front of the venue.

The woman says she will get family members to make him leave. She says this with a smile.

"See what she's like," he says, directing his attention toward me. "Man, the last time we broke up I got shot."

Eventually he decides to leave, but he says he'll be back later for his belongings.

5:10 p.m.—Drug Activity

Several younger men are supposed to be near the rear of a school selling drugs. I arrive to find nothing more than a half dozen teens playing basketball. They are not selling drugs. I ask if I can get into the game. The thought of a 5'10" white-boy cop shooting hoops with them draws a loud round of laughter.

6:42 p.m.—Disorderly Adults

The subjects who had been bothering the caller are gone before I arrive.

7:10 p.m.—Disorderly Juveniles

Several juveniles are walking down the street shooting a pellet gun in the neighborhood. When we arrive, the caller says they left in a car Eastbound. I check the area, but I'm unable to find the subjects.

7:18 p.m.—Shots Fired

A call for a neighborhood fight escalates into shots fired prior to police arrival. Several more officers respond when the call is upgraded. I am the fourth car at scene and there are about 20 people outside—adults and children - yelling at each other. After about 15 minutes of people screaming and carrying on, the street clears. As it turns out, the call originated because of two people arguing and escalated when their friends got involved. The report of shots fired was erroneously given to attract the police quickly.

8:00 p.m.—Drug Activity

The venue is a corner bordering the city and an adjacent township. There are several juveniles hanging out on the township side of the corner, but I don't bother with them. Technically, they are outside the city's jurisdiction. It is also too busy to get tied up shaking down these kids for drugs.

8:05 p.m.—Disorderly Juveniles

The kids who were reportedly were throwing rocks at passing cars are gone. Apparently no vehicles were struck as no victims have come forward to complain of damage.

8:10 p.m.—Family Trouble

I am disregarded off this call to handle another closer to my location.

8:13 p.m.—Neighbor Trouble

A dispute between neighborhood kids leads to a 15-minute counseling session by myself and the area officer. No report is needed. Everyone eventually goes separate ways and the problem is solved as easily as it could have been had anyone there showed some common sense and maturity.

9:50 p.m.—Panic Alarm

A residential panic alarm turns out to be false.

Friday, April 26

3:02 p.m.—Family Trouble

The woman who called looks tired and far too weathered for her years. She wants her boyfriend out of the house. She says she cannot take him being there anymore. She has seven kids to look after and having her boyfriend living with her is only complicating things. We tell her we can't make him leave. Fortunately, however, the boyfriend also has had his fill. He asks that we stand by as he packs his things.

Standing near the back door as the man packs a car, so many children walk in and out of the house I can't keep track of them. Behind me two semi-friendly, but not very clean, dogs roam a back yard nearly void of grass. In the driveway, a patio furniture set sits atop an eight-foot-by-eight-foot square of carpeting, still wet from the previous night's rain. We leave the house after about 30 minutes, which is 30 minutes too long. The depression surrounding this house sticks with me long after I leave.

4:35 p.m.—Parking Complaint

The vehicle in question has been moved prior to my arrival.

4:55 p.m.—Follow-up Investigation

Prior to the start of my shift, there were two drive-by shootings, one of them involved a man shooting at the van of an acquaintance. Hours later, the van's owner calls and tells Central Dispatch he found one of the bullets from the shooting stuck in a rear seat of his van. He thinks we might need this as evidence.

When I arrive, he casually hands me the slug. I survey the area where he said he found it and get his name. At police headquarters, I tag the bullet into the evidence room and write a supplemental report to the original case from earlier in the day.

5:55 p.m.—Larceny in Progress

There are several abandoned houses on the block where I am dispatched for an anonymous complaint of a man stripping aluminum siding off a vacant structure. At the house, I find the man puling siding off the back of the garage. I recognize him from the neighborhood. He is partially crippled and has burned skin covering much of his body. He says the house's owner gave him permission to remove the siding. We are unable to confirm this information because we cannot determine the identity of the homeowner. I don't believe the man's story, but I don't take him to jail because we can't find a victim.

The house itself, like many others on this block, stands with doors wide open to the world, inviting a glimpse into what used to be somebody's home. At one time, someone used to walk in the front door of this house into the living room - now strewn with trash, broken glass and empty booze bottles—and relax after a day's work. Someone used to worry about making the mortgage payment on this house. But that was many years ago, during distant and better days.

6:05 p.m.—Shots Fired

A report of shots fired in a neighborhood South of a local hospital leads to a three-car sweep of the area. Nothing unusual is located.

6:50 p.m.—Suspicious Vehicle

An anonymous caller tips off the police to a vehicle, which has been shot up and is now parked in a parking lot about six blocks from police headquarters. We locate the vehicle—a less-than-a-year-old SUV—and it is riddled with broken glass and bullet holes. The vehicle matches the description of one involved in a shooting earlier in the day. There is no blood inside and nothing of interest. I leave the scene and resume patrol as several other officers are dealing with this call.

7:35 p.m.—Family Trouble

The woman who called said she is at a neighbor's house, waiting for the police. She says her husband is at home and he threatened to hurt her so she fled. I arrive next door at the same time as another officer. We talk to the woman and then go next door to talk with her husband. Both are a bit on the strange side, to say the least. Both eventually admit that there were no actual threats made. At her request, we stand by with the woman while she packs some clothing to leave for the night. The entire call takes just under an hour.

9:10 p.m.—Malicious Destruction of Property

The young man I speak to lives with his son in an upstairs apartment in what used to be a very large single-family dwelling. Both the father and son are well mannered and courteous as the man tells of someone throwing a rock through his front window earlier in the night. He needs a police report for his landlord's insurance claim. After gathering his information, I turn to leave. It has already been a long day and writing this report will take me until near the end of my shift.

"Excuse me. Excuse me. Excuse me," says the man's five-year-old son. "I like to give cops hugs." With that the boy walks over and gives me a brief hug and tells me he wants to be a cop someday. We talk for a minute or two. I leave the apartment feeling better than when I entered.

Saturday, April 27

3:17 p.m.—Family Trouble

The female caller is a grandmother and she's confined to a wheelchair. She made the mistake of allowing her grandson to live with her a short time ago. Now her adult grandson has turned disrespectful and she thinks he's into drugs as well. Her grandson has left for the day, but she wants to know if she can put his things outside and lock him out. We talk for a short time about her options and what she should and should not do. She has incredible spunk for a woman in her physical condition. Somehow, I think she'll be able to handle the problem.

3:45 p.m.—Traffic Stop

I pull onto a busy road from a parking lot and immediately a car about 100 feet ahead of me changes into the slow lane and allows me to pass, even though the driver was not exceeding the speed limit. A check of the vehicle shows the male owner has several outstanding warrants for his arrest. The physical description of the owner appears very close to that of the driver. After several blocks, I pull the vehicle over and advise Central Dispatch the driver may have warrants for his arrest.

The driver of the vehicle has a baseball hat pulled down low. When I ask for a license and registration, I am surprised to find the driver is a female with her hair tucked under her cap. Obviously, she is not the man I am looking for. I inform the woman why I stopped her. She says the car belongs to her brother and he has been out of state for some time. We have a brief laugh over the circumstances and she is on her way within a few minutes.

3:50 p.m.—Family Trouble

A man in his twenties answers the door when I arrive with a back-up officer. He says everything is fine and the police are no longer needed. His girlfriend, sitting inside the dingy, one-bedroom apartment, holding a small child in her arms, confirms all is well. We leave with assurances they will work out their dispute calmly.

4:17 p.m.—Civil Dispute

Standing in front of one of several dozen duplexes lining the streets South of one of the city's auto plants, I listen to both sides of what turns out to be a civil dispute. Two residents say they called a locksmith to make a key for their car because their key broke. They say they paid in advance, but the key didn't work so they demanded their money back.

Turning to the locksmith, he gives the same story, except, he says, he informed the couple when he makes keys for cars, they don't always work. He says the couple agreed to pay up front for the service call. When they keys didn't work, they threatened him and he returned their money because he was scared. We inform the locksmith how to file a civil court complaint against the customers.

Now a relative of the couple chimes in. He is about fifty years old and has been listening to the conversation. He is black. The couple is black. The locksmith, the other police officer and myself are white. The man, who has not made a comment nor asked a question, turns his attention toward me.

"I'm going to call a detective," he says, naming a black officer who used to be a detective at our police department.

"No, I'm going to call a judge," he continues, naming a black Saginaw County District Court Judge. He pulls out his cellular telephone and looks at me as if I'm going to try to stop him. I ignore the man as he dials a number.

As the other officer at the scene finishes telling the locksmith how to file his civil complaint, I hear the previous man talking on his cellular telephone.

"We got some kind of white thing going on here," he says to someone on the other end of the line. "It's a white situation."

It is the kind of racially divisive situation that I have become accustomed to while working in Saginaw, a town where skin color seem to always be an issue, even when it is not an issue. I tune the man out and leave the scene disgusted.

5:01 p.m.—Breaking and Entering Alarm

The house checks out okay and the call is quickly cleared.

5:25 p.m.—Disorderly Adults

Checking the venue, I find the complainant. He says he and his son had an argument and his son left walking toward downtown. He asks me to find his son and have a talk with him. I locate the son about three blocks away and he says he is okay. He says whenever he and his dad argue over something he goes for a walk to cool off. I can't dispute his logic and I clear the call after a few minutes.

6:05 p.m.—Motorist Assist

Near the top of one of seven bridges, which span the Saginaw River a young girl waves me down. She is in her teens and she's nearly in tears. Looking at her car, I can see why. She hit the curb about 50 feet back and blew out both right-side tires. She says the car is her father's and she is in big trouble. We try to call family to come and help her, but no one is home. Finally, she agrees to have a tow truck come for the car. The service call and storage fees at the wrecker company will cost about $75. That doesn't include the cost of replacing two nearly new tires. It is assuredly not her day.

6:45 p.m.—Family Trouble

The woman who called wants her adult son out of the house. She's also very drunk. Her son stands in the doorway of his bedroom, staring at me. I tell the woman I cannot put her son out in the street because he is a resident of the home. He smiles and returns to his room. I explain to the woman she'll have to formally evict her son from the residence, but she's too drunk to listen. I leave having accomplished nothing.

7:05 p.m.—Breaking and Entering in Progress

The caller reporting this B&E in progress failed to tell us the venue is a vacant house. I hustle through traffic to find no one inside an abandoned house where there is nothing to steal.

9:15 p.m.—Family Trouble

This family trouble amounts to nothing more than name-calling between a sister, brother and father.
"Man she drinks all the time. She smokes dope," says a heavy-set, Hispanic man in his thirties, with an obvious dislike for the police. He is speaking of his

sister, who called the police on behalf of her father. The man turns his attention toward his father: "Grow some nuts. You don't have to call the police," he says.

The sister and her father leave after a few more unpleasant verbal exchanges. Neither wishes to press the brother any further. I can see why.

Monday, April 29

3:17 p.m.—Disorderly Adult

A disorderly adult complaint turns into an assault report, which keeps me tied up for over an hour.

4:24 p.m.—Breaking and Entering

The venue is an abandoned house, blocks from Potter Street, a former hotbed of saloons, fights and prostitution during Saginaw's lumbering heyday. The area used to be home to numerous bars and businesses, which surrounded the Potter Street Railway Station, a magnificent, sprawling brick structure, which now endures a slow and agonizing death, crumbling to the ground just a bit slower than the now-dead neighborhood it calls home. The vacant house to which I am sent is still vacant when I arrive. I check the house with another officer, but there is nobody inside.

5:00 p.m.—Disorderly Adult

The suspect is gone when I arrive, but the caller asks me to make a threats report for her. She says the suspect, who is her brother, threatened to kill her because he wants the rims from her car.

7:00 p.m.—Fight

The combatants are gone when I arrive. The call lasts less than five minutes.

7:10 p.m.—Disorderly Adults

Several problem youths at a local party store have departed before the police arrive. This is my last call of the day and I leave for the night anticipating a week long vacation, which starts tomorrow.

Thursday, May 9

I returned today from a week away from work, part of which I spent in Niagara Falls, Ontario, admiring the awesome power of nature. Some say there is no greater fury than the falls at Niagara. On this day, however, I will again bear witness to the fury of man, which can be even more brutal and unpredictable than anything offered by nature.

3:55 p.m.—Runaway

I have been to this house before for similar problems. Entering the kitchen I find a mother and daughter. Both are obese. Both yell at each other. Neither has much interest in anything I have to say. The mother says her daughter ran away from home and has just returned. She wants me to lock up her daughter. I explain I cannot do that, but I give her the number of two juvenile officers to call for guidance.

"Don't think 'cause this police be standin' here I'm not going to punch you in your mouth," the mother says, responding to another verbal onslaught from her daughter. After calming the two, I leave them alone to deal with their problems.

4:58 p.m.—Shooting

My attention turns toward the radio when I hear a Central Dispatch "alert tone," which is used proceeding a high-priority call to ensure all officers are listening. I had been at the front desk completing paperwork and I break into a jog toward my patrol car as Central Dispatch reports a shooting.

Within seconds I am driving southbound on East Genesee Avenue, lights and siren alerting traffic to my approach. The route to the venue is a five-lane major artery on the city's Eastside. At least three times I am forced into the turn lane by vehicles refusing to let me pass. At one point, a confused driver heading in the opposite direction, rather than pulling over to the right, cuts into the turn lane, nearly hitting me head-on. We miss each other by about 10 feet. By the grace of God, I arrive safely at the scene within about three minutes.

A Michigan State Police trooper has arrived first, about five seconds ahead of me. The scene is a block-long dead-end street with rows of single-story houses. The trooper immediately locates a victim lying face-up on the front walk of a modest-looking house with a well-manicured front lawn. The man is dead. He lies motionless with eyes wide open facing a deep blue spring sky, which he can no longer see. He appears to have a single gunshot wound to the head. A pool of fresh blood still leaks from underneath his head. Darker, jelly-like chunks of matter—possibly pieces of the man's brain—swim in the pool of blood.

I begin to rope off the block with crime scene tape as several more police cars arrive. The next 15 minutes or so is the usual confusion of a violent crime scene. Officers scour the neighborhood looking for witnesses while trying to keep bystanders out of the scene. I assist checking an abandoned home next to where the dead man was found to make sure no gunmen lurk inside. The house is empty. The suspect is long gone, but would later be located. After about half an hour, there is nothing left to do except stand around and keep the crime scene secure from onlookers.

Within an hour, I count at least 85 people standing at or near the edge of the crime scene tape. Most are milling about, talking on cellular telephones. A few people, who appear to be relatives of the victim, run up to the tape crying, only to be grabbed by other relatives and friends and escorted away to talk on the other side of the street. A while later, I notice people are bringing their children to the scene.

About a dozen kids sit on the curb just beyond the yellow tape. Several more people pull up and double-park their cars to walk up and have a look. Some break into greeting and hug each other the way one would at a family reunion.

A short while later, I hear the music from an approaching ice cream truck, which stops in an attempt to take advantage of the crowd. The scene is surreal. I spend the remainder of my shift here and eventually the crowd thins to about 25 people. The Michigan State Police crime lab team arrives a couple hours after the original call. A cold chill whips through the neighborhood, nearly blowing the yellow body cover off the victim, who still lies where he took his last breath on this Earth. As evidence technicians begin to photograph the scene, I realize I am getting hungry. With that thought it dawns on me, sadly enough, how little the death of a stranger affects me anymore. Checking the time, I notice the date display on my watch - it is May 9th. Eight years ago today, I arrived in Saginaw to become a police officer.

Saturday, May 11

3:12 p.m.—Breaking and Entering in Progress

When I arrive with another officer, we find nothing more than a few kids hanging out on the porch of the venue, which an abandoned home. For some reason, they run and we locate them a block away, hiding near a dirt pile. Neighbors quickly alert the kids' mother that we are talking to them and she arrives within two minutes. She scolds the children for being at the abandoned house, which she has warned them to steer clear of. She thanks us and says she'll take care of the matter.

3:40 p.m.—Suspicious Person

As I drive past a downtown officer building, I see a thin girl in her twenties walking up near the back employee entrance of the building. It's Saturday and the business is closed so I pull into the parking lot to question her.

She gives me a startled look when I park near the stairway where she is standing. She tries her best to act casual, hoping I'll go away. When I ask why she is there her response is not what I expect.

"I'm just checkin' the ashtray out here for cigarette butts," she says. "One lady that works here always leaves some good butts; only smokes half of 'em."

I recognize her now as a prostitute. A computer check shows she has an outstanding traffic warrant. I place her under arrest. She also has a crack pipe in her pocket. On the way to jail she begins to cry. Tomorrow is mother's day, she says. She's supposed to have a cookout with her children. I don't respond. I feel no sympathy toward the woman. I do, however, feel sorry for her children.

4:45 p.m.—Armed Robbery

When I contact the victim, who says he was robbed at gunpoint, the report seems legitimate. He says a man pulled a gun on him and robbed him of $25 as he walked through a parking lot. As I take down a description of the suspect, the man tells me the incident occurred more than five hours ago. When I ask why he is just now reporting the crime, he gives me several reasons why he couldn't get to a telephone. Within an hour I resume street patrol after filing another report of a crime which will never be solved.

5:28 p.m.—Breaking and Entering Alarm

The venue is an older two-story residence. We clear the call after about five minutes, determining it to be a false alarm.

7:20 p.m.—Breaking and Entering Alarm

Returning to the same house where I was dispatched nearly two hours ago, we again find the residence is secure.

7:54 p.m.—Family Trouble

A woman standing on the front porch of her home tells me her 13-year-old son is being disrespectful. The boy is standing five feet from his mother with a devilish smirk on his face.

"I can't be puttin' up with this," she says. "And I can't whip on him or you will take me to jail."

I tell the woman she can discipline her son as she sees fit, even if that means physically disciplining him. I advise her not to use weapons, and to keep it reasonable. Her son sneers at me, not liking the answer I provide. I advise the woman to call us back if she needs further assistance.

9:00 p.m.—Desk Duty

I am assigned to desk duty for the last two hours of my shift, which prove to be uneventful.

Sunday, May 12

3:10 p.m.—Breaking and Entering Alarm

The alarm location is a school on the city's North side. Central Dispatch advises me day shift officers already have responded to two false alarms there today. A third false alarm now awaits us as we eventually find the building secure.

3:20 p.m.—Family Trouble

No assault has occurred, but the man and woman continue to argue after I arrive with another officer. The woman is doing most of the talking. She says he drinks too much. She says he cheats on her. The man denies both accusations. I tell them this is none of my business as long as they are not going to harm each other.

"You wanna be my husband - that means no drinking!" the woman scolds. "That means no adultery! I pay the bills! I pay $100 a month for you to go to the casino! That's it!"

The man hangs his head, looking at the floor. They've got bigger problems than we can solve and we leave as the woman continues to lay the ground rules for their relationship, which I am sure is doomed by this point. I am glad to return to the relative quiet of my patrol car.

4:20 p.m.—Motorist Assist

A tow truck has already pulled on scene prior to my arrival and I resume patrol duties.

4:50 p.m.—Breaking and Entering Alarm

I arrive simultaneously with another officer. A check of the residence finds the property secure.

5:18 p.m.—Breaking and Entering Alarm

A woman at the home tells me she set the alarm off accidentally when she came in. I verify that she belongs at the home and depart within minutes.

6:10 p.m.—Disorderly Persons

Several people are reportedly hanging around an abandoned house. The caller thinks they are up to no good. I never find out, however, as they are gone when I arrive.

6:49 p.m.—Family Trouble

The suspect and victim were arguing over a set of keys. The male suspect has left, a woman tells me. She does not need the police anymore.

7:15 p.m.—Officers Need Assistance

Officers investigating a family trouble call for assistance at a West-side residence. I am the fifth car to arrive at scene. By the time I get there, two large men are handcuffed and sitting on the curb. Both have been pepper-sprayed during a fight with officers. Other family members stand on a porch, yelling at us as a small crowd gathers. I later learn that one of the original officers at scene was assaulted with a garbage can while trying to arrest one of the men. The situation is under control within about 10 minutes and I return to my patrol district.

7:30 p.m.—Disorderly Juveniles

A woman says several neighborhood youths have been throwing rocks at her house. The kids have a problem with her children, she says. When I ask her children what the problem is, I get the usual I-have-no-idea response.

"My kids don't do nothin'," the woman says impatiently. The answer is so common it almost appears scripted. Responding to literally dozens of problems like this every year, I nearly always find nobody's kids are at fault in the eyes of their parents.

No report is requested and I depart the scene having made little progress in solving the neighborhood dispute.

8:40 p.m.—Check the Well Being of Children Left Alone

An anonymous caller says several kids have been left alone at a house. The first responding officer finds at least two adults at the home. The kids appear fine and properly supervised. The officer is preparing to clear the call as I pull on scene.

9:44 p.m.—Family Trouble

I make it half way across town, but get disregarded when a district car clears to take the call.

Monday, May 13

3:10 p.m.—Family Trouble

Arriving at the home, I find a man crying in the driveway. He was having an argument with his father, but they got everything worked out. He apologizes for calling and says he does not need police help now.

3:23 p.m.—Breaking and Entering Alarm

Construction crews at a local art museum set off the alarm during renovations to the building. The call takes less than 10 minutes to clear.

3:45 p.m.—Family Trouble

A passing motorist calls to report a man beating on the front door of a home. The caller thinks there is a family trouble in progress. I arrive to find a boy in his early teens on the porch. He says everything is fine. He calls for his father to verify this. The father, a man in his forties, with sunken cheeks and a grizzled beard, comes to the door and says everything is fine and I am not needed.

4:08 p.m.—Family Trouble

The woman who called tells Central Dispatch her adult daughter is visiting her house. She says her daughter's boyfriend stopped over also and he is arguing with the daughter.

All three people are at the house when I arrive with another officer. The caller is in her fifties. She has the raspy voice of a life-long smoker. She launches into a detailed account of every fault of her daughter's boyfriend. I finally interrupt her.

"What do you want me to do for you?" I ask. "Do you want him off your property? I can do that for you."

"No, I just want him to treat my daughter better," she replies.

"I can't do much about that," I answer.

"Well ask my daughter what she wants done," the woman says. She walks over to her daughter, who is mowing the lawn. She motions for her daughter to turn off the mower. She tells her daughter I want to talk to her.

"What!" the daughter screams, her tone punctuating her annoyance at being bothered.

"Your mother said you wanted to talk to me. Do you need me here?" I ask.

"No," she says, turning the lawnmower back on.

Walking back to my patrol car, mom again approaches. "Listen, East," she says, using the name she read on my uniform. "I just want this guy to quit being so insecure. I mean, can you imagine a guy his age, being so insecure he has to check up on my daughter all the time?"

"That's your daughter's problem," I tell her. "I'm not the relationship police. I've got work to do now. Goodbye."

4:30 p.m.—Family Trouble

The woman who called said someone was trying to kick in her front door. She called from a pay telephone down the street, but she is going to return to the house to meet us.

When I arrive with another officer, we find the front door has been beaten with a hammer and also kicked in. The dead bolt lock has been re-engaged, but the door is not very secure. The woman arrives a minute after us and says she thinks it was her boyfriend kicking in the door. She says he assaulted her earlier in the day and now he forced his way into her house.

We get through the front with little trouble and find her boyfriend passed out drunk on the couch. When we finally get him to wake up, he can barely stand. He offers a few slurred words, which I cannot understand. After investigating her story, the man is arrested for domestic assault. The woman says he drinks all the time and he gets violent. Today is his birthday, she says, so this was bound to happen. She says she is tired of him beating on her. She also says he's done it several times, but she never follows through with prosecution. We take the man to jail. Before we leave the woman says she will not prosecute this time either.

6:10 p.m.—Suspicious Person

An anonymous caller says a man in a long brown coat has been living in an abandoned house in the neighborhood. The man is there now and he has supposedly been stealing things from people in the area.

When I walk up to the two-story vacant house, I can see the man through a broken front window. He spots me at the same time and says something to another man in the house. When I get inside, I order both men up against the wall. They comply and say they are just there drinking. My back-up officer arrives about a minute later. I have held off searching the men until the other officer arrived, choosing to stand about 20 feet from the men, gun drawn, but at my side. This is preferable to checking them by myself and risking a two-on-one fight.

We search both men and find no weapons. I locate a crack pipe just inside the bathroom, from which one of the men had emerged when I arrived. Both men are then handcuffed. A computer check shows one has an outstanding warrant. I am still trying to find where the other hid his crack cocaine. The man with the warrant says his friend had a rock of crack and the pipe when he went into the bathroom. I conduct an unpleasant search of the abandoned, filthy bathroom, but find no crack cocaine.

Before taking the man with the warrant to jail, I issue a citation to the other man for possession of drug paraphernalia. The charge may not hold up in court, but I know the crack pipe belonged to him and he's not getting away clean. I would have preferred finding his rock of crack cocaine and charging him with a felony. Today, however, a misdemeanor citation will have to suffice.

Saturday, May 18

The day starts on a bad note when I have to spend half an hour trying to get my patrol car started. The battery is dead and needs a charge. I finally get the vehicle going, but this day will only get worse.

3:42 p.m.—Dog Fight

A report of several men fighting pit bull dogs leads me to a downtrodden neighborhood near a local hospital. When I arrive there is nobody outside and no sign of a dog fight.

3:49 p.m.—Child Neglect

Workers from a child welfare agency ask for police assistance with a possible child removal. I arrive at the venue to find two case workers and another police officer at the door of the home, talking to the female homeowner. The conversation is not going well. The workers were at the home previously and have returned to follow up on the condition of the residence. The woman is yelling at them now, but eventually she lets us enter.

Once inside the home, it is obvious a removal will be necessary. The interior of the home is a mess. Trash is strewn about both bedrooms and there is no place to walk freely in either room. Plaster is falling off the walls and ceiling. The bathroom door, warped and splintered from a leaky ceiling, rests against the door opening as there are no hinges to hold it in place. Inside the bathroom, there is no sink—only pipes protruding from the wall. There is nearly no food in the house. When questioned about the condition of the home, the woman starts yelling again.

"Ya'll don't do nothing for me! You don't pay my rent! You don't pay my bills! All you do it pay my kids' medicaid!" she screams.

Her demeanor stays this way for the next half an hour until we leave. When we depart, we take her two children with us, having made arrangements for alternative care for them until a hearing the following day. We tell both children they will see their mother tomorrow. Neither seems to mind as we pull away from the home. They appear happy to leave.

6:15 p.m.—Disorderly Juveniles

A group of kids about 12 years old run around the street near a freeway off ramp. When I pull up and tell them to get out of the busy street, they comply and apologize. Their parents are no more than 75 feet away, sitting on the front porch of a rundown home. Only after I drive up do they start yelling for the children to get out of the roadway.

6:46 p.m.—Drug Activity

Several adults smoking drugs in a van are gone by the time I arrive to check out the dispatch call.

7:22 p.m.—Stolen Vehicle

An adult caller says he saw his stolen vehicle driving through an Eastside neighborhood. We are unable to locate the vehicle, however, after checking the surrounding area.

8:30 p.m.—Family Trouble

The house where we are dispatched is small, but clean. It is decorated with a country theme that seems to work well, giving the place a warm, intimate feel. Outside, standing on the front porch, a man in his early twenties says his father has assaulted him during yet another family argument. Within seconds the father walks outside and starts yelling. He is drunk and smells of a full day of boozing. He readily admits assaulting his son.

"Go ahead and put the handcuffs on me," he says. "If I gotta go to jail, I will." Seconds later, he gets his wish. The man is friendly enough and we talk as I help him into the patrol car. The home is only three blocks from where I lived just a few years ago. I tell him that my wife and I used to take our son trick-or-treating at his house on Halloween. He offers a sheepish smile.

At the jail, the man causes no problems in the booking area as a jail guard leads him to a cell. Inside the cell, a 20-year-old thug glares out through the glass. He has telltale gang tattoos all over his arms. He is not friendly. Undeterred, my prisoner walks into the cell and greets the gang-banger in a cheery voice: "Hey, how are ya!" The younger man gives him an annoyed stare. The look on the hoodlum's face immediately brightens my day.

Sunday, May 19

3:40 p.m.—Breaking and Entering Alarm

The alarm at city hall is the result of an employee not setting the system properly.

4:00 p.m.—Disorderly Adult

A woman at the home relates a story of her mentally ill son, who has a violent temper. He had just been at her house, pounding on the front door and making threats. He left before we arrived, but she asks if we can keep an eye on her house during the shift. We tell her we'll try to do this, knowing we probably won't be able to.

4:25 p.m.—Disorderly Juveniles

Several kids making threats to the caller's son have departed the area prior to my arrival. I check the neighborhood for the kids, but I am unable to find them.

5:20 p.m.—Suspicious Person

While on patrol, I see an older man standing next to a building, which used to house a downtown department store. There are about two dozen trees lining the side of the building. The man is cutting the branches off the trees with a small hand-held saw.

When I question the man, he says he has read about these trees. He says they need to have their lower branches cut off or they will cease to grow. He is obviously mentally ill, but he is friendly enough. When I tell him these are not his trees to cut, he agrees he should ask permission of the owner before cutting the trees. He says he will go to city hall tomorrow and find out who owns the trees. Fair enough, I tell him as we part ways.

8:52 p.m.—Man with Gun

A caller reporting a man with a gun in the street gives a distinct description of the gunman. Several cars join me in the area checking for the man, but he has vanished. We return to the waiting list of calls for service after not locating the man.

9:05 p.m.—Disorderly Adult

The disorderly person is gone before we arrive and the call is cleared quickly.

10:07 p.m.—Disorderly Adult

While en route to this call, I am diverted to assist officers about a mile away. They are chasing a mentally ill man through a South-end neighborhood. The man needs to be taken into custody as family members say he has become violent today. He also likes to fight with the police. Upon locating the man, it takes four officers to get him handcuffed after a brief fight. I am the fifth officer on scene, having arrived seconds after the altercation ended. My shift is over by the time I clear this call.

Michael S. East

Monday, May 20

3:40 p.m.—Fight

The first call of the day is a report of two women fighting in the street. The caller states the women both have children in strollers with them. As much as I would like to know why two women walking their children would break into a fistfight, I am relieved to find the two have departed before another officer and I arrive.

3:58 p.m.—Breaking and Entering Alarm

The call turns out to be a false alarm. The first officer on scene disregards me from the call.

4:00 p.m.—Drug Overdose

Two young children playing in the front yard greet me when I arrive. I am the third officer on scene. Inside the house, ambulance personnel are treating the victim - a male in his thirties - who apparently overdosed on heroin and prescription drugs.

Several adult relatives are also inside the house. They say they think the victim uses heroin, but they cannot be sure. The needle supposedly used by the victim comes up missing in the confusion following our arrival. Medical personnel want the needle and syringe to be sure what the man injected. No one will say where the items have gone, even when it becomes clear this may help the recovery of their family member. I leave, following the ambulance to the hospital, so I can monitor the victim's condition. About twenty minutes later, another officer from the scene arrives at the hospital. He says they found the needle syringe, after a family member eventually admitted hiding the items to protect the overdose victim from possible prosecution. There's nothing quite like family unity.

6:09 p.m.—911 Hang-up Call

A woman holding a small child tells us everything is okay and no one called 911. She appears nervous. When I insist on checking the house, she finally admits she dialed 911 after an argument with her boyfriend, who, she says, has since left. Still, I check the house. The man is gone and the caller apologizes. I tell her to call back if the man returns and causes problems.

6:50 p.m.—Disorderly Juveniles

A passing motorist says several kids are shooting a pellet gun at cars as they drive through the neighborhood. Checking the area, there are dozens of people milling about, but none match the descriptions given.

A block away, I see several men in their early twenties standing in a front yard, sipping beer from bottles wrapped in brown paper bags. They give a hard stare when I pull up and ask about the kids I'm looking for.

Three of the men continue their hateful stares. The fourth, a stocky guy with well-groomed facial hair, answers: "Man, you know I ain't gonna tell you nothin'."

"Yup. But you know I gotta ask," I respond in an annoyingly cheery voice. "It's my job."

The man lets out a quick laugh. The other three just smirk, as they look around to see who might be watching the conversation.

I leave without finding the pellet gun culprits. This unusually slow May evening ends quietly.

Thursday, May 23

3:20 p.m.—Guard Prisoner

At a local hospital sits a man in his thirties. He was arrested several days ago and on his way to jail, he began complaining of chest pains and other assorted problems. Because the jail would not accept him without medical approval, the prisoner was taken to this hospital. He has now sat for days, telling doctors he feels terrible, all the while ordering as much food as he can get his hands on. The wasted taxpayer dollars don't stop there, however. Because he is under arrest for a felony, our police department has to provide around-the-clock guards, cutting into much needed road patrol manpower. Today, it's my turn to baby sit.

When I arrive at his room, the man is sleeping. He is well over six feet tall and later tells me he weighs 300 pounds. He is also not handcuffed.

"I took the handcuffs off him," says the day shift officer I am sent to relieve. "He's an okay guy."

Looking at the officer in disbelief, I can only shake my head. A 300-pound man, possibly faking illness to avoid felony charges, sitting without handcuffs with a single guard on site. The scenario has all the makings of a disaster.

"Hey, we're putting the handcuffs back on," I tell the man when I walk into the room. He wakes up and looks at the handcuff dangling from his bed rail. He places the open handcuff on his wrist and clicks it locked without hesitation before closing his eyes to go back to sleep. I check to make sure the handcuff lock has engaged properly.

About 30 minutes later, a food service worker brings in a large plate of food. It's the prisoner's second meal in less than two hours. A short time after that, a nurse arrives to take his blood pressure. Moments later, a doctor comes in and tells the man he's being released.

"But I still don't feel good," he tells the doctor, a tray of empty food plates providing an appropriate backdrop for the conversation.

"There's nothing wrong with you," the doctor replies. "You're being released."

I call for a second officer to assist transporting the man to jail. Within half an hour, the man is in jail where he should have been days ago.

4:45 p.m.—Suspicious Person

The woman who called says a man with a tow truck came to her house to repossess her son's motorcycle. Payments are past due. She says she wants to be sure he's not trying to steal the motorcycle. After verifying the repo man's identity, I tell the woman he is legitimate. She surrenders the motorcycle to him without further problem.

5:57 p.m.—Neighbor Trouble

Several adults are arguing outside by the time I arrive. They are neighbors and the argument seems to stem from one neighbor's kids bouncing a ball outside and striking the other neighbor's car. They are all screaming and new complaints arise every minute. From improper lawn care, to people living together out of wedlock, all the dirty laundry is getting aired today. One neighbor, an older man in his seventies, yells until his face is a fiery red. He looks like he'll have a heart attack any second. After 15 minutes of yelling, both sides go back to their houses. The problem, I am sure, will arise again another day.

6:15 p.m.—Officer Needs Assistance

After pulling a traffic stop on the city's Eastside, an officer calls for assistance. The driver of the suspect vehicle jumped out and ran. The foot chase has gone for about three blocks by the time I arrive. By this point the suspect has run into an apartment and closed the door. I arrive as the two officers kick in the door. The man who lives in the apartment says the suspect ran into a bedroom. Entering the bedroom, there are two closed closet doors. We open the first one and before we can check it thoroughly, the second door pops open.

"Here I go," says a man in his late teens, walking out of the closet with his hands in the air. He is quickly taken to the ground and handcuffed. The man living in the apartment thanks us. He says the suspect just ran in the front door and asked to hide from the police. When the resident protested, the suspect hid in a closet anyway, says the apartment's owner, as he thanks us again for removing his unwanted guest.

8: 58 p.m.—Fight

A caller says there are several people fighting in the street. When I arrive, the street is empty, but a man walks down the road, waving me down. He says the girl who got beat up went into an upper apartment in a house on the corner.

At the house the man directed me toward, a girl in her late teens comes down to talk to me. She is wearing pants, which ride low and snug around her hips, and a tight tank top with no bra. She could be an attractive girl, but that potential ends when she speaks.

She has several scrapes and scratches, but says she doesn't need my assistance. "Naw, I'm all right. It was instigated by both parties," she says. "I'll take care of it.

I don't need no police." I leave her to handle her own problems, the magnitude of which she doesn't even realize.

9:10 p.m.—Disorderly Juveniles

After checking a neighborhood for several minutes, I finally locate three teenagers matching the description given by a caller. They had been throwing rocks at windows of a nearby business. No windows were broken. The three say they don't know why they were throwing the rocks; they just were. They are free to go after about 10 minutes of lecture, which is all I can muster at this point of the day.

Saturday, May 25

3:35 p.m.—Breaking and Entering Alarm

The alarm is false and is cleared within about five minutes.

6:05 p.m.—Family Trouble

The man and woman we encounter in a small apartment have lived there together for some time. They are in the middle of a break up and have been arguing. By the time we arrive, the man has decided to leave to alleviate the problem. He is packing some things. While he packs, the two of them exchange verbal barbs and give each other a hearty "fuck you" about every 30 seconds. After about 10 minutes the man leaves and we are, thankfully, no longer needed.

10:05 p.m.—Drug Activity

A slow day ends with me checking a usual drug corner for the usual drug dealers with the usual results. They are gone.

Sunday, May 26

3:22 p.m.—Breaking and Entering Alarm

The venue is a new truck dealership, which we seem to respond to a half dozen times every week for false alarms. Today's alarm produces the same results.

3:31 p.m.—Loud Music

Like the previous call, this complaint also turns up nothing as I find the neighborhood to be quiet.

4:03 p.m.—Family Trouble

An anonymous report of a family trouble leads me to an older two-story brick house. There are a lot of people out in the neighborhood. I arrive with another officer to find several women in their twenties, outside washing a sport utility vehicle. I explain to the female resident why we were sent.

"Naw, boo, nothin' like that goin' on here," she says, smiling. "You might want to check the next street. We heard some yelling over there."

We never do locate the family trouble. However, after asking around later in the day, I learn that "boo" is a street term for "baby" and the woman I had spoken to probably meant it as a compliment. At least today I learned something new.

4:17 p.m.—Shoplifter in Custody

At an East-side grocery store, employees have in custody a shoplifter they caught stealing fruit juice. I have been to the store dozens of times for similar complaints. It is one of precious few grocery stores serving this poor area of Saginaw. It's not as clean as a grocery store one would find in the suburbs, showing all of its years in cracked walls and peeling paint. I imagine the food probably isn't the highest quality either. Sales of alcohol and tobacco seem strong, however.

In the store's office, I speak to the suspect, an eight-year-old who is surprisingly respectful. I give him a brief lecture, adding to the one he received by a store manager. Management has decided not to prosecute and I load the youth and his bicycle into my patrol vehicle for the six-block ride home. At his house, I find his grandmother. I explain what happened and have her sign a custody form for the child. Several neighborhood kids have already gathered near my police car and they are laughing at the boy—not because he stole, but because he got caught. Grandma then takes the boy inside for what will probably be an unpleasant finish to his day.

5:20 p.m.—Breaking and Entering in Progress

A neighbor calls and says two men are breaking into a house down the street. I arrive to find the two men moving a refrigerator on the front porch. They have recently moved to Saginaw from Georgia and are moving into the house. They amused by the reported burglary and, after I confirm their story, they go back to moving.

5:36 p.m.—Fight

The fight call leads us to a decent-looking house in what is usually a quiet neighborhood. There is an outdoor party in the backyard. One man walks to the front yard. He is bloody and he is drunk. A second man follows the first down the driveway, taunting him. He is also drunk. They each relate how the fight started and they say they've settled their differences. Neither wants to file a complaint. After a few minutes they are hugging each other and talking about what great buddies they are. Shortly thereafter they stagger off to the back yard together for more drinks.

5:56 p.m.—Disorderly Juveniles

The call screen on my in-car computer says the woman complainant is reporting juveniles next door to her house breaking bottles in the street. The screen also says she will be waiting for the police on the front porch, where she is talking to the birds and her cat, "Sylvester." The screen further states the caller is possibly mentally ill.

At the house, I find the caller. She is a woman in her forties and she is definitely not all there. She explains the problem as half-chewed food falls from her mouth. "I don't know why these kids would do this," she says, not relating the exact problem. "I don't know if they're jealous of me or what."

There is no broken glass in the street and no sign of a problem. I promise her I will keep my eyes open for the disorderly kids.

6:08 p.m.—Breaking and Entering Alarm

After a 10-minute check of an Eastside school, we determine the alarm to be false.

6:30 p.m.—Breaking and Entering Alarm

Investigating another school alarm, we find it also to be false.

6:55 p.m.—Disorderly Juveniles

Several teens driving a dark-colored vehicle drove past, peppering the caller's house with paintballs. She knows the suspects, but only by their street names. She does not know where they live. I can do nothing more for the woman than file a report, as the suspects were long gone before I arrived.

9:59 p.m.—Fight with Weapons

Several people flee the street corner when they see my patrol vehicle approaching from two blocks away. Those who remained at the scene say there was a fight, but there were no weapons involved. Nobody still here was involved and nobody wants to be involved. I am preparing to clear the scene as back up arrives.

Monday, May 27

3:25 p.m.—Auto Accident

The two drivers are waiting patiently when I arrive. One is a man in his late thirties. The other is a teenager. Both say the teen caused the crash when he rear-ended the other car. After gathering all the information for an accident report, I issue a citation to the teen. His father, who owns the vehicle the teen was driving, has also come to the scene. I explain the citation to him as well. He thanks me and then directs a stern look at his son.

"What's wrong with your pants?" the man exclaims as he points to his son's baggy jeans.

The teen had been wearing his pants drooping halfway down his buttocks, exposing his underwear, which is stylish for his age group. He yanks his pants up without debate and the two walk over to again examine the vehicle damage. I leave the father and son as they debate the benefits of safe driving.

5:48 p.m.—Domestic Assault

The venue is a house where we respond often. The only thing the mother and father do more than drink is fight. Their children usually call the police when things get too rough. Today is no different.

After about 10 minutes of talking to everyone at the house, I arrest the man for domestic violence. He is well over six feet tall and he's drunk, but he puts up no fight when I handcuff him. As we pull away from the house to head to jail, he begins yelling.

"Fuck you, bitch. Let's ride," he says. "Talk about fuck me. Fuck you. Fuck you in your ass, you stinkin' ass motherfuckin' ho."

It's only a three-minute trip to the county jail. My backseat passenger makes it feel like an hour.

"Fuck you, you blue-eyed, white-ass motherfucker," he continues. "You peckerwood motherfucker. Fuck you."

Too drunk to think of anything original, the man repeats the previous tirade over and over. Once inside the jail, a county jail security officer checks the man again for weapons. When he asks me to take the handcuffs off the prisoner, the man exclaims: "Naw, I don't want that blue-eyed, white-ass motherfucker touchin' me. Let the Mexican do it," he continues, referring to a Hispanic intake officer standing nearby.

The man gives me a couple final "Fuck yous" before I leave the jail to complete the report.

7:40 p.m.—Assist Officers

Two officers at a traffic accident request a Preliminary Breath Tester (PBT) at their location. When I arrive with the PBT, they point out the driver, whom they believe is intoxicated. The man is friendly and offers no resistance to taking a PBT. He gives a half-ass breath of air when requested, trying to circumvent the effectiveness of the PBT. Before I can tell him again the proper way to give a breath, I see that won't be necessary. The display screen is rising rapidly, stopping above .40, which is four times the amount of presumed intoxication in Michigan. The investigating officers arrest the man. I clear after writing a supplemental report to their case.

8:40 p.m.—Fight

The fight is over by the time I arrive. Other officers, however, will be sent back two more times before the end of the shift to quell flare-ups in this neighborhood dispute.

9:20 p.m.—Family Trouble

For the past half an hour, there have been 15 calls for service holding and I have been the only car clear, unable to answer them without backup. When a second officer finally becomes available, we respond to a family trouble.

The building where we are sent is old. Some might call it historic. We walk the flights of stairs to the fourth floor because the elevator is too "historic" to ride safely. After listening for several minutes outside the apartment door, there appears to be no problem inside. We knock and find a young woman and man inside. Both say they had been arguing, but they are okay now and they don't need the police.

9:55 p.m.—Family Trouble

Another family trouble complaint leads us to another apartment where another man and woman say they don't need the police. Assured that no assault has occurred, we clear the scene for a shooting, which Central Dispatch has just been broadcast.

10:10 p.m.—Shooting

After a lights-and-siren drive across town, I arrive with four other officers to find a crowd of about seventy people in the street. Eventually we determine there was no shooting. The caller says she tried to get police response earlier because of all the people partying in the street. When the police didn't respond, she decided to call in a false shooting instead. I leave the scene to other officers and drive to headquarters to end my shift.

Thursday, May 30

3:35 p.m.—Mental Pick-up

Three mental health workers meet another officer and myself at police headquarters. They have a judge's order to pick up a supposedly mentally impaired man at a house a block away. They would like a police escort in case there are problems.

The venue is a three-story brick house, which has been sub-divided into apartments. It was reportedly once a mansion, housing one of Saginaw's many high-profile lumbering families of the 1800s. It has been reduced now to shelter for the poor and mentally ill. Inside the front door, I am nearly overcome by the smell of cat urine. It is quite humid and the staircase to the second floor is suffocating. Thankfully, we do not find the man at home, which expedites our departure.

5:08 p.m.—911 Hang-up Call

The call came from an assisted care facility for the elderly. A half dozen women in wheelchairs greet us just inside the front lobby. They are all in good spirits and happy to have visitors. After speaking to a nurse we determine which telephone the call came from. The elderly woman responsible has no recollection of calling 911, but she gives us a smile and says she's sorry.

Sunday, June 2

3:35 p.m.—Family Trouble

After a mild spring, temperatures in mid-Michigan have finally risen to normal seasonal levels. It's sunny and above eighty degrees when I pull up in front of a small, but well-maintained house on a corner lot. Several people are outside in the yard. None of them look happy.

A young pregnant girl approaches first and says her boyfriend, who is sitting in a car parked at the house, was arguing with her. He is the father of her child, she says, but she doesn't want to see him anymore. She keeps telling him to leave, but he will not. She says he did not assault her, but her lack of eye contact tells me otherwise.

When I speak with her boyfriend, he ignores me. He is dressed in baggy pants and has his baseball hat cocked to one side. His fake gold chains say a lot about him. I ask him a second time what happened and he tries to walk away to his girlfriend. When I take him by the arm and place him up against his car to talk, he finally looks me in the eye and says indignantly that nothing happened. Seconds later the backup officer at the scene says he has talked to witnesses who say the boyfriend tried to push the pregnant girl down some stairs prior to our arrival. The man is arrested for domestic assault and begins crying as soon as he gets into the patrol car.

During further conversation with the girl, she tries to protect her boyfriend, but then says he did indeed try to push her down some stairs. She says he has been violent with her in the past and she wants to leave him. I give her the names of a couple of agencies specializing in domestic violence and tell her to contact them for help. I know she will not. I cannot help but think her unborn child has a bleak future.

4:53 p.m.—Fight

The area where I am dispatched is currently one of the busiest drug selling corners in the city, bordering on neighboring Buena Vista Township. The fight is over by the time we arrive and another officer has located the victim, who says his family lives at a house on the corner, but they are in the process of moving because of all the drug activity and shooting that goes on night and day.

Today the victim came back to move some items from the home and found several young men tearing out the speakers from a car he had parked and had for sale in a side yard. The victim argued with the men briefly before the men fled the area. He says they had his speakers ripped out of the car and he cannot understand why because they are cheap factory installed speakers. There is obviously more to the story.

The other officer at scene knows immediately what the men were doing. They had been hiding crack cocaine inside the speaker wells and retrieving it when they needed it for a sale. It's much safer than holding it and running the risk of getting caught with the drugs. We check the inside of the car and find a large rock of crack cocaine near an empty speaker cut-out, which had presumably been dropped by the men before they fled. The victim is livid when he sees this. I tell him to be happy he's moving.

5: 20 p.m.—Breaking and Entering

A passerby reports he saw several youths running from a local soup kitchen. The building is closed at this time of day and he thinks the kids may have broken in.

I arrive with a patrol sergeant and we check the building, which appears secure. The place isn't much to look at, but I am sure it used to be. The single-story brick structure boasts a nice half-circle walkway on one corner, leading up to a large set of concrete steps, which pave a path to several large doors. Standing like aged sentinels along the front walk are two lampposts - their glass long-since shattered - and a 15-foot-high flag pole. The pole is rusted and stands slightly warped. It hasn't seen a flag in at least the better part of a decade.

The building itself appears to have once been a school or an administration building. Now it is where people come for a free meal and some second-hand clothes. It is a perfect example of all the splendor Saginaw once was and decaying waste it has become. On this day no one has broke into the building. They wouldn't find much of worth if they had.

5:47 p.m.—Family Trouble

Everyone at the scene advises there is not a problem. We clear the call in less than five minutes.

6:17 p.m.—Loud Music

Checking a call for a noise ordinance violation, I am not surprised to find all is quiet. The call has been holding for four hours.

6:25 p.m.—Injury Accident

I am the third officer to arrive at the scene of a child struck by a car. The child is okay, having suffered only a few scrapes. There are about 75 people at the site of the accident, watching the goings on. Many of them are children of about six years of age, the parents of which are nowhere to be found. Viewing this, I am surprised more of these children are not struck by cars due to lack of supervision.

6:45 p.m.—Family Trouble

We encounter a young couple in a small apartment in what used to be a large single-family house. They have both been drinking. They say they had been arguing, but they've settled their problems. Neither wishes for police involvement and we leave the scene without incident, wondering why they called in the first place.

9:22 p.m.—Fight

The house where I am sent for a fight is in the heart of a very rough Eastside neighborhood. When I arrive with a backup officer, the fight is still going on inside. We try to make entry, but several people are tussling in front of the front door. I call for more officers to assist as we finally make entry to find about 10 teenage girls fighting.

The physical confrontation quickly ends when we gain entry and take outside a girl who appears to be one of the main combatants. Back inside the house, I am bombarded with a half dozen different people trying to tell me their versions of the altercation. I pick the calmest girl to tell me what happened. Everyone agrees with what she said and the solution appears to be to get the girl outside to pack her belongings and leave the house. The girl outside agrees to this and we stand by to make sure another fight does not break out while she is packing.

Five officers are at the house now. As I fill them in about the call, one girl standing in the corner of the room catches my eye. She's trying to blend into the background, but that's hard for her to do—she's the only white person for blocks who is not wearing a uniform. When I question her she tells me she is 15 years old. She tells me the name of the town she is from. It is about 40 miles from Saginaw. She searches for lies to answer the questions I continue to ask. Eventually, I get her real name and find she has been a runaway for about five weeks and she is a ward of the state.

After things calm down at the venue, I take the runaway back to police headquarters so we can arrange for her to be transported to a juvenile facility. We talk a little during the ride. She tells me she ran away because her mother doesn't like what she does with her life.

"What do you do with your life?" I ask.

"I wanna do what I want. I wanna go where I want. I wanna hang with who I want and not go to school," she answers, defiantly.

I end the conversation, knowing I don't have enough time, energy or enthusiasm to change her perspective. She will continue on her course until she realizes it's the wrong path. The way she talks, I feel that realization will come much too late.

Monday, June 3

3:05 p.m.—Juvenile with a Gun

An off-duty officer who was passing an elementary school reports he saw a young teen loading a revolver near the school. By the time he was able to turn around and check, the juvenile was gone. Several officers arrive in the area within minutes and begin looking for armed youth. Despite a distinct clothing description and our quick arrival, the teen is never located.

3:50 p.m.—Assist Gang Task Force

Two members of the Saginaw County Gang Task Force (GTF) call for a marked patrol vehicle in the Northeast part of the city. When I arrive, they have two males sitting on the ground in handcuffs. The GTF members say they were going to a house on the corner looking for a warrant suspect, when these two started verbally harassing the officers. Upon checking the two, they found one to be carrying a gun and the other in possession of crack cocaine. Both were immediately arrested.

I place the adult male into my patrol car and the lip service starts immediately. A second patrol car arrives at my request to transport the other male—a juvenile—to police headquarters. After completing the necessary paperwork, I transport my prisoner to the county jail on a charge of cocaine possession.

"Fuck you. Ya'll motherfuckers don't do nothin' for me," he screams repeatedly as we drive to the jail. "I know ya'll think this is funny. You think I am just another stupid black kid! Well, I gotta get paid!"

He calms somewhat during the ride and I finally talk to him. He has already cried a couple of times between his cussing outbursts. Despite being a drug-selling street thug, I know he can be reached.

"Yup, I think you're a stupid kid, but not because you're black; because you're out here doing this shit," I tell him. "I quit taking this stuff personally a long time ago. I don't hate you. I hate what you do. You know why? Because you can do better than this. You're not stupid, but you're being stupid."

His eyes start to well up with tears.

"What I would really like to see is you come back to me in 10 years and show me you're making twice as much cash as me. Legitimate cash," I continue. "That, I would like. This might seem like the way to go, but you're gonna be in jail or a dead motherfucker within five years. There's a thousand other shitheads like you on these streets doing the same thing. The hard part is to find a way out and not take the easy way."

The rest of the trip is quiet. When we get to the jail, we do not talk. I see this as a sign that we made a connection, however weak it may be. I hope it was enough to get him to at least think about changing his life. Chances are it was not.

Tuesday, June 4

3:05 p.m.—Traffic Accident

Everyone at the accident scene is in good spirits when I arrive. This is surprising, considering they have been waiting for police response for nearly an hour, their smashed vehicles blocking a busy intersection. One driver immediately admits responsibility for causing the accident. It takes another hour or so to write the report and get the vehicles cleared from the intersection. Both drivers part on good terms, with a handshake and a smile.

4:18 p.m.—Assist Mental Health Personnel

Several days ago, mental health workers moved a client from his apartment due to poor living conditions. When they moved him, however, they left behind his cat. The client is apparently quite attached to this animal. They are going to back get the cat today and, since the apartment is not in the best of neighborhoods, they have asked for police assistance.

I remember the apartment well, having been here last week looking for the client. The common hallway of the building reeks of cat urine. It is hot and humid today, which only compounds the stench, making the building's interior that much more suffocating.

We reach the apartment we're looking for on the building's second floor. It is small, dirty and poorly ventilated. One of the mental health workers spots the cat hiding underneath a bed. She tries to coax it out, but the cat makes it clear he does not want to leave, hissing and growling menacingly. When I kneel down to get a look under the bed, the workers warn to watch out for cockroaches. This instantly brings me to my feet. I see several roaches are crawling near my boots. Having to stay mobile to keep the roaches at bay, we resort to prodding the cat with broom handles and any other available objects. After about 15 minutes, we back the cat into a pet carrier. The other officer and I leave with the cat to get some fresh air. The two mental health workers follow a short time later with a few other items their client had left behind. The entire call takes about half an hour. The smell of the apartment stays with me much longer.

5:25 p.m.—Breaking and Entering Alarm

The building, a former tire store converted into a storage facility of some sort, is found to be secure. I doubt there is much of value inside to steal.

6:16 p.m.—Family Trouble

When I pull up to a dirty blue house on a two-block-long street, I recognize it immediately. It's a rental unit. I've been here several times in past years, but there always seem to be different people living here. They are different in name and appearance only, however, as they all share the common bond of poverty and hopelessness.

Several kids about 10 years old appear from the back yard. "Here she go, back here," one says, directing me to the rear of the house.

When I reach the back yard, a 14-year-old girl starts yelling to me that her boyfriend is arguing with her. She is holding an infant. Her boyfriend, a skinny 15-year-old boy, is standing near the back door wearing a cocky grin.

"Who is he to you?" I ask.

"That's my baby daddy," she responds before breaking into a screaming fit about the boy.

Seconds later the boy's mother emerges from the house and says her son and the girl have been arguing and the girl began tearing up the house during the argument. The woman, who lives at the home, says the girl has to leave. The younger girl is still holding the woman's grandchild. She says she lives around the corner and she agrees to leave as soon as she gets the baby's belongings from the house.

I stand outside while the woman gathers the belongings for the younger girl. Several children, ranging from about five to 15 years old, play in the back yard. One girl in her teens has been staring at me.

"What's you're name?" she asks in an indignant tone.

"It's right here on my name badge if you need it," I answer.

"I can't read. What is it?" she responds. I don't bother to answer.

The 14-year-old mother has emerged from the house now and she's putting the baby in a stroller as she yells now at a couple of the kids in the back yard.

A boy about 10 years old responds to the girl's yelling. "You better shut up, bitch, or I'll bust you in your mouth," he says. His words catch me off guard and I cannot hide my disgust for what I've witnessed in the past 20 minutes. The girl leaves with her baby. The despair of the scene lingers with me for hours.

7:05 p.m.—Assault

I respond with another officer to an assault report, which is usually a single-officer call. The primary officer has asked for backup, however, because of the neighborhood where he is sent. Gunfire and street-corner drug sales are common here and the sight of one officer alone might be too inviting for the local thugs to pass up.

Our response is uneventful. While the first officer gathers information for the report, I keep an eye on the neighborhood. Seven or eight young children gather around, pointing to items on my utility belt, asking the purpose of each. Several of the kids are eating cheese puffs from a bag and they leave orange fingerprints on my uniform. Their friendliness is refreshing. They haven't been taught to hate the police yet. Sadly, most of these kids will not be so friendly toward cops within 10 years. Innocence fades quickly on streets like this one.

7:20 p.m.—Family Trouble

The suspect is gone when I arrive. I take a domestic assault complaint from the caller, who says her boyfriend kicked her in the shin during a fight.

9:38 p.m.—Disorderly Juvenile

The first responding officer handles the call. The disorderly person turns out to be a disoriented older man, who was reported missing earlier in the day.

10:00 p.m.—Dog Fight

I see no evidence of fighting dogs while checking a neighborhood on the city's far North side.

Wednesday, June 5

3:25 p.m.—Warrant Arrest

While assisting another officer at a family trouble complaint, we learn one of the men at the scene has a warrant for his arrest, issued by another department miles from Saginaw. We take the man into custody. After sending several messages to the department that issued the warrant, we get no response. Twenty minutes later we set the man free as the other police department has failed to confirm the validity of the warrant.

4:06 p.m.—Stolen Vehicle

The man I meet at a gas station on the city's Eastside is tall and thin. His face shows the wear of years of drug abuse. He is from a small town about 30 miles from Saginaw. He relates a story of leaving for Saginaw yesterday, running out of gas, having no money, finding money for gas, stopping to use a restroom and then getting his car stolen by an unknown person. His story makes no sense and I know he traded his car for crack cocaine. He insists, however, the lies are true. He has probably told similar lies so often he might even believe them himself. Several days later, one of the police department's auto theft detectives tells me he located the car. As expected the guy found driving the stolen car said the vehicle had been obtained through a trade for crack cocaine.

5:29 p.m.—Disorderly Adult

A woman in her sixties or seventies calls to report a disorderly adult in her apartment. We arrive to find the man has departed. The elderly woman says the subject who left used to be her man. Now he just stays over sometimes. She says she'll call us if he comes back and bothers her again.

5:51 p.m.—Sexual Assault

The two girls I encounter are juveniles in their mid-teens. One girl has called for the police. She says she and the other girl were walking down the street when two males approached them and started grabbing their buttocks. The men went into a house down the block and told the girls they would kill them if the girls called the police. The second girl will not confirm the story. She wants nothing to do with the police.

A few minutes later I take both girls down the street to drop one off at her aunt's house. When I explain the nature of the call, the aunt yells at her niece for calling the police for such a trivial matter.

Two other officers arrive and they talk to the suspects. I stay in my patrol car, talking to the girl who made the complaint. She lives a couple miles from this neighborhood, but she says she comes here often to visit her friend. I can tell she gets into trouble often. She says she has been locked up in the juvenile center before for drinking alcohol and also for being in a stolen car. She relates these facts in a disinterested tone of voice.

A short time later the other officers return with the suspects' information and their version of what happened, which is a totally different story than that told by the girl in my car. The neighborhood is buzzing now. About 20 people are walking around, watching what is happening. Several complain openly about the police being on their block.

When I take the victim home to turn her over to her parents, her mother is livid. Before the two break into a full-scale argument, I ask the mother to sign a juvenile custody form, which she does. The house smells of body odor and urine. I advise the mother how to follow up on the case. Getting into my patrol car, I look back to see a boy about 10 years old leaning out of an upstairs window of the home. There is no screen and his elbows drape over the windowsill. He pays no attention to me. He is staring far off into the distance. I presume him to be imagining a better place.

8:00 p.m.—Larceny

Before I arrive at scene, the primary officer advises I can disregard the call.

8:59 p.m.—Fight

The report is for a fight in the middle of the street. I find nothing when I arrive.

9:16 p.m.—Assist Officer

Arriving to assist another officer with a traffic stop, I find he already has one suspect in custody for driving on a suspended license. Due to the strong dislike for the police in this neighborhood, I stand by while the officer completes his investigation and impounds the suspect's van. We endure a lengthy wait for a tow truck to arrive. My night ends with this call.

Sunday, June 9

3:20 p.m.—Stolen Bicycle

The caller has waited more than an hour for police response regarding his stolen bicycle. Not surprisingly, he is gone by the time I arrive.

3:30 p.m.—Assist Citizen

The man who called is moving out of an apartment he shares with his girlfriend. He has asked for two officers to accompany him to get his belongings so there is not a confrontation when he leaves. When I arrive, I remember being at the same apartment a few months ago. The man and woman share the apartment and they have a young child. This apartment also used to be a well-known haven for drug sales. Neither the man nor the woman answers the door when we knock. We clear the call without contacting anyone. Just as well, I think.

3:42 p.m.—Open Fire Hydrant

Following a summer ritual, I am dispatched to an open fire hydrant where kids are playing in the powerful water spray, which is quickly filling the intersection as well. From about two blocks away, I hit the siren in my patrol car and gun the gas pedal for a couple of seconds, quickly getting the attention of the 10 or so children playing near the gushing hydrant. They look with big eyes and run scrambling through back yards to get away. I do not chase them.

The fire department has already been dispatched to shut off the hydrant. For several years they have asked for police assistance when performing this task as some folks have been known to get violent when the fire department arrives to shut down their summer fun, resulting in assaults, thrown bottles and rocks and some mini-riots. Most of the time the presence of the police helps alleviate the problem. Today, the kids who ran return about five minutes later, creeping closer and closer to the hydrant while keeping an eye on me as well. When they realize I'm not going to chase them, they play in the hydrant for a couple more minutes while two adults also walk down to the corner to supervise. When the fire department finally arrives, the kids leave without protest.

5:22 p.m.—Fireworks Complaint

The woman who called says kids on the next block are shooting fireworks at her house, using some kind of homemade cannon. She points out the problem house and I go to talk to a large group of kids sitting on the porch of a rickety house on the next block. Some of the kids are black. Some are white. They appear to range in age from five years old to about 13. They all share the common bond of poverty.

When I ask about the problem, some say they know nothing about it. A couple kids, however, point me toward the weapon, lying in some tall grass behind the house. It is the hollow leg of a swing set, cut down to about three feet in length. There are a couple of holes drilled into the pipe and it smells like gunpowder. Carrying the mini-bazooka to my patrol car, I encounter a parent on the front porch. The woman is overweight, dirty and missing several teeth. When I ask about the fireworks, she gives the response I expect.

"It ain't none of mines doin' it," she says. She also says there are some kids from down the block causing the problem. They ran off, she continues, unable to tell me where they live or what they look like. She is in mid sentence when I walk away, not willing to waste any more time on the woman's lies.

5:40 p.m.—Man Down

The man I find lying near a fence looks familiar. He is trying to stand by propping himself up on the fence. He is too drunk to do this. On the ground his shirt and socks and comb litter the yard of someone he does not know. An ambulance arrives to take the man to a hospital to dry out. It's not his first time through this process. While he sleeps off a bad drunk, I spend more than an hour on paperwork for the report I must write.

8:15 p.m.—Domestic Assault

We are dispatched to a small, but nicely decorated and well-kept house, for a disorderly juvenile. His mother is the caller and she says the juvenile assaulted her last night. We are now at the home of the juvenile's grand parents. The woman says the police were looking for her son last night to arrest him, but he ran away and today ended up at his grand parents' home.

Inside the house, the grandfather addresses me. He speaks firmly, but courteously. He tells me he is retired and he is too old to be caught in the middle of these family problems. He says his grandson is too much for him to handle and the grandson cannot stay at this house. The grandfather is in good physical shape, but his eyes show the fatigue of his many years of work. I guess to myself he has retired from an auto plant.

The grandson enters the living room when called. His posture says he thinks he is tough, but his voice tells me that's an act. He is respectfully evasive when he talks, as if he doesn't yet know who he is—street thug or honor-roll student. Via radio, I ask a sergeant to review the previous night's assault report and advise if the teen can be arrested. Moments later I arrest the juvenile without resistance as ordered by the patrol sergeant. I lodge him at a juvenile detention facility until his trial, which will be the following day.

The boy's mother seems grateful he is being arrested. She says he has been drinking, doing drugs and becoming violent. She is looking for any way to get him back on the right path. The grandfather gives me a firm handshake and a sincere "thank you." He is still tough enough to keep his grandson in line if he has to, but not for long. His grandson grows bigger, stronger, and probably meaner, by the month. Soon grandpa will have no control, just like the boy's mother. I can see this in the older man's eyes. It doesn't sit well with him.

Tuesday, June 11

3:06 p.m.—Disorderly Adult

Security officers from a local hospital call for assistance with a disorderly person. The venue is a community center built by the hospital for use by area residents. The facility provides free computers and laundry facilities, among other amenities. Today, a man has become angry when staff asked him to not use all four washers at once because other people needed them as well. He has made threats to kill staff members and the security staff.

When I arrive with another officer, we find the man packing his clean laundry into an army duffel bag. He is a jerk from our first words and tries to start an altercation. He appears to be mentally ill. We decide to let him pack up and leave. He is given a trespass warning and continues his verbal tirade as he leaves.

3:45 p.m.—Disorderly Person

A disorderly adult begging for money outside a local convenience store is gone when I arrive.

4:00 p.m.—Disorderly Juveniles

Similar to the previous call, the disorderly juveniles have departed prior to our arrival.

5:00 p.m.—Breaking and Entering Report

The call involves another instance of someone breaking into a dumpy house where there is nothing of real value to steal. The report ties me up for more than an hour.

7:25 p.m.—Man with Gun

The man in question was shooting a pellet gun, not a real gun as reported by the caller. He agrees not to shoot it anymore, as there is a city ordinance prohibiting discharging pellet guns within city limits. He has caused no damage to property and I release him with a verbal warning.

7:32 p.m.—Fight

The fight is over and everyone is gone before my arrival.

7:52 p.m.—Family Trouble

A younger woman greets me at the front door. "Sorry, you guys are too late. I don't need you now," she says, indicating the problem is over. She says this like I will be disappointed because I missed out on a confrontation. Nothing could be further from the truth.

8:58 p.m.—Armed Robbery

A report of an armed robbery of a fast food restaurant turns out to be false. Approaching the building, it appears to be business as usual. When I enter the business, my handgun drawn but held down near my thigh, no one takes notice. I ask for the manager, who comes out to the lobby. He smells of chicken grease. He is annoyed when I try to confirm there was no attempt to rob the business.

9:10 p.m.—Disorderly Juveniles

Like more than half of my calls today, the problem has worked itself out before I arrive. With not nearly enough officers on the street, today offers a perfect example of how hard it is hard to perform effective policing without proper staffing.

9:20 p.m.—Juvenile Assault

Speaking to the mother of a teenage girl who was just assaulted, it is clear the mother does not really care. She spends more time yelling at the girl than she spends talking to me. I wrote a report of the same girl being sexually assaulted about two weeks ago. The only thing more bleak than the girl's current surroundings is her future. This call ends my day.

Wednesday, June 12

3:03 p.m.—Fight

The caller reports a fight and says someone is using a board to assault another person on the city's West side. When we arrive there are dozens of people - mostly teenagers - out and about in the neighborhood. The arrival of the police is greeted with mass indifference. No one gives us a second look. The people we ask about the fight say nothing is going on without even making eye contact. We clear the call without finding a victim.

3:20 p.m.—Family Trouble

I can hear the screaming from my car when I pull up in front of the small, three-bedroom home. When I reach the front door, a woman comes out demanding I make her husband leave. She is a large woman and her voice carries throughout the neighborhood.

I enter the home with another officer who has just arrived. In the kitchen is the husband, a man of equal physical stature to that of his wife. He is angry also, but controls his voice and speaks in a reasonable manner. They both agree no assault has taken place and they are engaged only in a verbal argument. She again demands that I make her husband leave.

"How am I supposed to relax, living up in here with a crackhead!?" she exclaims. "Bringing me sexually transmitted diseases; what kinda man is that?"

"Awe, that was years ago. And I ain't no crackhead," he refutes, as their not-yet-ten-year-old son slinks into the kitchen and sheepishly taps his father on the arm.

"Can I have some pizza?" the boy asks. His father opens a cardboard pizza box sitting on the kitchen table and motions the boy forward. The child, now smiling, takes some pizza and retreats to a bedroom, away from the noise.

Unable to convince either person to leave, we have no choice but to depart, leaving the two of them together. We ask both to stay clear of each other and call back if things get out of hand.

4:02 p.m.—Disorderly Juveniles

I am dispatched to an anonymous call for kids skateboarding on the steps of city hall. They are gone when I arrive.

4:25 p.m.—Abandoned Vehicle

I take half an hour writing a report and tagging as abandoned yet another of the army of discarded cars littering the streets of Saginaw. This car apparently has been sitting in the street for three weeks and someone in the neighborhood finally got tired of looking at it. Having been tagged for removal, it will be towed away after a mandatory 48-hour waiting period.

5:26 p.m.—Loud Music

I find no loud music when checking the address given by an anonymous caller.

6:15 p.m.—Auto Accident

I arrive to find a younger male standing in the street in front of his wrecked car. He says his girlfriend had been driving, but she decided not to wait around. He is nervous and cannot make eye contact. I know he was really the driver of the car. Eventually, he admits this. He has no license and he didn't want to get a ticket. He isn't able to maintain his lie very long, deciding honesty is his best course of action. Because of this I do not take him to jail for providing false information. He gets a traffic citation, which he will have to answer within two weeks. The other driver, who was actually at fault, receives two citations. No one leaves happy.

8:58 p.m.—Panic Alarm

While investigating a residential panic alarm, I find the cause was only children playing with the alarm keypad. The adult homeowner says she'll take care of the problem. From the tone of her voice, I think one of the kids will have trouble sitting down tonight.

10:05 p.m.—Loud Music

Once again, the music has been turned down by the time I am able to check the complaint.

Sunday, June 16

Summer has arrived in full force and with it comes the annual takeover of tall grass and weeds. It's only mid-June and many city lots are already overrun with grass, which now stands between two and three feet high. Most of the overgrown lots are abandoned and the problem is compounded by the city's lack of financial resources to pay for upkeep of the now vacant parcels. At several street corners, waves of grass block my view of oncoming traffic, forcing me to slowly creep into the intersection to see if it is clear to proceed. At times it seems the only thing more dominating than the thugs and drug dealers in some neighborhoods is the uncut greenery that threatens to swallow up entire city blocks.

3:13 p.m.—911 Hang-up Call

No one answers at the home when we arrive. There does not appear to be any trouble and we clear the call.

3:38 p.m.—Breaking and Entering Alarm

The homeowner advises she set off the alarm by mistake.

4:05 p.m.—Man Down

I arrive at the same time as another officer to find a man lying in the grass about 30 steps from a bar. He is drunk and has been sleeping in the lawn for a while. When we wake him, it is clear he does not like cops. He tells us to leave him alone. When he finally stands, he squares off in a semi-fighting stance with me.

"You're a punk," he says, trying to stare me down, but unable to maintain focus. "Man, if it comes down to it, I got people who will pop a cap in a cop."

He continues a meandering verbal assault, ranging from bragging about the time he's spent in prison to several of his relatives, whom he insists are cops. When ambulance personnel arrive to check him out, he's not much friendlier with them, but at least they've diverted his attention for a while. The day is slightly more than an hour old and already I am ready to call it quits.

4:59 p.m.—Family Trouble

The man we encounter sitting in his driveway is pleasant enough. I can immediately tell this isn't the first time the police have been to his house. His wife is the complainant and he says she's inside the house drunk again. He doesn't bother getting up as he waves us into the house via the side door.

Inside the home we find the man was right. The woman is drunk; very drunk. She babbles on about how she doesn't like her husband and how he has physically abused her in the past. She says he hasn't assaulted her today, but she wants him to leave anyway. She raises her voice when we say we cannot make him leave. She spits as she slurs through several incoherent sentences. We leave after about 10 minutes. There is nothing we can do for her.

5:33 p.m.—Disorderly Children

The call results in a talk with some neighborhood kids and an ordinance violation citation for a 17-year-old, who decided to make threats to a police officer at the scene.

7:45 p.m.—Cutting

The first arriving officer locates the victim at a gas station. He is cut deeply across his chest and arm. He tells the officer the address where the cutting occurred and I respond to that house with another officer right behind me.

The street is a familiar one. It is only a block long and sits in the shadows of an auto plant on the city's East side. There are only about a dozen houses on the street, but the police are called to this block nearly every week. Twenty or so people are standing around in the street and yards near the venue. Most quickly walk away when we pull onto the block. Everyone knows why we're here, but nobody saw a thing. Eventually we determine the suspect has fled the scene. We check for him at another address in neighboring Buena Vista Township, but he is not located. Hopefully, detectives will have better luck locating him.

As we are looking for the suspect, a hostage call goes out on the city's West side. Half of the available city officers respond and are later assisted by the Saginaw County Sheriff Department and the Michigan State Police. This call goes on for hours, tying up valuable manpower and making the night that much busier for the rest of us.

7:10 p.m.—Dog Fight

I check the address given by the caller, but there is no dog fight—only one large pit bull, sleeping in the back yard.

7:25 p.m.—Breaking and Entering Alarm

The alarm is at a small church. It goes off at least once a week. The church appears secure when I check the perimeter.

8:00 p.m.—Fight

Several teens are playing in the front yard when we arrive, but there is no fight. Most likely, the call came from a neighbor who didn't like the noise the kids were making.

8:15 p.m. - Breaking and Entering Alarm

Again, we find the premises of this alarm secure.

8:28 p.m. - Disorderly Adult

The disorderly person turns out to be a wife, who has turned up at the duplex home of her husband's new girlfriend. During the next hour of sorting out the problem we are treated to numerous stories of who is cheating on whom and why. There are also two young girls and an infant at the scene. They all get to hear the countless curse words being thrown back and forth. Finally, the man tells his wife to leave. He is staying with his girlfriend. He wants his wife to leave their kids with him, however.

"I don't want them here with that girl he's fucking!" she exclaims.

Everyone then agrees the kids should go with mom. She is in tears as she turns to leave. Her oldest daughter starts crying also.

"Do you want to tell your dad 'Happy Fathers Day' like you've been crying to all day?" she says to her daughter. The girl runs to her father crying and gives him a hug. I wonder how she'll remember this Father's Day when she grows older.

Monday, June 17

3:10 p.m.—Cutting

The caller reports two brothers fighting. One has cut the other. When I arrive, I find the victim, who has no more than a tiny puncture wound on the palm of his hand. His brother has fled the scene, but he says he wants to file charges for the assault. Several witnesses say the caller was actually the aggressor. This information is included in the report, which will be sorted out by detectives if the victim does not drop the case when he calms down.

4:25 p.m.—Fight

All parties are gone when I arrive.

4:48 p.m.—Missing Person

The mother who called said her adult daughter left the night before and hasn't returned home. She says her daughter has been dating a man she does not know very well, but she has heard the man beats her daughter. She does not know where the man lives. After half an hour of checking, I locate the man's address from past case reports involving him. Within an hour, I locate the woman's daughter. She is fine. I tell her to call her mother, who is worried about her. She agrees to call, but she never does. Two hours later, the mother contacts me to inquire about her daughter. I inform her that her daughter is okay and she is with her boyfriend.

Tuesday, June 18

3:10 p.m.—Family Trouble

The call is dispatched 50 minutes after it is received. We are unable to locate anyone at the address to which we are sent.

3:20 p.m.—911 Hang-up Call

Upon investigating the call, we find several children who were playing on the phone have accidentally dialed 911.

3:28 p.m.—Breaking and Entering Alarm

A quick check of the residence and we determine the alarm to be false.

3:35 p.m.—Family Trouble

This call also has been waiting for nearly an hour. By the time we arrive at scene the caller is angrier with our slow response time than she is with family matters. We are told the police are no longer needed.

3:50 p.m.—Fight with Weapons

The dispatcher puts out as call of a man with a knife assaulting a woman as they walk down the street. I arrive in the area with another officer within minutes of the dispatched call. We check several blocks surrounding the area and cannot locate the dispute. Several people we question in the street say they saw no fight.

The day is now less than an hour old and I have responded to five calls. Eleven calls are still waiting to be answered when I check my in-car computer screen. The start of my day has been entirely non-productive. None of my first five calls was actually dispatched within a reasonable time frame from when it was received. I think back to a conversation I recently had with a former Saginaw officer, who left to work for another police department in suburban Detroit just more than a year ago. He had laughed as he talked about working an entire shift without being sent on a call for service. Sometimes I would give anything for a day like that.

4:05 p.m.—Fight with Weapons

Two parties have called from different homes complaining of an assault. One caller says her niece fought with another woman's daughter. As is often the case, it never ends with two kids settling their differences. Eventually, relatives got involved. Then, supposedly, a gun was pulled.

When we arrive at the venue, the female homeowner comes outside to talk. It is eighty degrees and sweat is rolling down my back. The woman, who is wearing an over-sized baseball jersey and pink, fuzzy bunny slippers, is apparently not bothered by the heat. She says she did open her front door with a handgun when several adults came to confront her daughter. She brought it out to protect her family, she says. The gun is registered to her and she did not point it at anyone.

At the house of the other caller, I arrive to find several adult males in the driveway washing a car. They are talking about the incident. About 10 people are in the front yard. I speak to a woman who appears to be in her forties. She agrees the altercation started as a fight between kids and the whole thing is sort of stupid. As we talk, an older man and woman pull into the driveway. They appear to be grandparents. The woman gets out of the car and several people begin to tell her what has happened.

"They want to pull out guns! We can pull out guns!" exclaims the older woman. "Ya'll let me know if you want some guns." With that, she gets back in her car and drives away. She is not exactly the classic picture of a grandmother. The call ends when both families agree to stay clear of each other.

5:01 p.m. - Fight

A neighborhood dispute involving several teenagers results in nothing more than a 10-minute lecture from the police. The lecture will accomplish nothing.

6:06 p.m.—Neighbor Trouble

The woman I encounter is in her fifties and is pleasant to talk with. A young woman has recently moved in behind her and keeps parking her car in the caller's back yard. When I go to speak to the neighbor, she does not answer the door. I tag her car to be impounded if she fails to remove it as she has left it on the caller's property.

6:45 p.m.—Disorderly Adult

The argument revolves around a drug sale gone wrong. Wisely, neither person wants to pursue police involvement.

9:25 p.m.—Suspicious Situation

An anonymous caller says she drove past a local fast food restaurant and the doors were locked. The drive-through window was open, but no one was there. Then she heard yelling inside. She thinks they're being robbed.

I arrive on scene simultaneously with another officer. We take positions on opposite sides of the building. Eventually, we determine everything is okay. The workers have closed up the dining room for the night. The yelling came from the workers playing as they closed up, they say. That's preferable to a robbery, I think to myself.

Wednesday, June 19

3:20 p.m.—911 Hang-up Call

Before I can reach the scene, a plainclothes detective in the area handles the call.

3:30 p.m.—911 Hang-up Call

The call originates from a church. There is no one at the venue when we check and the call is cleared quickly.

3:43 p.m.—Neighbor Trouble

The caller says kids in the neighborhood have been damaging her flowers. She says she has handled the problem with the kids' mother. I'm not sure why she called in the first place, but I'm happy to not be involved in such a trite matter. There are many situations where involving the police only makes things worse. This is one of them.

4:30 p.m.—Breaking and Entering Report

The elderly man I meet at the venue carries the stench of someone who is too old to care about regular bathing. I am glad our conversation takes place outside. He is in his eighties and meanders his way through providing information about a theft from his business. He owns a small brick building and storage yard full of old machinery parts. I would call the place junkyard. It is no longer open. He keeps me there for nearly 25 minutes, talking about the old days and how great things used to be. He follows me to my patrol car and keeps talking right up to the minute I close my car door to leave. The report itself is simple and takes only about 20 minutes to complete. Being patient enough to endure the loneliness and idle chatter of the old man keeps me tied up much longer than I should have been.

6:30 p.m.—Family Trouble

The call involves a typical demand from a mother that the police take her child "somewhere" because she cannot control her daughter anymore. When we inform her we cannot provide surrogate parents, we get the usual "you cops don't do anything" response. We leave the mom to figure out her own solution to her parenting problems.

9:50 p.m.—Disorderly Juveniles

The elderly woman who calls runs a neighborhood candy store of sorts out of the back of her home. Today, she says, a young boy from the next block over tried to start her house on fire. The woman doesn't want the young boy to get into trouble. She would like us to talk to the boy and his mother and tell the boy to stay away from her house.

When we arrive at the young boy's house, there are several kids playing in the front yard. Mom does not even say hello before denying her child's involvement in the incident. She starts blaming several kids down the street. She does not know their names or where they live. The officer handling the call suggests she speak to her son to find out firsthand if he was involved. Tired from the long day and disgusted by the woman's excuse making, I lean against a fence post at the edge of the yard. I notice a teenage boy on the front porch. It doesn't take long for him to start running his mouth.

"Man tell them they ain't supposed to talk to them kids. How you gonna question him? He ain't nothin' but nine years old," the teen says.

When I tell him this is none of his business, his response comes quickly: "I'm on private property. You can't do nothing to me. I'm on private property," he says, as if reading directly from a law book. I decide he's too stupid to argue with and I let him ramble on, without rebuttal, about his rights. After speaking with the juvenile suspect and his mother for about 10 minutes, we leave having not accomplished much of anything.

10:00 p.m.—Suspicious Person

On my way back to the police station to call it a night, I see a woman in her fifties sitting on a bench behind a downtown business. I've dealt with her before. She's a prostitute.

When I pull up to talk to her, she smiles the kind of smile you expect from your grandmother, greeting you at her front door at Thanksgiving. I walk up and ask if she's working.

"Yeah, I'm working, but no one is stopping. Nobody wants to stop for an old lady like me," she says with a laugh. I sit on the bench next to her to look at her identification and check her for warrants.

"I used to do alright out here," she says. "Now, I still get a few regulars from Bay City and Midland, but not many. You got a cigarette?"

She has no warrants. Rather apologetically, I tell her I don't smoke, almost feeling bad that I don't have a half a pack to give her. She laughs and says she didn't think I was a smoker. Two other officers have since stopped to check on me. They are also non-smokers. I tell the woman not to sit too long in one place because we'll start getting complaints. She thanks me and bids us all a good night. I tell her to be careful. Sensing my sincerity, she winks and says "Thanks."

Saturday, June 22

3:25 p.m.—Abandoned Vehicle

Surprisingly, the day starts on a slow note as I'm dispatched to tag an abandoned vehicle for future removal. With no in-progress calls holding when I check into service, I hope for the low call volume to continue.

4:10 p.m.—Neighbor Complaint

The man who calls is in his forties. He says neighbors around the corner have been dumping their garbage in an abandoned home which shares a property line with his home. Among other items, he says dirty diapers and old food are being discarded in the garage. Fueled by the hot summer temperatures, the stench hangs over his property like a cloud.

When I arrive at the neighbor's house, I see through the screen door an overweight woman in her mid-twenties, sitting on a sofa in the living room. She does not answer the door when I knock. A clearly annoyed "Who is it?" rings out from the darkness of the living room. Once inside, I find the heat nearly unbearable. Several children run around yelling. As expected, the woman vehemently denies throwing trash in the garage next to her house. I leave without much satisfaction. Walking to my patrol car, there are at least five abandoned homes within a block. Ironically, the garage full of rotting trash meshes well with the landscape.

4:25 p.m.—Assault with a Weapon

An anonymous caller reports someone being sprayed with chemical mace by someone else. When we arrive at the venue, nobody answers. A woman leans out the window of an upstairs apartment and says there had been a fight, but everyone left. We clear the call without contacting a victim. Within an hour I hear other officers being sent to the same home for the same call again.

4:50 p.m.—Runaway Report

I am dispatched to the same house where less than an hour earlier a woman had denied illegally dumping trash. She wants to report one of her children ran away earlier in the day. When I ask why she didn't tell me of this when I was here before, she said because I didn't ask her about it. I take information for the report, which ties me up for nearly an hour.

7:50 p.m.—Malicious Destruction of Property Report

The caller reports several neighborhood kids smearing dirt on her house. She does not know the kids. There is nothing I can do except write a useless report for the woman at her request.

9:00 p.m.—Assault

When I arrive to check on the complaint of several kids assaulting another in the street, I locate no one. A pleasantly quiet evening ends with this call.

Sunday, June 23

3:15 p.m.—Breaking and Entering Alarm

The alarm originates from a church, which we find to be secure upon checking the premises.

3:33 p.m.—Assault

The mother I speak to is livid because her son has been assaulted by another child. The suspect apparently punched her son in the nose for refusing to help him steal some things. The neighborhood we are in is terrible and this assault is not surprising. I write a report for the woman and forward it to a juvenile investigator.

5:10 p.m.—Attempt Suicide

The woman we encounter on her front porch says her son is in the bedroom with a razor, threatening to slit his wrists. He has tried several times before, she says. She also says he has several knives in the room with him.

The home is small, but well decorated. There is a man in the kitchen cooking food, as if nothing is happening. He is the boy's father. The woman directs me to a small bedroom where I find her teenaged son lying on a couch. He has small cuts on his throat and arms. He says he wants to kill himself. For our safety, another officer and myself get him off the couch and check him for weapons. He has none. In a Bible sitting next to the couch, I find a razor blade tucked between the pages. I find two knives underneath cushions of the couch on which he had been lying. Fortunately, he never used any of these weapons against us. The teen is lethargically cooperative and is taken by ambulance to a hospital for psychiatric evaluation.

Before we leave, we get a sincere "thank you" from his mother. The father stands vigil over his cooking food. He doesn't say a word.

6:15 p.m.—Family Trouble

Everyone has departed the scene before we arrive.

6:39 p.m.—Assault

Pulling into the parking lot of a rundown grocery store on the city's Eastside, I am greeted by a tall, dirty-looking, white man in his thirties. His face is covered with blood. He is drunk. He tells me a Hispanic man with a knife tried to stab him during a fight over some beer. He says the suspect is at a house a half a block away.

The suspect I encounter is drunk also, as are three of his friends, who come over to plead the man's innocence on his behalf. A computer check shows the victim in this case has two warrants for his arrest. Both are from jurisdictions too far away to concern us. Both are alcohol-related. Eventually, we arrest the suspect for felonious assault. He has been indignant from the start and gets worse on the way to jail.

While bringing the man into the booking area of the county jail, he becomes more rowdy for the benefit of the inmates who are watching. He weighs all of 140 pounds and is so drunk he is staggering, but he manages a final threat: "Man, fuck you police. I'll see you in the street when I get out," he says, portraying himself as a man to be reckoned with.

9:58 p.m.—Attempted Suicide

A man who drank far too much has taken several prescription medications in an attempt to commit suicide. Medical personnel have the situation under control before police arrive and they handle the call with minimal assistance from us.

Saturday, June 29

3:10 p.m.—Fight

I am greeted by blank stares when I knock on the door of a run-down, two-story home and inquire about a fight, which has been reported at the residence. After about a minute of silence, one adult says there was no fight and the police are not needed.

On my way down the front walk, cutting through a front yard, which hasn't seen grass in years, a teenage girl emerges from the house I have just left.

"How I get a job?" she says, with a smirk on her face.

I stare at her with an obviously puzzled look.

"How I get a job with the police?" she repeats, becoming slightly more specific.

I begin to explain the process, but she loses interest after less than a minute and returns to the house.

3:35 p.m.—Assault in Progress

Two female officers arrive at the venue several minutes ahead of me for a reported domestic assault in progress. When I arrive, a girl in the front yard points to a back door of the apartment building. "You better get up there. They need a man up there!" she bellows.

Running up a narrow stairwell, I can hear yelling coming from the apartment. When I reach the apartment door, it is locked and there is a three-foot-square hole in the middle of the door. I reach in through the hole to unlock the door from the inside only to find it will not open without a key from the inside as well as from the outside. A woman runs past the door inside the apartment and ignores my demands to unlock it. She mutters something to me and it is apparent she is drunk. The door crashes open seconds later as I give one solid kick to the knob and I enter to find the two original officers on scene searching the apartment for a male suspect.

The temperature is in the 90s and the apartment is sweltering. One officer tells me the suspect had kicked a hole in the door, entered the apartment and assaulted his girlfriend. She says when officers arrived, they heard the suspect beating a woman. The man ran down a hallway and disappeared when officers entered the apartment. He has to be hiding somewhere in the apartment, but they cannot find him.

After checking the main floor, we ascend into a walk-in attic. Several other officers have arrived on scene to watch the exterior of the building. We do not locate the suspect in the attic, but before going back downstairs, another officer looks out a small window, which leads to a third-story roof. She spots the suspect there, crouching in a ball, hoping to go unnoticed. After several commands to come inside, the man complies and is taken into custody without a fight.

Like everyone else involved, I am sweating profusely by now. My uniform is soaked and uncomfortable. I can taste the salt of sweat as it pours from the top of my head, stinging my eyes as I wipe my face. The suspect begins complaining that he too is hot. I pay him little attention, instead focusing on my own misery.

6:10 p.m.—Neighbor Trouble

The primary officer has the call pretty much in-hand by the time I arrive. We stand in the hallway of the apartment building, talking to a female complainant. As we talk, a man in his early twenties walks up to me and says he is frustrated over problems with his neighbors. He then punches the wall near me four or five times, causing his knuckles to bleed.

"I like to punch things when I'm mad," he says, as if this has earned my respect. I don't look at him or say a word. He walks away without a final statement. The first responding officer takes care of the report and I return to patrol duties.

6:51 p.m.—Shots Fired

Checking a neighborhood about a half a mile south of the downtown area, I am unable to find a suspect or a victim. The report came in through an anonymous cellular caller, so there is no way to obtain more information about this call.

8:56 p.m.—Shooting

The call for a shooting in the parking lot of a local party store turns out to be a prank, continuing a recent trend of false reported shootings. Several patrol officers made quick time getting to the scene, risking their own safety, only to find they are not needed.

9:09 p.m.—Drug Activity

The suspect we locate walking down the sidewalk on the city's south side is a twenty-something female in a flowered dress. She is also a prostitute. We inform her a caller reported she is selling drugs. She consents to a search of her purse and her person. No drugs are found and she is back to her business within five minutes.

9:42 p.m.—Neighbor Trouble

The female complainant I encounter is a large woman. She is rightfully mad about a young boy in the neighborhood who walked into her house and threatened one of her children. She wants the boy locked up and she is not happy when we tell her we cannot accommodate her.

"I'll tell you what I'll do if he comes back into my house," she says, her children standing within earshot. "I'll lock the front door. I'll lock the back door and me and my kids will beat that motherfucker!"

While this would undoubtedly solve the problem, I advise her not to do this. She cusses at us as we leave.

Monday, July 1

3:10 p.m.—Suspicious Situation

Another officer and myself respond to a house where an anonymous person says drug dealers have supposedly taken over the residence. At the house, several boys in their early teens are hanging out on the front porch. One of the youths says he lives there with his grandmother. All of them deny selling drugs at the house. They are all mildly evasive as we question them.

Within moments the elderly woman who owns the home pulls into the driveway. When I tell her why we are there, she laments that her grandson brings his drug-dealing friends over every day when she leaves. The woman yells for all the teens to get off her property and to not come back. She gives us permission to check anyone standing on her porch during the day when she isn't home. I thank her, but considering our current lack of manpower, I know I won't have time to do this. Like cockroaches, the teens will be back on the porch the first time the woman leaves her home.

5:00 p.m.—Disorderly Person

The complainant has no telephone and had to send her child to the neighbor's house to call for police assistance. However, the disorderly person has left by the time we arrive.

5:10 p.m.—Drug Activity

The vehicles described as being involved in drug sales outside a neighborhood store are gone when I arrive.

5:15 p.m.—Auto Accident

The accident causes a lot of damage to one of the involved vehicles, but nobody is injured. One of the vehicles has no insurance and an improper license plate. The driver argues when I give him citations. I instruct him how to set up a court date to fight the tickets. Completing the accident report and citations eat up more than an hour of my shift.

6:50 p.m. - Fight

The first arriving officer disregards me from the call before I arrive on scene.

7:11 p.m.—Family Trouble

The woman who called is in her twenties. She is having problems with her mother's husband, who is a thin man with a hot temper. The man tells us to put his wife's daughter out of his house. He becomes irate when he is told we cannot make her leave.

"If she comes back in here, you're gonna have to call out the S.W.A.T. team—bank on that," he says.

The caller decides it is best if she packs her things and leaves. Apparently, she believes the implied threat. I also believe the man and I am happy with her decision. No one gets hurt and no one goes to jail. It's a good ending to a potentially bad situation.

7:28 p.m.—Shooting

This call occurs only blocks from where we just left the previous family trouble. The call turns out to be a prank.

8:55 p.m.—Breaking and Entering Alarm

The alarm originates from an adult foster care home. The female worker inside says she set it off accidentally and everything is fine.

9:08 p.m.—Suspicious Situation

The caller states several drug users have entered an abandoned house via an open back door. When I arrive with a second officer, we enter the house to check for the suspects. We survey the house with guns drawn, not knowing what we may find. The house is empty with the exception of a small puppy sitting on a rickety staircase. The puppy doesn't flinch when the other officer picks him up by the scruff of his neck. In fact, his eyes light up from the attention. We take the dog back to police headquarters to be turned over to animal control. Oddly, the five minutes I spend playing with the dog at headquarters turn out to be the most rewarding of my day to that point.

9:50 p.m.—Family Trouble

The call for a family trouble involves a teenager who has fled the scene on foot. The boy's mother is the complainant and she says the boy has a juvenile pick-up order—the equivalent of an arrest warrant. I check the area for the boy and find him walking about four blocks from the scene. I expect him to fight or run when I pull up next to him to take him into custody. To my surprise, he does neither. He offers no resistance and is very respectful. I explain the juvenile pick-up order and he doesn't argue. Another officer, who has also responded to the scene, takes custody of the boy and transports him to a juvenile detention facility.

In some of Saginaw's more desperate neighborhoods, it is hard to find a house that is not abandoned or on the brink of abandonment.

Many of the city's churches were left to rot as the population of Saginaw plummeted. This structure later met the wrecking ball.

Once a staple in a town rich with automotive history, several vacant gas stations now litter Saginaw's landscape, providing a constant reminder of better times.

One of the city's few bright spots is the current re-vitalization of the South Washington Avenue corridor, which cuts right through downtown Saginaw. This avenue (foreground) has drawn several investors, including a major medical facility, which should open in 2003.

With many large, older buildings remaining from Saginaw's heyday, the city's skyline is fairly impressive for a city of only some 62,000 residents.

The Potter Street Train Station, which used to welcome visitors to Saginaw by the hundreds, now stands silently crumbling, despite recent preservation efforts by area citizens.

Once a street said to be rife with saloons, gunfights and prostitutes, Potter Street now houses nothing more than crumbling buildings, some of which still carry the monikers of businesses long since departed.

Despite efforts by city government, an army of abandoned homes still dot the landscape of Saginaw. Many of these structures become magnets for prostitutes, drug addicts, and alcoholics.

Saginaw's North side seems to have suffered the most from the city's rapid decline. It is an area of town where driveways often lead to decaying structures, or sometimes just fade off into a grassy abyss where a house might have once stood.

Tuesday, July 2

3:12 p.m.—Drug Activity

Responding to a report of juveniles dealing drugs from the front porch of a residence, I find no one at the venue. The call has been waiting some time and not surprisingly, the bad guys have moved on.

3:35 p.m.—Abandoned Vehicle

The half—striped van I locate abandoned has been there for days, according to the caller. The vehicle sits roadside, a few yards from an abandoned church. The lawn between the church and the van is nearly three feet high, parting only for a cracked sidewalk, which splits the sea of uncut lawn. The scene paints a picture of a neighborhood suffering a slow, urban death. It is an all-too-familiar part of my daily work experience. I tag the vehicle for future removal.

4:55 p.m.—Neighbor Trouble

The dispute between neighbors is solved quickly and without incident.

6:32 p.m.—Landlord-Tenant Dispute

Before I arrive at scene, the first-responding officer handles the call. I am disregarded and clear quickly.

6:38 p.m.—Breaking and Entering Alarm

The alarm at a residence turns out to be false. The house appears to be secure when we check it.

6:50 p.m.—Assault Report

The call is made by a local hospital, whose staff is required to report all assaults to the police. The victim is not seriously hurt, but she is also drunk and uncooperative. She doesn't want to file charges against the man who assaulted her. I take information from her and write the case anyway in case she changes her mind when the booze wears off.

7:50 p.m.—Panic Alarm

The alarm is from a residence. An older woman tells me everything is okay. She set off the alarm by accident.

8:07 p.m.—Family Trouble

The woman caller says her boyfriend chased her with a bat during a fight and then took her car. She says he is angry because he thinks she is having sex with other members of the family. She never denies that his suspicions are true. I check several places for the suspect, but I am unable to locate him. The felonious assault report takes about an hour to complete.

9:40 p.m. - Assault

A clerk at a West-side convenience store calls to report a man bleeding heavily in the store's parking lot. When I arrive I find the man splattered with blood. His nose is broken and he is missing several teeth. He is extremely intoxicated and cannot remember too many details of the assault. As we talk and wait for the ambulance, the man keeps trying to walk around, nearly falling headfirst into the parking lot each time. I continually tell him to sit down, but he is distracted.

"Can I go in the store and get a beer, officer?" he asks. He doesn't argue when I tell him he cannot.

When the ambulance arrives, the man grudgingly accepts medical assistance. As the ambulance pulls away, I think about how excruciating the pain will be when his buzz wears off. Then again, he probably never lets that happen.

Tuesday, July 9

3:10 p.m.—Family Trouble

The suspect is a teen who just got released from the juvenile detention center. Today, during an argument with family, he threw a large rock at his sister. He also kicked in the door of his mother's car. The assault is enough to get him another trip back to the juvenile center and he is taken into custody.

At police headquarters, as we arrange for the suspect to be lodged at the Saginaw County Juvenile Detention Center, I get a chance to talk with the teen. His mood swings from polite to yelling and pounding his fists in fits of anger. After a while, he opens up a little. He says his dad is in prison. His mother, who called the police today, deals drugs out of their house, he says. Within minutes he is crying. I can't blame him. We talk for a while and I offer advice. Despite this, I know very well that he has little chance of leading a productive life. Jail and/or premature death likely await him. This thought clouds my mind the rest of the day.

6:08 p.m.—Hit-and-Run Accident

The damage to the victim's vehicle is minor. I am unable to locate the suspect or his vehicle. The call and the related paperwork keep me tied up for more than an hour.

7:00 p.m.—Threats Report

A boyfriend/girlfriend relationship has gone bad. Today, relatives of the two have gotten involved and threats are being made. Mostly, it is just a case of adults acting like children. The report takes another hour out of my day.

9:40 p.m.—Fight

Checking the street corner for a report of a large fight, I find nothing. Several people standing on their front porches smirk as I drive past. They know the fight is over and the cops again arrived too late. No one approaches to tell what happened or to ask for help. I am as happy to leave their neighborhood as they are to see me go.

Wednesday, July 10

3:25 p.m.—Larceny

I am dispatched to a larceny from a business shortly after checking into service. The business is located in a small strip mall, a distinction the structure carries in name only. The building is nearly three-quarters void of tenants. The few businesses scattered here and there appear to be surviving day to day.

A young man behind the counter is pleasant, but visibly disgusted at the long delay in police response. He says two teens stole about $100 worth of merchandise and ran from the store, but that was an hour ago. He points to a display where the stolen merchandise had been. Looking over my shoulder I see the display, like nearly every inch of the store, is packed full of second-rate merchandise. The store itself seems to have no order to how it is stocked. At the young man's request, I write a larceny report, the only purpose of which may be to estimate theft losses at year's end.

4:30 p.m.—Larceny

Central Dispatch puts out a call for a larceny, which just occurred at a downtown bus station. When I arrive, two officers are already handling the call. I stay at the scene because there are at least a half dozen people involved. Eventually, things get worked out and nobody goes to jail. All the parties know each other and there was a dispute over ownership of some items.

5:20 p.m.—Animal Complaint

The caller states a vicious pit bull is on his front porch and will not let him out of his house. As ridiculous as the call sounds, that is exactly what the first officer on scene finds. She lures the dog into her vehicle even before I arrive. Eventually, the dog is taken to police headquarters to wait for someone from animal control to arrive.

6:20 p.m.—Disorderly Adult

The adult foster care home where I am sent is familiar. The police respond to calls here often, mostly from disgruntled clients who say they want to go live with family. Looking at the house as I walk from my patrol car, I recall being here for a similar call on Christmas Day six or seven years ago. As officers that day were walking a disorderly client downstairs, the man pulled out a small razor blade he had hidden between his fingers. Before the officers were able to stop him, he slashed one arm wide open. I had just reached the front door of the residence that day when I heard the officers' yells and the ensuing tussle for control of the razor blade. Fortunately, today's visit offers no such drama. Another unhappy client eventually agrees it's best if he remains at the home.

6:43 p.m.—Armed Robbery

The robbery occurred in neighboring Carrollton Township, which borders Saginaw to the north of the city limits. Our department places officers at several entrance points into the city in case the suspects might try to enter our jurisdiction. I am dispatched to the city side of a train bridge spanning the Saginaw River. Central Dispatch advises this was the escape route the last time there was an armed robbery in Carrollton Township. The suspects are not located, though, and I eventually return to patrol duties.

7:11 p.m.—Dog Fight

Several recent reports of animal fights at the residence produce the same results as today—nothing.

9:18 p.m.—Vehicle Accident

This accident is a rarity as everybody involved is polite, both vehicles are properly registered and both are insured. The person who caused the accident freely admits responsibility and apologizes to the owner of the car he struck. I quickly complete a traffic accident report.

9:40 p.m.—Criminal Sexual Conduct

The woman who complains of being raped calmly relates the incident as we stand in the street in front of her friend's house. She says she was raped twice nearly 40 hours ago. She gives several reasons why she waited so long to call the police. She says she only called at the urging of friends. I take the report and tell her an investigator will be in contact. She refuses my request to go immediately to the hospital and get a physical examination. This case will have little chance in court based on the time lapse and what the victim has told me occurred.

Thursday, July 11, 2002

It is sunny and in the mid-80s when I check into service. It would be a great day, except there are 19 calls for service holding when I check my in-car computer screen. The next eight hours will offer little time to enjoy the summer sunshine.

3:10 p.m.—Suspicious Situation

The man I am sent to see is in his eighties. He's friendly with a genuine smile. His home is clean and very orderly. His wife stands by with a worried look on her face as the man relates the incidents of earlier in the day.

The elderly victim says he met a younger man while waiting to pick up a prescription at the pharmacy. The younger man claimed to be from out of town and he needed some assistance. Before long the victim offered to give his new found acquaintance a ride.

Soon they met up with a third man, who was supposedly a stranger to them both. The three ended up betting on a card game as the victim drove the other two around town. Three queens turned face down. The cards are moved around and you must pick the Queen of Hearts to win. The victim says he won a few games at first. They picked up some whiskey and started drinking as they played. Eventually, the victim lost the $100 he had with him. The two men then talked the victim into withdrawing $2,000 from the bank, which they also swindled from him.

"Even if you find them, they ain't gonna have my money, are they?" the man asks, already knowing the answer. I tell him he is probably right. His wife is soft-spoken. She says her husband is on medication and doesn't think clearly. I tell the woman her husband should not go out alone in his condition. It has been an expensive lesson to learn today.

3:46 p.m.—Officer Needs Help

The officer calling for help had just enough panic in his voice to make the hairs on my neck stand up straight. He had chased a suspect into a house and the two are now fighting. He says the man has a gun. I am about three miles away and I am responding through fairly heavy traffic. My overhead lights and sirens are screaming, but many cars do not yield. Some drivers are simply not paying attention. Some vehicles boom loud music, which drowns out the blare of my car's siren.

The officer's struggle continues seemingly forever. Central Dispatch is now trying to raise him on the radio. They get no answer. The first officer on scene says he can't find the officer calling for help. I think he's been shot. Reaching a traffic jam, I have nowhere to go so I take to the sidewalk, driving past several houses. Eventually, I run out of sidewalk and I'm forced back onto a side street, turning Northbound. I need to be going Eastbound. With traffic at a stand still and no alternate route, I have to circle back and try to get going the right way again on a less traveled street.

Several officers have now arrived on scene, but they still can't find the officer is trouble. The officer needing help has come on the radio twice trying to describe the house he is inside. He is out of breath and still in trouble. By now, I am going the right direction. Several blocks later, I am caught by a train at a railroad crossing. Too far away to do any good and with no roads left to travel, I shutdown my lights and siren, swear loudly and pound my steering wheel several times. I can feel the stares of people in cars near me. I listen to the police radio and, feeling helpless, hope for the best.

Soon, officers advise they have everything under control. The suspect has been disarmed and is in custody. Nobody is hurt. Within a minute, my relief is tempered, however, as another officer asks for assistance a block away from the incident.

Walking through a yard to retrieve the original officer's patrol car, he has been bitten by a dog. There is a crowd gathering now, becoming disorderly.

Arriving at the venue within five minutes or so, the scene is chaotic. There are police cars parked here and there for a block. A large crowd has gathered, taunting every officer within earshot. Many are unaware of what has transpired. They're just here to yell because everyone else is doing the same thing.

Talking to several officers there, I learn we are waiting for animal control to come out and take possession of the dog that bit an officer. It will be necessary to take the dog due to the severity of the bite. The dog's owner is on the front porch of the home, screaming obscenities and racial taunts. Some people in the crowd have brought out their video cameras, yelling for us to beat someone. There are several references to a recent police case in Inglewood, California. The scene is disgusting beyond description. It seems to me standing here today that the country's post September 11 affection for police was short lived. We're back to being targets for hatred again.

"Man, look at all you motherfuckers come out when one of your boys is in trouble!" yells one man from the crowd.

When an animal control officer finally arrives to take possession of the dog, things really boil over. As the officer is trying to slip a harness around the dog's neck, the owner yells something to the dog and it tries to attack the officer. Considering this use of a weapon against the officer, we ascend the porch to arrest the owner, but he has retreated into his house and locked the door. Suddenly, he doesn't like the scenery outside anymore.

I reach the door along with a sergeant and give the door a hard kick. It gives easily, swinging wide open and rebounding back halfway after striking a living room wall. As we enter the house, the suspect runs out the back door and is taken into custody by two awaiting detectives.

I tell the detectives to put the man in my patrol car and I'll transport him to jail. He is screaming obscenities. A young girl runs up behind me starts yelling at me: "I hate you motherfuckers!" she screams. She is no more than 12 years old.

We leave quickly for the county jail. It's not a quiet ride. The man we've arrested wants to debate the arrest. He wants to debate race. He wants to debate my toughness. I don't engage him in any of the topics. They are all impossible arguments because he has lost his ability to reason. I am glad for the quiet when I finally leave the jail.

Acquaintances have asked me why some police officers become such bitter and negative people. That question can easily be answered by experiencing the sights and sounds of the previous two hours' events.

6:49 p.m.—Family Trouble

There are at least a dozen people on and around the front porch of the venue. Nearly all of them are drunk. The first arriving officer is talking to the caller. I stand back and listen.

"Hey man, get over here! I want to talk to you!" yells a drunken man in his fifties, staring at me from the porch.

"Don't talk to me like I'm a dog. I am not your dog. You wanna talk, bring your drunk ass down here and we'll talk," I tell him, taking a tone I usually try to avoid. Today, however, I am in no mood for the man's ignorance.

My response has drawn laughter from his friends and puts the drunken man on the defensive. He mumbles some obscenities under his breath, but he won't leave the porch or come near me. Meanwhile, the other officer is wrapping up the call. We leave after about 15 minutes with the drunk still mumbling on the porch.

7:25 p.m.—Cutting

An intoxicated customer came to a local convenience store and tried to return a cellular telephone he had previously bought. When the store manager wouldn't refund his money, a fight ensued and the manager suffered several cuts to his face. The suspect has fled. I write a report of the felony assault, which will be turned over to detectives in the morning for further investigation.

8:40 p.m.—911 Hang-up Call

Everything turns out to be okay when we check the residence.

8:50 p.m.—Malicious Destruction of Property

The caller advises someone carved a threat into his front door. He requests a report, which I say I will write. He knows the suspect. He says the threat involves a girl the caller used to date. The report takes me about 45 minutes to complete.

9:36 p.m.—Officers Need Assistance

For the second time today, officers are calling for assistance. By the time I arrive the suspect is in custody. He had assaulted his girlfriend and when officers arrived at scene, he challenged them to a fight. In the end, the suspect and several officers ended up getting sprayed with chemical mace. Fortunately, no one is severely injured. I leave for the night after this call. There are still 14 calls for service pending. Today, I am especially glad I do not work the midnight shift.

Friday, July 12

4:30 p.m. - Parking Complaint

Just half an hour before the start of a downtown festival, not to mention the end of the workday for employees in the downtown area, I get a call for a vehicle parked in a traffic lane. I arrive to find a truck parked in one of only two available Northbound traffic lanes. Traffic has already bottlenecked and is backed up for blocks. The truck is parked directly in front of a sign marked "No Parking Any Time."

After waiting 20 minutes for a tow truck, the vehicle owner arrives just as the car is being pulled onto the flatbed wrecker. With some pleading, the wrecker driver unhooks his vehicle, but still charges a service call rate. The embarrassed vehicle owner also does not argue the parking ticket he finds on his windshield.

5:23 p.m.—Panic Alarm

No one is home and the residence appears to be undisturbed.

6:30 p.m.—Family Trouble

A male in his twenties advises us that everything is alright. He had called about a problem with his girlfriend, but he has decided to leave for the night, which solves the problem.

6:47 p.m.—Check the Well Being of Child

The caller states a young child has been left alone at a residence. The caller also states the child's mother is dealing drugs. When I arrive, the child and his mother walk over from the porch of a neighbor's house, where they had been sitting. The child looks fine. I explain why I am there. The woman says she has been having trouble with a relative calling the police on her as payback for a previous family dispute.

9:10 p.m.—Breaking and Entering

The woman who called is in her twenties. She is sitting on her front porch with her two children when I arrive. She is crying. She says a young girl in the neighborhood told her the neighbors across the street had broken in the back door shortly after the woman left her home. They stole all the meat from her refrigerator.

When I cross the street to confront the suspects, they will not open the door. The woman says they are home because she just saw them prior to my arrival. With no further recourse, I write a report to be forwarded to an investigator, if any have the time to handle the complaint. My day ends with this report and thoughts of a family vacation, which begins tomorrow.

Monday, July 22

3:10 p.m.—Warrant Suspect

Acting on an anonymous tip, I arrive, along with several other officers, at a rickety house on the city's Northeast side. A man wanted for suspected child abuse is supposed to hiding inside the house. He is described as 6'7" and 300 pounds, which is why there are four officers here now.

The people we find inside the house are surprised by our arrival. They say they do not know the man we are looking for and they give us permission to search the house, which is sweltering from the summer heat. Fortunately, the search lasts only about 10 minutes. There are very few places a guy this size could hide in the house. We do not locate the suspect.

4:00 p.m.—Abandoned Vehicle

The caller is anonymous, reporting a vehicle abandoned somewhere in the block. The description given is a dark-colored car. There are three in the block that match the description. Unable to determine which one the caller was referring to, I tag none of them for removal.

4:50 p.m.—Loud Music

The venue is a street corner, well known for its blatant drug selling activity. Several people scatter when they see my police car from three blocks away. Arriving at the corner, no one remains outside and the corner is quiet. They will all be back five minutes after I pull away.

5:30 p.m.—Traffic Stop

A woman passes me more than 20 miles per hour over the speed limit, going the opposite direction. Despite the high volume of dispatch calls, I make a quick traffic stop. She apologizes and says she wasn't paying attention. I give her a verbal warning to slow down and return to answering calls.

5:35 p.m.—Loud Music

There is no loud music to be heard when I check the area.

5:38 p.m.—Warrant Arrest

Responding to a request from another officer for back up, I drive to the far North end of the city. When I arrive, the officer is placing handcuffs on a large man in his twenties. The man has a warrant. Shortly after being taken into custody, the bitching begins. Despite having a valid warrant, the man feels we should have turned the other way and he should have been let go.

6:10 p.m.—Disorderly Person

The man I encounter outside a bank looks like he just woke up from a three-day drunk. His hair is messy. His eyes are bloodshot. He smells of old sweat. Bank personnel called because he refused to leave the lobby.

The man tells me he is trying to clear up a problem with his car payments. His car was stolen a while back. Well, truthfully, he says, the car was traded for drugs. Now the man has no car and the bank keeps taking payroll deductions out of his checks to cover the car payments. He has been to several different branches of the bank to argue about the issue. I skip the lecture about drugs and responsibility and give him a trespass warning. He agrees to leave.

6:35 p.m.—Drug Activity

The reported drug activity has ceased prior to my arrival.

8:00 p.m.—Breaking and Entering Alarm

The premises appears secure when we check. The call takes less than five minutes to clear.

8:55 p.m.—Juvenile Assault

The report stems from one juvenile throwing a firecracker at another. No one was injured. It's the kind of stupid thing kids sometimes do, but one parent wants to file assault charges. The call takes me about an hour to clear.

10:15 p.m.—Officer Needs Assistance

Two Michigan State Police troopers call for assistance in an Eastside neighborhood. The original call they responded to was that of a fight, but it escalated when they arrived. By the time I get to the scene, there are at least 100 people roaming the street near the scene. Some are yelling. Some are just watching. There are also 15 police cars there from three jurisdictions. The neighborhood quiets as the crowd slowly disburses. I clear about 15 minutes later and leave for the night shortly after departing the scene. There are 13 calls for service awaiting the midnight shift's arrival.

Wednesday, July 24

3:15 p.m.—Runaway

The day starts on a mundane note, taking information for one of hundreds of runaway reports filed in the city of Saginaw every year. The child who has run away from home eventually gets entered into a statewide computer database filled with the names of thousands of similar kids.

5:20 p.m.—Disorderly Person

The caller is a woman in her thirties. When I arrive she is sitting on her front porch with several children. She says a teenage girl has been driving an SUV recklessly through the neighborhood and the woman is afraid her kids might get hit. She says the girl lives somewhere a couple of streets over. I check the area, but never locate the driver.

6:15 p.m.—Family Trouble

Arriving at the scene of a reported family trouble, I find the venue is a vacant house. Central Dispatch double checks the address and says I am at the right place. A neighbor says nobody has lived here for months. I clear the call without ever finding a victim.

6:20 p.m.—Hit-and-run Follow-up Investigation

The vehicle accident I am investigating occurred several days ago. The department's Traffic Services Division has returned the report to me for further investigation. When I arrive at the home of the suspect vehicle's owner, two females have just pulled into the driveway. They tell me the suspect used to live here, but he has since moved.

6:40 p.m.—Attempted Suicide

The call turns out to be a sick person. The caller is mentally impaired and her description of the circumstances led Central Dispatch to believe there had been a suicide attempt. Ambulance personnel end up handling the call.

7:02 p.m.—Verify Return of Runaway

I am sent back to the location of my first call of the day to verify the runaway has returned. Driving through an Eastside neighborhood en route to the call, I see a young boy about five years old walking down the sidewalk. We immediately make eye contact. I slow down because the boy has turned his body facing my passing car to say something. To my surprise, he raises both his five-year-old middle fingers in my direction and mouths the words "fuck you." It's the type of scene never aired on police television shows. In the midst of all the shootings, cuttings, and assaults, I find these fleeting moments of overwhelming negativity the hardest to deal with. I continue to my call without stopping to talk to the youngster.

7:50 p.m.—Assault Report

The victim is at a local hospital. A man she has been living with has assaulted her. She calls him a "tenant." The woman is frail and shows signs of years of alcohol and drug abuse. She is what many people would call "white trash."

We talk for about 10 minutes. She says she argued with the suspect over past-due rent. The suspect then became angry and beat the woman and bit her ear, before pulling out her telephone wires so she could not call the police. After taking photos of her injury, I give the woman a case report number and advise her how to follow-up with prosecution. My sorrow for the woman is tempered somewhat as I gather my things to leave. A nurse tells me the woman has been through the emergency room uncountable times with the same type of injuries. I write the report anyway.

Thursday, July 25

3:20 p.m.—Disorderly Adult

The call requires two patrol cars and is the result of nothing more than one adult who had been staring at another. One of the parties demands a report. I clear the call after about 15 minutes. The other officer remains tied up some time longer writing a useless report.

4:00 p.m.—Attempt Suicide

By the time I am able to respond to the call, the ambulance has already located a supposedly suicidal female who may have overdosed on prescription medication. She will not speak to me, however, and makes no suggestions that she is suicidal. She apparently has made suicidal threats to her boyfriend, however. He agrees to sign a petition to help her seek psychological help. I file a report to explain why I did not petition the victim myself, in case there are any questions about the call in the future.

5:40 p.m.—Family Trouble

Arriving at the venue, I find a woman in her twenties, sitting in a car at the house, braiding the hair of a young child. She says the people involved in the dispute have left and the police are not needed anymore.

6:00 p.m.—Neighbor Trouble

I am the third car to arrive at the scene. I immediately make myself available to Central Dispatch because the other officers at scene are handling the call. From what I can gather before I leave, the call involves a property line dispute. The teenage daughter of one of the involved parties is walking up and down her driveway with a Bible in her hand the entire time I am at scene, repeating the words: "Praise the Lord. Thank you Jesus" over and over again. She seems oblivious to her surroundings. I depart after about 15 minutes.

7:40 p.m.—Homicide

The call goes out as a cutting in a West-side neighborhood. Within seconds of the first officer's arrival, it is clear this will be a homicide. Nearly every available car in the city makes it to the scene. The assault, which led to the victim being killed, was ignited by a dispute over someone's reckless driving. Several people allegedly came back to the scene after the dispute and chased the victim through the neighborhood. After he fell, the victim apparently was stabbed several times.

I locate a couple of witnesses who saw the original confrontation, but not the actual stabbing. While talking to one of the witnesses, the victim's newlywed wife arrives at the scene. Someone apparently notified her of the assault and she came home from work. The woman asks a sergeant what happened. He tells her that her husband was stabbed and informs her what hospital to go to. Unaware of the extent of her husband's injuries, she seems more angry and inconvenienced than concerned at this point. She has no idea that her life has just changed drastically. I cannot stand looking her in the eye, knowing myself what she has yet to find out.

The next day, I see the woman on the noon news, devastated by her loss. I change the channel quickly. Being there in person was more than enough. I would rather not re-live the tragedy again.

8:24 p.m.—Dog Fight

I cleared the homicide scene as quickly as possible, as calls for service have started to stack up. My involvement was minor, having interviewed only two witnesses. I have returned now to responding to less dramatic calls. The animal complaint I am sent to has long since broken up and no action is required on my part.

8:34 p.m.—Disorderly Juveniles

The juveniles have moved on and the neighborhood where I am dispatched is relatively quiet now.

8:50 p.m.—Loud Music

The venue is quiet when I arrive. Catching up on some paperwork near the house where I was dispatched, I stumble over the irony of one of my thoughts. Just more than an hour ago, a young man lay bleeding to death in the yard of a stranger, thinking the thoughts to which only the dying have access. Meanwhile, the biggest concern for a person across town is that a neighbor is playing his music too loud.

Thursday, August 1

4:30 p.m.—Purse Snatching

The woman I meet in the lobby of a downtown bank is neither shaken nor overly concerned. She relates a few details of a purse snatching, but her thoughts are scattered. She says she has mental problems and rambles on about several topics not related to why I am there. From the few details I am able to extract, I write a report for a purse snatching which I am not even sure occurred.

4:58 p.m.—911 Hang-up

No one answers at the apartment where a 911 call originated. The door is unlocked and swings open as we knock. The inside of the apartment is empty, with the exception of some scattered furnishings. Unable to find a problem, the call is cleared within 10 minutes.

5:25 p.m.—Unarmed Robbery

The female victim says she got into a fight at a party store with a girl with whom she has had a long-standing feud. During the fight the suspect's boyfriend stole the victim's gold chain, yanking it from her neck.

Finding the suspect's address, I arrive with another officer at an old three-story apartment building. Of course, the suspect lives on the third floor. Climbing 60 or 70 rickety wooden stairs on an exterior staircase, I am half winded by the time I reach the top. The apartment door is open and we enter to check for the suspect. The smell of rotting food fills the apartment, gagging me immediately. There are hotdogs on the counter, slowly turning green in the summer heat. Thankfully, no one is home and our stay is brief.

6:37 p.m. - Officer Need Assistance

Two officers pursuing a stolen vehicle call for help after the driver bails out of the car and runs into a residence. While they call for assistance, a struggle is audible in the background. I am the fifth officer to arrive and I find the front door being blocked by several bystanders. One large man stands directly in front of the door, looking inside, refusing my orders to move. I shove him aside and can hear him yelling "fuck you, man, don't shove me" as I enter the house.

In a bedroom to the right of the front door, the scene is chaotic. Several officers are struggling to handcuff the suspect, whom they have had to physically drag from underneath a bed. He is about 6'2" and weighs well over 250 pounds. Someone has sprayed him with mace, but he still will not comply. The mace has now affected everyone in the room and it takes several minutes to get the man handcuffed. Once handcuffed, the man resorts to passive resistance, going limp and refusing to walk on his own. As we get him outside, he yells to a sympathetic crowd that he is being beaten though he clearly is being carried.

"We're going to get our video cameras," yells one woman from the crowd. The rest of the crowd of 50 or so yells surprisingly few insults. One man says he is going to contact the FBI to have the police investigated. He says the arrest is racially motivated. With the man finally inside a patrol car, he is taken away to have medical personnel check him over due to the use of mace at the scene. He later goes to jail.

7:13 p.m.—Fight with Guns

Two men who had been fighting now reportedly have guns and are going to shoot each other. Arriving at the scene, there is no one outside matching the description of the combatants. They are never located.

8:35 p.m.—Assist on Traffic Stop

I stop to offer assistance to another officer who has pulled over a vehicle. The driver has a suspended license and will be going to jail. I stay tied up only until the driver is in custody. The remainder of the night is uneventful.

Saturday, August 3

3:17 p.m.—Vehicle Accident

Despite having to wait in the hot sun for more than half an hour for police response, everyone at the scene is surprisingly courteous and understanding. Clearing the roadway of one disabled vehicle and writing the actual accident report consumes more than an hour of my workday.

Burden of the Badge
A Year in the Life of a Street Cop

4:54 p.m.—Disorderly Adult

An intoxicated man who was refusing a store manager's demands to leave the premises has departed after hearing the police were called. From the description given, I recognize the man as a homeless trouble-maker who likes to fight with the police. During previous run-ins with him over the years, he has made claims to be a Vietnam veteran, a Detroit Police Department undercover officer and a federal law enforcement officer. He is never easy to deal with and I am not disappointed at being unable to locate him today.

5:01 p.m.—Breaking and Entering Alarm

The community center where we receive an alarm is a large building, located in the heart of one of Saginaw's most violent neighborhoods. Several children and adults wandering in the area of the building stare as I check doors and windows for signs of entry. None of them say a word; few people speak to the police around here. After about five minutes of checking, another officer and I determine this to be a false alarm.

5:14 p.m.—Man Down

One of the city's more recognizable homeless men has decided to take a nap in someone's front yard, prompting several calls from motorists who think he might be dead. The man is an alcoholic and today he is drunk again. A sergeant has arrived on the scene before me. He handles the call and sees to the man's well being.

5:45 p.m.—Family Trouble

The man and woman having a dispute both are in their thirties. There is a thick air of animosity between them and they trade verbal barbs while talking to the first arriving officer. Each seems to be trying to sway our opinion, although the matter is civil in nature and there is nothing we can do for either of them. Eventually, the woman goes back inside their apartment. The man continues to drone on about his mate's character flaws and the fact she has run up $30,000 worth of debt on his credit cards. It sounds like they should have split up long before now.

5:59 p.m.—Breaking and Entering Alarm

The venue is a church, which takes up an entire city block. I haven't been to this particular church in years and I admire the building's architecture as I check doors and windows, eventually determining the alarm is false.

6:50 p.m.—Breaking and Entering

Assisting another officer, I arrive to find her listening to the victim say a neighbor has broken into her house and stolen her stereo. We go to the neighbor's house and find stereo parts inside an open back door in plain view. The neighbor is not home and, after summoning a sergeant to the scene, we enter the home, looking for the remainder of the stereo.

There are few belongings inside the house. In the dining room, we find a single-seat church pew in front of a makeshift alter, overlooking a lighted candle and a picture of Jesus Christ. Despite the religious overtones, the scene is creepy, reminding me of the sort of place where sacrifices are made. I shake off the goose bumps as we press on to check the house. We locate nobody inside the house, but we do find the victim's stereo in an upstairs bedroom.

On the way to the back door, the female officer checking the house with me lets out muted scream in the kitchen. When I reach the room she is laughing and looking in the kitchen sink where a mouse had just run from the countertop into the drain, prompting her scream.

We return the stereo to its owner. The case will be forwarded to detectives, who will try again to contact the suspect at a later time. A lengthy report follows and this is the last call I take for the evening.

Wednesday, August 7

In roll call, we are told two teens died in a car accident in the city early this morning. Apparently their vehicle went out of control, flipped over and landed in someone's front yard during the early morning hours. Some people in the neighborhood, used to hearing cars racing down their street, as well as the noise from passing trains, said they heard a commotion, but did not give it a second thought. The overturned car and its two deceased occupants were not located until morning when a shocked homeowner awoke to find the car in her front yard, several hours after the accident occurred.

3:25 p.m.—Breaking and Entering Alarm

Checking a garage for signs of entry, we find everything secure and clear the call within about three minutes.

3:33 p.m. - Disorderly Juveniles

The woman I meet at a small house of the city's Southeast side is calm and friendly, despite the fact neighborhood kids just broke out her window. She asks for a police report for her insurance claim. I give her the assigned case number and write a simple report, which takes less than half an hour to complete.

4:35 p.m.—Man with a Gun

The caller gives a description of a man with a gun outside a local party store. He tells Central Dispatch that the man pointed the gun at him, but he does not want to file charges. I check the area and a sergeant assists me. We do not locate the suspect and clear the call after about 10 minutes.

5:00 p.m.—Civil Dispute

The dispute involves a landlord and her tenants and the status of a condemned house. After several calls to city inspections, we determine police involvement is not needed. The process of determining this is a lengthy one and the call keeps me and another officer tied up for about 45 minutes.

6:24 p.m.—Vehicle Inspection

The call involves verifying the vehicle identification number on a car so it can be re-titled. When I arrive, I find the caller in the back yard of a rundown two-unit rental. Junk cars are strewn about the back yard where grass hasn't grown in years. At least a half dozen men are milling about, drinking beer. I can immediately sense their dislike for the police when I enter the yard. I make sure to not turn my back when completing the inspection. While this is a very basic call for service, I can sense danger here. It's a sense I imagine most cops develop quickly. My wife calls it paranoia. There is no help nearby if this drunken group turns on me. I leave as quickly as possible after completing the required paperwork.

6:51 p.m.—Check Fraud

A store clerk has called to report a man who has written two bad checks in his business today. Both parties are there when I arrive. The check writer is a man in his fifties. He's half drunk and he's not a listener. As I try to get both sides of the story, the man keeps talking over me and I have to tell him to shut his mouth several times. Eventually, after checking the suspect for warrants, the problem is solved between the store clerk and the suspect.

8:55 p.m.—Malicious Destruction of Property Report

The female caller has had numerous problems with her ex-boyfriend. Today, the man came to her house, destroyed some items in her bedroom and stole a video game player. I have advised her to seek a personal protection order in the past, but she has not. She always meant to, she says. She tells me she will this time. I am certain she will not.

Thursday, August 8

3:22 p.m.—Breaking and Entering Alarm

Several neighborhood kids gather when I pull up to the residence, asking what is wrong. After checking the house for signs of entry, I talk with them for a while. They want to know why I carry a gun. They ask about everything on my equipment belt. Their youthful enthusiasm is refreshing and I stay talking to them about 10 minutes longer than I should.

4:04 p.m.—Fight

One of the combatants is pulling away in a car when I arrive, but the other person involved—a well-dressed girl in her twenties—tells me everything is okay. She says she does not need the police.

5:17 p.m.—Prisoner Transport

Detectives, who have just finished interviewing a suspect, request two patrol officers to take him back to jail. The suspect, dressed in an orange county jail jumpsuit, does not talk during the ride. The task is an easy one and kills about half an hour of my day.

9:08 p.m.—Fight

I arrive to find everyone involved in the fight is gone. The caller is drunk and makes little sense when talking. We clear the scene with no report and no contact with anyone actually involved.

9:20 p.m.—Family Trouble

The caller is in her sixties. The suspect, who has left the scene on foot, is the caller's middle-aged daughter. The woman who called says her daughter is a drug user and today damaged some of the caller's property during an argument.

I locate the female suspect walking with a man about three blocks from the venue. The man wants no part of dealing with the police and asks if he can leave. I dismiss him and turn my attention toward the woman. She is slightly built, jittery and will not quit talking. She is an obvious crack cocaine user.

Before placing the woman into my patrol car, I check her for weapons. Despite the warm weather, she wears several layers of clothing. I pull from her pockets numerous wads of tissue, a lighter and some other small items. Sitting in the back seat of my patrol car, the woman continues talking. I find she has a valid warrant and put her in handcuffs.

During a more thorough search, after she is handcuffed, I find several items I had missed on the first search: another lighter, matches, a nail, a crack pipe, a box cutter, several candies and other miscellaneous junk. I am embarrassed to have missed so many potential weapons in my rush to get the woman secured in my car. The other officer at scene, despite having considerably less time on the job, gives me a well-deserved disappointed look. My complacency is inexcusable and could have caused either of us to be hurt. I transport the woman to jail, vowing to myself to be more careful. Considering the monotony of day-to-day police work, I know it is a vow I will eventually break.

Friday, August 9

3:10 p.m.—Vehicle Accident

The woman who caused the accident is what I consider a typical middle-class woman from a small town. She happened to be driving through Saginaw and got into an accident. Now she thinks her problems are my problems. As I try to gather information from both drivers, the woman continually complains. Her summer is going terribly. She has family problems. She just paid this vehicle off, and so on, and on. Ignoring her whining, I keep prodding her for her vehicle information. Eventually she complies and I start my report while awaiting a wrecker to tow away her vehicle.

Wallowing in the despair of life's less-fortunate every day, I find it nearly impossible to listen to the overblown complaints of people like the woman I deal with at this scene. I would like to take her to work for a full shift. Eight hours of submersing in poverty, drugs and violence would do wonders for her outlook on life and her appreciation for how fortunate she really is.

After about 15 minutes of waiting—and listening—a wrecker arrives. I give the other driver his case report number. He has been very patient, but I can tell the woman is getting on his nerves also. Not surprisingly, the woman argues over being found at fault for the accident. Despite her protests, I won't change the report. The wrecker driver agrees to transport the woman to a town in Eastern Saginaw County. She is his problem now.

4:40 p.m.—Prostitute

Driving through the downtown area, I see a known prostitute approaching a vehicle. When she sees me, she walks away from the car. I have taken her to jail before and have a decent rapport with the hooker. She comes to my car when I wave her over. She's thin, somewhat unkempt and has decaying front teeth. I tell her to keep her business more low key and ask her to tell the other area prostitutes to stay away from this particular corner because it's too high profile. She agrees and moves on quickly. With a shortage of officers and calls for service pilling up every day, we don't have much time to police prostitutes. I hope this soft approach will at least keep them off the busier corners.

5:36 p.m.—Panic Alarm

We check the residence to find nobody home and the property secure.

5:42 p.m.—Shoplifter

The party store I respond to is usually the scene of disorderly persons, drug dealing and an occasional shooting. Today, Central Dispatch advises, the storeowner has called because he caught a seven-year-old boy stealing candy cigarettes. I find the irony amusing.

After locating the caller and the pint-sized suspect, I leave the store to take the kid home. We have some good conversation during the five-minute drive. He is a pretty smart kid for a seven-year-old. Most of his smarts are street smarts, though. Seeing the way the boy handles his mother when I drop him at home, I can tell he is a good manipulator. This will not be his last run-in with the police.

6:05 p.m.—Breaking and Entering Alarm

The alarm is at a local zoo. I check the exterior of the facility. It looks secure.

8:50 p.m.—Disorderly Adult

The complainant says a man is walking through a business district, threatening people. The caller tells Central Dispatch the name of the disorderly man. He is a well-known, somewhat unstable guy that our officers have dealt with since before I was hired. When I locate him walking down a sidewalk, he is more scared than agitated.

"Don't take me to jail, man. Please don't take me to jail," he repeats as I walk up to him. He gives me his version of the argument he just had with a pedestrian. He says he was antagonized. He says he's going straight home. I release him with a warning.

9:12 p.m.—Breaking and Entering Alarm

The woman I encounter when I walk in the front door is dressed nicely. She says she is the homeowner and she just got back from church services. She tells me her son is in from out of town and he does not know how to set the alarm properly. After confirming her identity, I leave as she continues to apologize for troubling the police. Her pleasant demeanor is refreshing. If everyone were this nice, my job would be much more enjoyable.

9:28 p.m.—Gambling Complaint

There is no on gambling on the front porch of an abandoned house as the caller reported and the call takes less than five minutes to clear.

9:58 p.m.—Family Trouble

I arrive in the area simultaneously with a back-up officer, but there is no such address as the one reported to Central Dispatch. We are advised the call came in from a pay telephone, so it cannot be traced back to an actual address. After several minutes, no one approaches for help and we clear the call.

Saturday, August 10

3:25 p.m.—Breaking and Entering in Progress

The complaint originates from a warehouse on the city's West side, where a neighbor says several teens are trying to break in. The primary officer arrives at scene a couple of minutes before me and determines the suspects have left without gaining entry.

5:12 p.m.—Breaking and Entering Alarm

The venue is a flower and gift shop located in a residential neighborhood on the far Eastside of the city. When I arrive, a young boy is trying the knob on the front door. There is a sign proclaiming the business is open. But the door is locked. The boy says he has been trying to get the door open for a couple of minutes because he wants to buy some candy. I explain the store is closed and he set off the alarm by pulling on the door.

As I get back into my patrol car, the boy comes over to talk. I ask if he is ready to go back to school and he shrugs his shoulders.

"When does school start for you?" I ask.

"I dunno," he replies. "I think we go back in December."

The boy is about eight years old and he should know school doesn't start in December. Sadly, he does not. I wonder what his home is like. But I already have a pretty good idea.

6:55 p.m.—911 Hang-up Call

The call comes from a retirement high rise. When I enter with another officer, we find several elderly people in the lobby. They direct us to the manager's apartment, where we find nobody is home. Eventually, we determine the call came from a lobby telephone. Everyone we speak to says there is no trouble. We clear after about 25 minutes, never finding out who placed the 911 call.

7:16 p.m.—Breaking and Entering Alarm

A quick check of the premises, a modest, one-story house on a court where all the houses look the same, and we determine this is a false alarm.

7:53 p.m.—Disorderly Adult

Responding to a call from the clerk at a party store, we locate a customer outside the building. He is livid. He says he was inside the store and bought a dollar beer. The man says he gave the clerk a $10 bill and got only $4 back. When he argued that he received the wrong change, the clerk insisted the man had only given him a $5 bill.

Inside, the clerk - a man in his late twenties—insists the customer originally gave him only $5. He refuses to give any more money to the customer. Frustrated, the customer decides to cut his losses. He reaches for the change trough underneath a bulletproof partition that separates he and the clerk, expecting to find the $4 he had left there when he went outside to cool off. The trough is empty. The clerk says he does not know what happened to the $4. He says there was another customer in the store when the man left the money and walked outside. The clerk says that customer may have picked up the $4.

"Man, I bought a dollar beer and now I'm out ten dollars!" screams the man, fists clenched, barely able to maintain control of his anger.

I think for a moment that he will charge the counter and try to break through the bulletproof partition, compounding the costs of his quest for cheap beer. The man, however, regains his composure and leaves the store, making a few veiled threats at the clerk as he reaches the door.

8:09 p.m.—Man Down

A citizen approaches another officer and I as we talk a block away from our previous call. He says there is a man lying on the sidewalk in front of another party store down the street. He thinks the man might be hurt.

When we arrive, I recognize the man in his fifties lying on the ground. I have dealt with him before and he is never pleasant. As we try to wake him, he looks up in a state of groggy, booze-induced confusion. We call for an ambulance to transport him to a hospital, where he can be placed into protective custody.

The man is carrying a variety of tools and sharp objects in his pockets. When I begin to remove the potential weapons, he offers some mild verbal resistance at first, but springs to life when I reach for a pair of needle-nosed pliers in his front pocket. With all the energy he can muster, the drunken man tries to grab my testicles with his left hand. Clamping onto his wrist just before impact, I pull his hand back as he then lunges toward my thigh, mouth open, trying to bite my leg. The ambulance pulls up as I am holding his head near the sidewalk to keep his mouth away.

When the ambulance driver brings a gurney over, I let go of the man's head and take a quick step back. A handful of gray, greasy hair falls to the ground from under his baseball cap. He manages to cuss out each of us as we lift him on the stretcher. Most of his anger is directed toward me.

At the hospital, the man's anger boils over again when a nurse tries to get him into a hospital gown. When I come in the room to help the nurse, things get worse the minute he spots me.

"You fucking faggot. I'm going to kill you, you faggot-ass motherfucker. Stick this up your ass, motherfucker," he screams, holding his middle finger as high as his weary, drunken body will allow.

The nurse decides this is enough and, with the help of another nurse and a hospital security guard, we place the man into leather restraints. He passes out within 10 minutes.

Wednesday, August 14

The big news today is that one of my co-workers has apparently had a contract put out on his life. The officer in question has been causing a lot of problems for some of the city's North-side drug dealers. Tired of the pressure he has put on their business, one of the dealers has allegedly offered $800 for anyone who will kill this officer. With the recent murders of police officers in Hazel Park and Detroit, everyone takes the threat seriously, even though the officer who is targeted tries to downplay the situation.

3:22 p.m.—Fraud

I am dispatched to local public health care center for a fraud report. There are at least 50 people in the overcrowded lobby when I enter the building. Small children sit crying. There is not a smile to be seen. I am relieved when the complainant finally arrives and we head for an office to discuss the report of a forged prescription. Gathering the information and writing the report takes a little more than an hour.

5:05 p.m.—Abandoned Vehicle

I check a rundown neighborhood for a report of an abandoned vehicle parked roadside. The car is gone.

5:30 p.m.—Disorderly Juvenile

A disorderly juvenile who has been hanging around a local gas station is gone when I arrive. The clerk says he has been offering to pump gas for customers if they will pay him a dollar. I tell her to call if he returns.

5:39 p.m.—Fight

The fight is over and everyone is gone when I arrive at scene.

7:19 p.m.—Family Trouble

We apprehend a teenage boy who threw bicycle parts at his mother during a family argument. He is charged with domestic assault with a weapon. There are several juvenile forms to be completed. There is evidence to tag. The boy is eventually lodged at a juvenile detention facility, which is half an hour round trip from the police station. Another officer and myself spend at least two hours completing this case report.

Thursday, August 15

I am assigned to a two-person car today. Our task is to patrol the North side of the city, where drug dealers have recently made threats to kill one of our officers.

Our primary job is to deter street corner drug sales, putting pressure on the sellers and buyers. The area is surprisingly quiet. Most people vacate the street corners when they see a two-person car ride through. They know all of our patrol cars are single-officer units unless we're trying to be especially proactive. Word spreads quickly on this day as there are very few people hanging out on the corners during our shift.

6:00 p.m.—Officer Needs Assistance

Responding to an officer in a foot chase with a wanted felon, we arrive in time to help set up a perimeter on the block where the suspect was last seen. My partner and I check a couple of abandoned houses while the K-9 Unit uses a dog to track the suspect. We fail to locate him, but the man is well known in this part of town and he is not liked. Someone will undoubtedly turn him in soon.

8:52 p.m.—Domestic Assault

We arrive to find the suspect has left on foot. The victim says the suspect - her boyfriend - assaulted her with a baseball bat and a rum bottle, striking her repeatedly in the upper body and head. Her injuries are far less severe than they could have been, but she goes to the hospital to get checked out anyway. The suspect is not located by other cars searching the area for him. The ensuing report takes a little less than an hour to complete. The remainder of the night is uneventful.

Friday, August 16

3:20 p.m.—Motorist Assist

A vehicle abandoned on an expressway, which runs through the city, has prompted several calls from passing motorists. I arrive to find the vehicle blocking part of the passing lane. The driver has left.

With my patrol vehicle parked at an angle behind the broken down car, I wait for a tow truck to arrive and remove the car. Despite the illumination of my overhead lights and hazard lights, many cars passing by do not change lanes, clearing my patrol vehicle by mere inches while traveling at 60 to 70 miles per hour. I decide it is best to wait for the tow truck while standing outside my patrol car. The thought of getting rear-ended at these speeds is not a pleasant one. After about 20 minutes a wrecker finally arrives and the vehicle is taken away.

4:00 p.m.—Stolen Vehicle

An officer calls for assistance after spotting a stolen vehicle parked at a local party store. I arrive within minutes, but I'm the fourth officer on scene and three suspects have been taken into custody without incident. Fortunately, a Michigan State Police trooper happened to be nearby and assisted the city officer until back up arrived.

6:00 p.m.—Neighbor Trouble

The woman I speak to originally said her neighbor commanded a dog to attack her. The woman changes her story quickly, however, and says the dog came after her, but maybe it wasn't ordered to do so. The woman says she has had problems with her neighbor for months. I assume this is why she exaggerated the claim of a dog attack. The woman insists a report be made and I oblige her, knowing the report is basically useless as no crime has been committed. The 30 minutes I waste writing the report is nothing compared to the hours involved in an internal investigation if the woman makes a fuss that I refused to take her complaint. Sometimes it's best to choose your battles. This is one of those times.

6:55 p.m.—Prisoner Transport

Halfway between our jurisdictions, another officer and I meet a Bay County Sheriff Deputy to take custody of a prisoner he has picked up on a Saginaw Police Department warrant. We talk for a few minutes and allow the prisoner, handcuffed in front and supporting himself on crutches, to stretch his legs.

After a moment of listening to our conversation, the prisoner asks if any of us smoke, which we do not. About 30 yards away, a man is fishing in the banks of the Saginaw River. I walk down to the riverbank and ask if he can spare a cigarette for our prisoner. He gladly offers one. The handcuffed man is grateful for one last smoke before heading to jail. I have dealt with him several times during my career and have taken him to jail at least twice. He has never given me a problem. A single cigarette, I think, is the least I can do to repay him for never fighting with me.

8:40 p.m.—Officer Needs Assistance

On the South end of Saginaw, an officer has located an armed car-jacking suspect. A lengthy foot chase ensues and the officer is calling for assistance. I am coming from the North side of town and hit speeds of nearly 100 miles per hour en route to assist. Fortunately, there is little traffic and the majority of the short trip I travel a four-lane road, which offers some room for error. I arrive safely seconds after the suspect has been apprehended. The gun allegedly dropped by the suspect is located near where the foot chase started.

9:10 p.m.—Attempt Suicide

The house where I am sent is small, but very well kept. Family photographs cover the walls. A woman in her late thirties sits in a chair, crying. She says she has taken some pills and has downed about 12 beers. A neighborhood friend consoles the woman while medical personnel check her over. Several children, one of them also crying, dart in and out of the house. The woman says she needs psychological help and she wants to check herself into a hospital. She is cooperative and the ambulance and rescue personnel say they do not need police help. I leave without ever speaking to the woman.

Michael S. East

Saturday, August 17

Twenty-one calls await my shift as I check into service on a sunny and warm summer day.

3:10 p.m.—Car Accident

The woman I find waiting in her vehicle on Southbound Interstate 675 is surprisingly pleasant. She has been waiting for 70 minutes for an officer to respond to the single-vehicle accident in which she was involved. I apologize for the delay and get her on her way within about 10 minutes. Writing the report itself adds 40 minutes to the call.

4:10 p.m.—Prisoner Transport

I am sent, along with another officer, to meet a Midland County Sheriff deputy for a prisoner exchange. There are now 27 calls for service holding in the city. We normally wouldn't even bother with picking up a prisoner on a busy day like this, but this person's warrants are of a serious nature. Picking up this prisoner takes two officers away from answering calls for well over an hour.

5:39 p.m.—Warrant Arrest

A man with an outstanding warrant is about to be released from a local hospital. Another officer and myself arrive as the suspect is about to be discharged. His mood gets considerably more glum when we enter his room. He knew about the warrant, but had hoped no one else did. We take him into custody without incident and transport him to the county jail.

6:52 p.m.—Shooting

A shooting directly across the street from a local high school throws a neighborhood into chaos. I arrive as the fifth or sixth car on scene. Officers have already located the victim, who is alive. Several witnesses have also been rounded up and are being interviewed. I leave the scene to check a neighborhood about a mile to the West of where the shooting occurred. The suspects are supposed to live in this area, but I am unable to locate them or the suspect vehicle. I clear to assist with other in-progress calls, which are quickly stacking up.

7:20 p.m.—Disorderly Persons

Several persons throwing rocks at cars from a freeway overpass are gone when I arrive.

7:26 p.m.—Drug Activity

A report of area drug dealers hanging out in a North-side neighborhood yields nothing when I check the area. The call is nearly an hour old and they have moved on.

7:39 p.m.—Man with Gun

The woman who called says her brother pulled a gun on her. I am only a few blocks away when the call goes out and I locate the supposedly armed man, along with two women, inside a van parked two houses from the venue. Several other people are milling around the van. I have no back up when I pull on. There is no easy way to approach this situation. At gunpoint, I order everyone away from the van and tell the occupants to get their hands where I can see them. Nobody is quick to follow my commands as they grudgingly comply. Several people sit on their front porches watching. I am extremely vulnerable as any one of 10 people could have the gun by now—if there even is a gun.

I get the male suspect out of the driver's seat and check him for weapons. This means holstering my own gun and I am now more vulnerable than ever. The man weighs at least 260 pounds and I am unable to handcuff him with my one set of handcuffs. I walk him backward toward my patrol car, using him as a shield separating myself from the other potential suspects at the scene. Finally, another officer arrives and I used his handcuffs to double-cuff my suspect and place him into my patrol car.

Returning to the van, the other officer and I remove the two females and check them for weapons. No weapons are located on the women. Neither is a gun located in the van when I search it. Several of the people who had been standing around the van have left the area, as I was unable to contain everyone when I first arrived.

I begin the task of sorting out the story, talking to a rather loud-mouthed victim, who has now come down the street yelling at the man and women who had been inside the van. I also talk to witnesses and get some conflicting information.

The victim says the suspect, who is her brother, has pulled a gun on family members twice today. She says he had a gun several seconds before I arrived. I begin to doubt this. After collecting everyone's accounts of the altercation, I release the man and the women who had been inside the van. Considering the conflicting witness statements, and the fact no gun was located, I make no arrests. The case report I write will be sent to detectives for further investigation.

9:30 p.m.—Suspicious Situation

A woman calls to report a child walking down the street in the dark, crying. The caller is unsure if the child is lost or has possibly been assaulted. When I check the neighborhood, I speak to several other children within a two-block radius. They all say they saw the child and I follow each of their directions to where they saw him last. I never locate the child. There are no further calls regarding him.

Before checking out of service a short time later, I see on my computer screen there is a family trouble call still holding from 1:16 p.m. During the shift, it was downgraded from an in-progress call to a report call. Still, more than nine hours later, no one is available to respond.

Thursday, August 22

3:23 p.m.—Suspicious Person

The first responding officer arrives moments before me and I am disregarded as the suspicious person has apparently left the area.

3:26 p.m.—Family Trouble

I can hear a man and woman yelling from inside the residence even before getting out of my patrol car. Moments later, standing between the two, the yelling is much more intense, with the woman making most of the noise. Her husband, who appears to be suffering from a huge hangover, bounces between quiet humility and verbal tirades of his own. He tries to hug the woman several times and is met with a barrage of profanity. Finally, he decides to leave so his wife can cool down. There has been no assault. My back-up officer and I leave as the man walks away down the sidewalk.

3:47 p.m.—Abandoned Vehicle

The venue is an aging auto repair shop. Like many of these slowly crumbling, locally owned garages, this place used to house a nationally known, full-service gas station. The ones that aren't falling down and vacant are now home to mechanics trying to make a living being their own boss. The owner is a polite, soft-spoken man in his sixties. We talk for a few minutes as I tag two vehicles that have been abandoned on his property. They will be impounded in two days if the owner does not return to remove them.

5:17 p.m.—Disorderly Person

The dispute is between an adult brother and sister. It is the type of petty call that should never involve the police—or anyone outside the family for that matter.

6:06 p.m.—Prisoner Transport

A trip to Bay City to pick up a prisoner proves uneventful. The man is wanted on a warrant issued by the Saginaw Police Department. The entire trip, including dropping the man off at jail, takes about an hour.

8:20 p.m.—Retail Fraud

A 14-year-old boy with a history of petty theft has been caught shoplifting by the owner of a small party store. The boy stands defiantly and lies his way through a story when I question him. His mother is there and looks at her son disgustedly as he defends his actions. The storeowner bans the boy from returning to the property.

I release the juvenile to the custody of his mother and write a report to be forwarded to juvenile detectives in the morning.

Saturday, August 24

3:17 p.m.—Malicious Destruction of Property

The venue is a beautiful church, standing tall and proud in a drug-infested, poverty-stricken area of the city's Eastside. The female complainant says she was inside the church offices when she heard several teens passing by outside. Moments later she heard shattering glass and came outside to find her car window smashed and her checkbook gone. The woman keeps her composure while giving me information for the police report. I can tell she is a religious and forgiving woman. I can also see today's incident is testing her faith somewhat.

5:00 p.m.—Loud Music

Driving through one of the rougher neighborhoods on the city's North side, I pass a group of 20 or so older men and women, milling around in front of a corner "social club," which is a building where everyone hangs out, but nobody seems to actually own. Several people are standing on the sidewalk drinking beer. Some try to hide their bottles as I slowly pass by. Blues music wafts from the stereo of a newer pickup truck parked on the grass. It's the kind of scene that would have had me writing a dozen tickets for open intoxicants and loud music when I first took the job.

"We ain't doin' nothin' wrong, are we?" asks a man in his sixties when I pull my patrol car up curbside.

"Nope. Nobody's complaining, but that is some good music," I reply.

The man, realizing I am not there to harass him, looks more at ease now. Several of his friends are not so sure. They eye me suspiciously, wondering what I am up to. Halfway down the block there is a white girl in her 30s, wearing leather pants, standing on the sidewalk. She is a prostitute. Across the street a disheveled white guy with greasy hair walks past. The three of us are the only non-blacks of the 40 or so people who are out and about on the block.

"What's with all the white folk up here today?" I ask the older man. "Usually I'm the only white guy up here."

"I don't know who that girl is with the leather pants; ain't seen her before. That guy is probably from the mission on Norman Street," he says with a quiet laugh.

"Just checkin'. Thought maybe the neighborhood was changing or something," I reply, as a call comes in over my police radio. "I'll see you later. Gotta go back to work."

The man offers the slightest of smiles as I pull away. He has to be careful of appearances when talking to the police. Anybody seen around here being too friendly with the cops will quickly be labeled as a snitch.

5:10 p.m.—911 Hang-up Call

The call comes from a pay telephone outside a party store well known as a haven for dope dealers. Nobody is on the phone when I arrive. The store clerk gives me the cold shoulder when I ask about the call or if she saw anybody at the phone.

5:38 p.m.—Disorderly Adult

Responding to another party store for a call about a disorderly person, I arrive to find another rude store clerk, who does not even acknowledge my presence. There is nobody acting disorderly that I can see so I clear the call quickly.

6:30 p.m.—Family Trouble

The house where we are sent is just a few blocks from the river on the city's West side. The surrounding neighborhood is becoming rundown. Talking with the people involved, I am immediately struck with the irony that the decay of this city block is comparable to the decay in each of their smiles. The suspect, victim and several witnessed all display mouths of rotting, black teeth when they talk. The sight is so appalling I have a hard time concentrating on their words while taking statements.

Eventually, we sort through the problem and nobody goes to jail. Several visiting family members say they are leaving to go home in a few moments so there will be no further problems. Climbing back into my patrol car, I am happy to leave.

9:15 p.m.—Abandoned Vehicle Follow-up

The day has proven to be fairly slow. I take time at the end of my shift to impound an abandoned vehicle, which I had tagged for removal a few days prior. Between waiting for a tow truck and completing the appropriate paperwork, this call takes nearly an hour and is the last call I take before calling it a day.

Sunday, August 25

3:32 p.m.—Assault with Weapon

The call is dispatched as a family trouble, but I am advised halfway to the venue that it has been upgraded to weapons call. I arrive at the venue and park several houses away to better conceal myself from potential gunfire. Most of the houses is the neighborhood are modest, yet well kept. There are, however, well-known trouble spots on this particular block. Gunfire is not uncommon to residents of this area.

As I approach the house, a woman comes outside. She says a neighborhood drug dealer assaulted her 18-year-old daughter. She says the suspect forced his way into the house. He also had a gun. Surveying the inside of the house, I can see where the man tore the house apart, breaking items in the kitchen and the daughter's bedroom.

The daughter, who is pregnant, says the suspect actually had been staying at this house, but when she discovered he was dealing drugs, he was asked to move out. The victim says this is why the man tore up the house. Looking around the room, there are several broken items lying on the floor. There is graffiti painted on the walls. The words "Fuck me" are scrawled twice on the wall over a bed. I am not sure who wrote the words and I don't care to know.

The other officer who had been dispatched to the scene checks the surrounding area and is unable to locate the suspect. The report I write will be sent to detectives in the morning.

4:52 p.m.—Disorderly Adult

Three businesses in the same neighborhood have called about an intoxicated man in a black leather jacket causing problems. When we finally track him down, the man is sitting on a stool at a local bar, drinking a draft beer. The man is physically imposing and appears to have mental problems. Fortunately, he offers no resistance when we ask him to come outside to talk.

Standing on the sidewalk outside the bar, I get the man's identification and check him for warrants. While I do this he begins to tell his life story to my back-up officer. He says he was a "roadie" for a well-known band in the 1970s. Within seconds, he breaks into a rock song, singing a very animated version as rush-hour motorists pass by and stare. He has no warrants and we give him trespass warnings for the businesses where he caused problems. He says he will stay away from the area. My contact with him was odd, yet pleasant. I walk away laughing as he walks the other way still singing a very off-key rock song.

5:28 p.m.—Fight

A couple of officers arrive before I make it to this call. I am disregarded while still miles away.

5:48 p.m.—Abandoned Vehicle

I tag for impound an old car with two flat tires, sitting on private property.

6:48 p.m.—Missing Child

While we investigate several calls for missing children every month, this call is more urgent than usual. The child is apparently lost in a rail yard on the city's North side. Several family members are looking for the child when I arrive.

At least six other officers are dispatched to assist. Central Dispatch has already made contact with the person in charge of the train yard and all rail traffic in the yard has been halted. Fortunately, within 10 minutes the call is cleared when the boy's family finds him walking in a residential neighborhood South of the train yard.

7:15 p.m.—Prostitute

The woman I spot walking around a block in the downtown district is an obvious prostitute. She is overweight and balding, but still trying to make a living at what may be her only job skill. For fun, I observe her from a few blocks away. She knows I am watching her and she stops to look in empty store windows as she walks. I finally pull up to talk to the woman after 10 minutes of watching her window shop at vacant stores. I can hardly keep a straight face when I approach her. She is slightly amused as well and offers no lies about what she is doing. I check her for warrants and advise her to leave the area, which she does.

7:39 p.m.—Family Trouble

The woman I contact at the venue says she is fine. She had an argument with her husband. She does not need the police now, she says. She appears to be okay and I clear the call without further discussion.

8:12 p.m.—Panic Alarm

The house where I arrive is one of the nicest in the neighborhood. I contact an elderly man who says he just got the alarm installed and he's not sure how to use it. I disregard the other responding officer and try for a few minutes to assist the man with his alarm system. I have no better luck with the alarm and clear the call without fixing the problem.

9:35 p.m.—Family Trouble

A man in his thirties meets me at the front door of an older house not far from the expressway. He says his daughter is acting up and he would like me to talk to her. The overweight, 14-year-old girl he brings onto the front porch is crying uncontrollably. She won't talk to me and she won't listen either.

A minute later, the other dispatched officer arrives. He knows the family well and this gives him a little more leeway than I have. He grabs the girl by the arm and leads her to his patrol car, placing her into the back seat as she screams that she doesn't want to go to the juvenile center.

At the father's request, we let the girl stew in the back seat for a while, thinking she is going to the juvenile detention center. Finally, the father comes over and feigns giving her a second chance. By the time the girl is out of the patrol car, "yes sir" and "no sir" is all she can manage. She goes inside the house at her father's command. He thanks us for the help and with that my night is through.

Sunday, September 8

3:00 p.m.—Suspicious Situation

Returning from a long and relaxing vacation, I am thrown back into the reality of police work within seconds of checking into service.

The caller is a driver for a local towing company. He has spotted a strung-out-looking male hiding in bushes along a busy road on the city's North side. The man waved down the tow truck driver and asked him to call police.

Talking to the man now, he continuously looks over his shoulder while he tells a paranoid tale of being up all night, smoking crack and being chased by drug dealers with guns. The man is sweating profusely. He says he ran from a nearby neighborhood and into the woods, trying to escape his pursuers. Finally, an ambulance arrives. The man gladly jumps in and is taken to a local hospital.

To be on the safe side, another officer and myself check the neighborhood where the man says he had been smoking crack the previous night. The house he described is nowhere to be found. And, while there are dozens of crack dealers and users in this neighborhood, not surprisingly, none of them approaches us to inquire about a disheveled-looking, paranoid white guy who had been running through the area, hiding behind trees.

3:47 p.m.—Fight

Before I can arrive, two Saginaw County Sheriff Deputies arrive at the scene and handle the problem.

4:10 p.m.—Breaking and Entering Alarm

The venue is a former gas station, which has since been turned into several other businesses. It is now a used tire store of sorts. The building's alarm goes off nearly weekly. We find the building secure upon checking it.

4:20 p.m.—Larceny of Bicycle

By the time I arrive the complainant has found out who stole his bicycle and he has retrieved it. He says he does not wish to file charges against the suspect, but he'll call if it happens again.

5:02 p.m. - Cutting

Although I have never had to respond to this house, another officer who arrives with me says there is a history of domestic problems here. This time, the female caller says her knife-wielding boyfriend has cut her. I get no answer after several knocks on the door and step back to kick the door in. Despite being a large, solid-looking door, the wood doorframe is old and the door gives way easily on the second kick.

Inside the house, we can hear a man and woman arguing in an upstairs bathroom. After separating them and listening to both their stories, we determine the man will be jailed on a felonious assault charge. The woman was not cut as she had claimed when calling 911, but we determine the man did threaten her with a knife.

6:40 p.m.—Animal Complaint

Switching gears from domestic disturbances to bothersome dogs, I respond to a report of a vicious dog, which has trapped a woman inside her vehicle. When we arrive, the woman has gotten away, but the dog—a large brown-and-white creature, with far too much excess saliva, is running around loose behind the venue. He is actually very friendly, too friendly, in fact as he jumps on me several times, getting dirt, fur and drool all over my uniform. We finally coax the animal into a patrol car and transport him to the police station to await pickup by animal control officers. The smell of the dog is now part of my uniform and stays with me for the rest of my shift.

7:21 p.m.—Suspicious Situation

The caller says two men have entered a vacant house where a lot of drug activity has taken place lately. The house, however, is empty when I check it.

9:11 p.m.—Breaking and Entering

The complainant is a woman in her twenties. She is crying when I walk into the living room. While she was out earlier in the day, someone broke into her apartment and stole a television set and, more importantly, all of her daughters' new school clothes. There is little I can do to console her. I gather information for the report. She is still crying when I leave.

Monday, September 9, 2002

3:08 p.m.—Breaking and Entering Alarm

The alarm is one of many dispatched in recent months at a newly constructed home on the city's Eastside. Upon checking the residence, the house appears to be secure. Recent requests to the homeowner to have the alarm system checked have apparently fallen on deaf ears.

3:15 p.m.—Assault

When I arrive at a busy intersection near a local high school, a frantic woman in her twenties waves me down. She talks to me through tears while holding her infant child. She had been stopped at a traffic light next to a school bus, when several teenagers inside the bus began pelting her car with small apples. The woman says she got out of her car and yelled at the kids to stop because she had a child in the car.

"We don't give a fuck!" was the response of several teens, says the woman. As she got back into her car, one of the assailants threw another apple through her open car window, striking the child. Fortunately, the child was not hurt. The teens apparently then ordered the bus driver to open the door and they fled the scene, knowing the police would be called. The bus driver didn't even wait for my arrival, telling the woman he had to finish his route. The assault report I write for the woman will probably not result in prosecution, as the suspects will be nearly impossible to identify without the cooperation of other kids on the bus. From past experience, I know the chance of that happening is slim.

4:35 p.m.—Family Trouble

A 15-year-old girl is the caller. She is having an argument with her mother's boyfriend. The adults at the house, including the girl's mother, say the girl instigated the problem. After listening to a five-minute tantrum from the girl, we leave her to work out the problem with her family.

5:01 p.m.—Family Trouble

I arrive at the venue simultaneously with my back-up officer. The house we enter is neat and tastefully decorated. The furnishings and interior colors convey a feeling of warmth, which is shattered shortly after our entrance when the caller begins yelling, ordering us to remove her husband from the home.

It takes several minutes to explain to the woman that we cannot force her husband to leave. She does not understand my explanation, mainly because it's not what she wants to hear. As expected, the woman begins to tell me all of her husband's faults, despite my protests that this is none of my business. We are interrupted once when a well-dressed, carefree girl comes in the front door, holding her day's homework assignment.

"Go on out on the porch and play," the woman instructs her daughter, who appears to be about seven years old.

When the girl leaves, the woman begins to re-hash her previous speech. I stop her mid-sentence and reiterate that we cannot make her husband leave just because she is mad at him. We bid her good day and turn to leave. The husband, slightly embarrassed, thanks us for coming.

5:38 p.m.—Abandoned Vehicle

The abandoned car I am sent to remove is already gone.

5:46 p.m.—Abandoned Vehicle

Continuing the never-ending task of cleaning up the city's junk cars, I find this one right where the dispatcher said it would be. The vehicle is tagged for removal and the report is written within about 45 minutes.

6:15 p.m. - City Council Meeting

Mainly due to past disruptive citizens causing problems at city council meetings, the police department is now required to pull one officer from patrol duty and place them at meetings for security purposes. The assignment is rotated through the second-shift patrol ranks. Today, it is my turn. The meeting lasts hours and is my final assignment of the day. Ironically, I spend half of my day providing security against disgruntled citizens who often complain about Saginaw's lack of police protection.

Thursday, September 12

Fall is in the air as I take to the streets. The day is mild and sunny and reminds me of a college football Saturday. Before this beautiful day ends, however, death will come swift and unsuspecting to someone who, as I start my shift, has no idea he is living out his final hours.

3:50 p.m.—Vehicle Accident

There are no injuries at the scene and my report is finished within an hour.

5:15 p.m.—Breaking and Entering Alarm

The alarm proves false, but I am disregarded as I drive to the scene.

5:19 p.m.—Family Trouble

The venue is an apartment complex where the police are a regular fixture and family trouble calls are a part of life's routine. The apartment we are standing in is somewhat cramped, yet well decorated. I locate the suspect—an 11-year-old boy—upstairs in his bedroom. He is sobbing, but I can tell he is trying to get sympathy.

After bringing the child to the living room, we listen to his mother relate the story of an argument between her and her son. He interrupts her sharply several times, blowing his cover of an innocent, crying child. Before we leave the son gets a 10-minute lecture about his behavior. We refer the mother to a juvenile officer who can help her more thoroughly than we can today. She is appreciative when we depart. However, I am sure officers will be back for the same problem in the not-to-distant future.

5:59 p.m.—Armed Robbery

I am the first officer to arrive at the robbery of a muffler shop. Three victims, who had been locked in the bathroom by a gun-wielding robber, are relating the events of the robbery when other officers finally arrive. Over the police radio I give a better description of the suspect. Two city officers and a Michigan State Police trooper are checking the area for the suspect. My request for a tracking dog is denied. There are no dogs available in the county at this time.

A search of the area proves futile. Being locked in the bathroom, the victims are unsure if the suspect fled on foot or in a car. They are visibly shaken by the incident. I gather information to forward to detectives, not knowing whether the suspect is in a car speeding down the expressway or sitting in a house a block away. The report is a lengthy one, which takes hours to complete.

9:30 p.m.—Breaking and Entering/Fire Alarm

When I arrive at the venue, a building belonging to the local school district, the fire department and another officer are already checking the premises. Shortly thereafter, we determine the call to be a false alarm.

9:40 p.m. - Shooting

When the venue - a party store on the city's North side—comes over the air as the scene of a shooting, several officers besides those dispatched, decide to respond. The store is a magnet for drug activity and this is likely not a false call.

I am the second officer on scene, arriving seconds after a sergeant. The victim is sitting slumped over inside his pickup truck, which he apparently had driven backward up an embankment after being shot. The cab of the truck is coated with blood. The sergeant checks for a pulse and finds none. The man appears to be dead, but we ask Central Dispatch to have medical personnel expedite their response.

Within a couple of minutes the scene is more chaotic. Dozens of people, attracted by the lights and sirens, have gathered around to watch. The scene is cordoned off by one of several officers who have arrived. Others are checking the area for evidence and, more importantly, witnesses. The crowd thins as we ask if anyone saw the shooting. As expected, everyone wants to watch, but few want to become involved.

It appears the suspects were gone long before police arrival. The victim and a friend, who was in the truck with him at the time of the shooting, are not from Saginaw. A witness says the shooting occurred during a drug deal gone awry. This witness is secured and taken to police headquarters where a long night awaits.

Eventually, I am relieved and I return to police headquarters to begin writing a report of the shooting. I have the victim's wallet, which was left at the scene. It will be secured in the evidence room. As I sit at a computer screen a short time later, writing the details of the homicide, I am numb to the scene I have just left. After a few homicides, senseless death no longer seems to be a big deal. People get shot. People get stabbed. People Die. It's becomes just another fact of the job.

Moments later, as I reach for an evidence envelope to place the victim's wallet into, the wallet itself falls open. Inside are several photos: a four-person family picture, a young boy posing in a baseball uniform, a teenage girl in a dance costume. The reality hits me now that these are the real victims. These are the people, probably home in bed sleeping right now, who had no say in the events of this evening. A wife, a son and a daughter, who are unknowingly only a telephone call away from having their hearts broken forever.

The sadness now darkens my mood. I get home nearly two hours late and thank God for my own family. I hope they will never have to be awakened by a telephone call like the one that will be made tonight to this victim's family.

Sunday, September 15

3:30 p.m.—Drowning

Roll call runs late today and the minute I check into service I am greeted with a report of a man drowning in the Saginaw river, underneath the Court Street Bridge. Several officers respond and I arrive third on scene, covering the nearly three-mile distance in less than two minutes.

Standing underneath the bridge, wrapped in a blanket, the victim has already been pulled from the river by a friend. Both men are bums who have been living underneath the bridge. Both reek of liquor. Ambulance and fire department rescue personnel have already arrived and begin to treat the victim, who is probably a little more sober for the experience.

While the man is being treated, I walk down to the cement embankment underneath the bridge. Another bum, a disheveled, smelly man in his sixties, sits quietly and tries not to make eye contact. Empty liquor bottles litter the area. There are also a couple of backpacks, some clothing, a rolled-up tent and a wicker chair. I ask the man for identification and he hands it over without a word. His hands are leathery. Yellow, cracked fingernails extend from each finger. His beard is mangy and graying. A warrant check shows he is not wanted by any law enforcement agencies. I give him a trespass warning and tell him he has to leave the area. He nods his head in silent understanding.

Several members of the Saginaw County Dive Team have already arrived when I return to where the victim is standing. When told the circumstances, one dive team member rolls his eyes. I am sure it's not the first time he has had a Sunday afternoon with his family interrupted by a drunk falling into the river. Eventually, the victim is loaded into an ambulance and taken to a local hospital due to his level of intoxication. He obviously is a danger to himself. The man offers no resistance when told to get into the ambulance. He looks like he could use a warm bed and hot meal.

5:01 p.m. - Runaway

The woman reporting her daughter as a runaway says she hasn't seen the girl in a week. She thought her daughter had been staying at an aunt's house. The aunt had called today and said the runaway was not with her. I take the report and the child is entered into the computer system as a juvenile runaway.

6:00 p.m.—Felonious Assault

The two combatants are a woman in her twenties, and the boyfriend of the woman's now-deceased mother. They are living together in the dead woman's house under a pre-death arrangement both agreed to.

Today the man says he argued with the woman because she was using a drinking glass, which the man considers his own. He says when he confronted the woman she threatened him with a knife, then a baseball bat, then a glass bottle. The man says she eventually came after him with a pan of hot grease. The story seems a little far-fetched. Speaking to several witnesses all of them say the assault never happened and the man is lying. Since the man is claiming to be the victim of a felony, I write the report for him anyway.

8:23 p.m.—Fight

Arriving at the scene of a fight in front of a West-side coffee shop, we find all parties have departed.

8:40 p.m.—Assault

A woman who wishes to remain anonymous tells me she watched her neighbor pull into his driveway at a high rate of speed and park in front of his garage. She says a second car pulled in immediately after the neighbor had arrived. The second car backed up twice and struck the first car, knocking in through the garage door. She says the second car's driver then chased her neighbor into his house, but was unable to catch him. She is concerned, but does not wish to be directly involved.

I check out the garage and find a late model SUV sitting halfway through a shattered garage door. After several knocks on the door of the residence, a man answers the door. He is nervous yet looks puzzled to see us. The man is immediately defensive and insists the assault did not occur. He is obviously lying. He says he does not need our help. I ask him several times if he is sure and he says he does not want the police.

An hour after departing the residence, the man calls police headquarters and makes a complaint that I had refused to take a report from him.

9:35 p.m.—Stolen Vehicle

A stolen vehicle report keeps me tied up for the balance of my shift. The report involves nothing unusual; it's just another stolen car on another day in Saginaw.

Monday, September 16

3:12 p.m.—Disorderly Adult

The owner of an Eastside grocery store tells me there is a mentally impaired man in his parking lot, asking customers for money and cigarettes. The man refused to leave when asked. When I locate the man, I find he is the same man I have had to kick out of the police station lobby several times in recent weeks for the same behavior. He departs without argument when I tell him he must leave.

3:38 p.m.—Car Accident

The persons involved have been waiting more than an hour for police response. By the time I arrive, they are not only mad at each other, but also mad at me. I don't even bother to explain the call volume and our lack of available officers. I am sure the fact that I have been in service for only 26 minutes would not interest them either. I listen to them complain as I gather information. I depart the scene as quickly as possible and find a quieter environment to complete my report.

4:50 p.m.—Larceny from a Vehicle Report

A construction worker employed at a downtown development project had his car broken into. Fortunately, he keeps very little of value inside his work vehicle, so his losses were minimal.

5:29 p.m.—Juvenile Assault

It takes nearly 20 minutes to interview both persons involved in the assault. Predictably, neither admits responsibility for starting the altercation. Both are obviously lying to some extent. I document their lies on an assault report, which will be sent to a juvenile investigator.

6:45 p.m.—Felonious Assault

The woman I meet at a rickety home alongside the expressway looks familiar. I recall having been here before for similar problems. Several boys threatened to hit her son with a whiskey bottle, she says. She does not know the boys or where they live. I check the neighborhood for them, but have no success locating the suspects.

7:30 p.m.—Larceny

A juvenile says another boy stole his earring. The victim is a pudgy 12-year-old boy. He relates the details of the larceny, which occurred more than half an hour ago. I write a larceny report for him. I again am unable to locate the suspect or the stolen earring due to the lag in dispatch time.

Thursday, September 19

3:15 p.m.—Car Accident

A man who runs a stop sign causes an accident, but fortunately nobody is injured. After verifying each driver has a clear driving status and up-to-date insurance, I tell the drivers they can leave and I complete the written report at another location.

4:25 p.m.—Abandoned Vehicle Follow-up

I finally get time to impound an abandoned vehicle I had tagged for removal nearly a week ago. The impound sticker has been scratched off the car's window, presumably by the owner, in an attempt to thwart the impound. Nonetheless, the vehicle is towed away.

6:03 p.m.—Gambling Complaint

The intersection of the residential neighborhood where I am sent is clear of any gambling activity. I assume the roving dice game has found a new location.

6:10 p.m.—Assault Report

I locate the victim awaiting treatment in the lobby of a local hospital. She is in her twenties and probably has a pleasant smile, but today she is not smiling. She says she was assaulted after another woman cut her off while driving on the city's Southwest side. A fight ensued and she lost. She requests an assault report, even though she does not know her assailant and we have no means by which to identify the suspect.

While the report is basically useless, at least it will allow the victim the illusion of feeling like she did something about being beat up.

6:52 p.m.—Unknown Disturbance

The call is occurring at a low-income high-rise, but it is unclear what is happening. Central Dispatch advises there was a 911 call with a lot of yelling in the background and someone asking for the police to be sent. When I arrive, a younger man greets me in the lobby. He says the problem, which was a dispute over stolen jewelry, has been solved. A short time later a woman enters the lobby and confirms that she is the caller and the police are no longer needed.

As we talk, a privately employed, uniformed security guard assigned to the building comes over to hear the discussion. Upon sight of the guard, the woman starts yelling for him to leave because he is useless. She verbally berates the man for nearly five minutes as he stands with no response. The guard is young and naïve. He is one of many I have seen at this facility. They don't last long, usually starting off eager and full of self-confidence. But most soon learn they are defenseless to the verbal and physical assaults that occur here daily. The woman finishes speaking her mind to the still speechless guard, turns and thanks me, and I leave.

8:28 p.m.—Disorderly Adult

As I look at the caller, he seems to be the picture of a worn out blue-collar laborer, discarded onto life's scrap heap, like so many other once-proud men in this industrial town. Sitting on his front porch in the dark the man, still wearing a work shirt with his first name embroidered on the pocket, tries to tell us his live-in sister stole money from him. The man is drunk and can barely talk. A couple of empty 40-ounce beer bottles litter the porch near the broken down chair on which he sits. His hair is thinning and messy. His fingers are long, with dirty, yellowing fingernails extending as he points while yelling out his complaints. The man has a large frame, but years of drinking and working the night shift have left him thin, with little muscle tone. He is a far cry, I think, from the man he once was.

Meanwhile, the sister is busy moving some belongings from the house. Tired of his accusations, she is leaving. She is at least sober and moderately pleasant toward us, but she is obviously uneducated and very rough around the edges. The brother and sister continue to bicker as she retrieves belongings from a house that appears on the verge of collapse. After about 10 minutes of refereeing, we depart. There is nothing we can do for the man.

10:10 p.m.—Officer Needs Assistance

A car chase on the city's North side ends when the suspect car crashes and the driver flees on foot. There are three passengers inside the car and the pursuing officer takes them into custody. I arrive second at scene and take off on foot into a train yard where the driver fled. Within a minute, I am joined by at least a half dozen other officers and we begin a search for the suspect.

The train yard is vast and dark. There are a dozen sets of tracks running both East and West in front of us, with long trains blocking at least the first four sets of rails. We check from car-to-car and train-to-train. The train cars number in the hundreds. Central Dispatch advises they contacted the train yard and all rail traffic has been stopped. I fear, however, one train may lurch forward at any time, knocking me over and hacking off a limb under the heavy and dull edge of a boxcar's wheel.

At this moment, a rail yard employee runs up and says the suspect jumped inside an open-air train car, which he points out. Checking the car, we find it empty. We check the next five, as well, and they are empty too. The search goes on for nearly half an hour. During this time we split up and check rows of boxcars, flatbed cars and chemical-filled tanker cars. A sergeant climbs to the top of a train and surveys the yard from above. In the quiet darkness, I check car-to-car with gun drawn, yet close to my body in case I get jumped. There are a million places for the suspect to hide in here. On this night, with the odds stacked in his favor, the bad guy wins this game of hide-and-seek. I leave the rail yard and return to the police station, ending my shift on time.

Sunday, September 22

4:41 p.m.—Armed Robbery

The person who called is a smallish man in his twenties. He is jittery and doesn't want to listen. He only wants to talk, even when I try to get details of the incident he is reporting. He talks over me, not listening to my questions. The victim says a man came into his house and stole, at gunpoint, nearly $2,000, which he had in his pocket. His story is strange, at best. It is a total lie, at worst. Still, I treat it as an actual armed robbery and advise two other responding units of the suspect description. According to the victim, the suspect is supposed to be, at this very minute, standing on a street corner four blocks away. The suspect, however, is not there when we check. The entire incident smells of a drug transaction gone bad. I write up the case report and forward it to the detective bureau for further investigation.

7:30 p.m.—Violation of Personal Protection Order

The victim has come to police headquarters and I am dispatched there to take a report for her. She relates to me how an ex-boyfriend is violating a personal protection order by contacting her on the telephone. The woman is hysterical and I can barely understand her as she talks. Eventually, I get enough information to write her report. There is not enough evidence at this point to make an arrest, however.

8:44 p.m.—Family Trouble

The call of a family dispute came from a pay telephone at a party store. Predictably, nobody is there when we arrive.

9:31 p.m.—Man with a Gun

The caller is anonymous and reports a man walking down the street on the city's Eastside, carrying a gun. Checking the area, we are unable to locate the suspect, if there ever was a suspect at all.

10:03 p.m.—911 Hang-up Call

The Eastside residence where I am sent sits mid-block in a fairly quiet neighborhood. The woman who answers the door gives me a puzzled look when I inform her someone called 911 from her home. Several children stand behind her in the entranceway. I ask if everything is okay. She looks at me as if I just told her there is an elephant standing on her roof. Finally, she says everything is fine. When I ask if one of the children might have called by mistake, she says they did not, although I can see she isn't sure. Again, I verify she is okay. I turn to leave and she offers neither a thank you, nor an apology for the inconvenience.

Monday, September 23

3:25 p.m.—Disorderly Persons

A November vote is looming to raise property taxes in the city of Saginaw. At issue will be raising monies to maintain current police and fire department staffing levels. Today there is concern over a planned protest outside city hall. When I arrive, there are three older men with hand-made signs standing on the sidewalk in front of the castle-like building, which houses several city offices. The sight is almost laughable. What is not funny, however, is the likelihood that this tax issue will be defeated and more of my co-workers will lose their jobs in the next year.

3:25 p.m.—Traffic Stop

While driving on the city's West side, the car next to me begins creeping into my lane and eventually cuts me off altogether, forcing me to quickly maneuver into the turn lane to avoid a collision. The teen behind the wheel is dumbfounded when I pull him over. He says he never saw me. The teenager is, at worst, an inexperienced driver, but has a clean driving record thus far. He thanks me for not issuing a ticket before he leaves with a verbal warning.

3:45 p.m.—Vehicle Accident

The person reporting the accident says one of the drivers may be drunk. When I arrive, however, I find the supposedly drunken man is Hispanic. He speaks somewhat labored English, but he is not drunk. The accident is a simple one to write and I am clear within about 45 minutes.

4:59 p.m.—Breaking and Entering

A neighbor reporting a breaking and entering turns out to be mistaken when we find the homeowner had simply left his door open by mistake when he left home. We secure the house and clear the call quickly.

5:37 p.m.—Breaking and Entering Alarm

The residential burglar alarm turns out to be a false alarm. We find the premises to be secure when we arrive at scene.

9:25 p.m.—Drunk Driving Accident

Assisting another officer who has been dispatched to an accident involving a drunken driver, I find a woman arguing with the officer when I arrive. She is sitting in the back seat of his patrol car, yelling. She is clearly intoxicated. I give the officer the Preliminary Breath Test (PBT) hand-held machine, which he had requested I bring to the scene.

The woman refuses to take the PBT. She continues her verbal assault. Her accusations run from racial to gender discrimination, as she says the officer is picking on her for no reason. Eventually, we have to transport the woman to a local hospital and seek a warrant from a judge to draw her blood. She continues to yell the entire time and, eventually, has to be placed into restraints at the hospital. I end my shift with the sound of her yelling still ringing in my ears.

Thursday, September 26

3:15 p.m.—Reckless Driver

A neighbor complaining of a reckless driver in the area prompts me to be dispatched to a neighborhood on the city's North side. I am unable to locate the suspect vehicle when I check the surrounding area.

3:35 p.m.—Family Trouble

The call turns into nothing more than a counseling session between a mother and a daughter who cannot get along. I finally depart as they promise things are okay between them. I leave with the feeling that I did not accomplish much.

4:22 p.m. - Neighbor Trouble

An older couple in their sixties are sitting on their front porch when I arrive. They say they are having problems with several neighbors who live about three houses away. Looking at the problem house, there are about a half a dozen juveniles hanging out in the front yard. Several are staring at me as I talk to the couple.

When a second officer arrives, the two of us walk to the problem house to hear the other side of the story. One girl immediately walks away, saying: "I ain't talking to no police." The woman in charge of the home waves us over to an open living room window, where she speaks through a sheer curtain. Apparently the problem is not big enough for her to come outside.

As she is talking, one of the teens in the yard starts running his mouth, yelling toward the elderly couple I have just left: "Man, you wanna call the motherfucking police. Meet me in the street, bitch," he yells. "Gotta call the police. Shit!"

The woman continues to speak to the other officer, not at all concerned with the language of the young man in her yard. Looking around the neighborhood, it is obvious this house is the scourge of the neighborhood. There is trash blowing around the yard, which is a yard only by name. The front lawn is mostly dirt with deep ruts worn into the ground from too much foot traffic. The outside of the home is dirty and the smell of body odor seeps out of the house through a couple of open windows. We eventually clear the call, not having accomplished much by the way of keeping the peace. Ignorance, it appears, has prevailed on this day.

4:47 p.m.—Drug Activity

Checking one of the usual drug corners, I find the drug dealers described by the caller have already moved on to another location.

5:00 p.m.—Disorderly Person

Personnel at a downtown bus station have called about a disorderly, drunk man, hanging around the bus station. I recognize the man on sight as one of the usual drunks in this area. Today, however, he is still in control of his senses. After checking him for warrants, I release the man with a trespass warning. He agrees to not come back to the bus station and walks on his way.

5:43 p.m.—Injury Accident

The accident occurs at a busy intersection. The injuries are minor, but the damage to the vehicles is enough that the fire department is also dispatched to assist with cleaning the fluids leaking from both cars. The scene is chaotic and another officer arrives to help direct traffic. Slow tow truck response keeps us at the scene for more than an hour, directing traffic around the wreckage.

I am unable to determine the cause of the accident, as both drivers have stated they had the green light in their direction when entering the intersection. One of the drivers is lying, but without witnesses, I cannot determine which. One man also has a driving history, which includes several speeding tickets and another citation for disregarding a traffic control device. While I believe he is probably responsible for the accident, I am still unable to prove who is at fault.

Saturday, September 28

3:11 p.m.—Larceny from a Vehicle

Upon leaving an Eastside church, a young couple attending a wedding discover their vehicle has been broken into and their cellular telephone stolen. They are from a small town about 50 miles from Saginaw. Both are in surprisingly good spirits. "We used to live here. This is why we left Saginaw," the man says with a grin. The call takes me about an hour from start to finish.

5:02 p.m.—Civil Stand-By

A teenage girl who was kicked out of her mother's house wants to go back and retrieve her clothing. She has asked for the police to stand by with her in case there is trouble. When we arrive at her mother's home, the doors are locked. There are noises coming from inside the home and it is obvious her mother is inside, but she won't answer the door. The teen is frustrated, but remains calm. She is an attractive, well-spoken girl, who says she's moving out of state soon to attend college. She seems like the dream child. Obviously, for this mother, she is not. We leave without her clothes, as her mother never opens the door.

6:20 p.m.—Man with a Gun

A woman in a rough Eastside neighborhood called to report a man with a gun walking down the street. She says he is a drug dealer and he just threatened to shoot her. The first car on scene locates the man and checks him. He has no gun. I am the third officer to arrive and by this time, several of the suspect's family members are yelling at us for harassing the man. When they are told the nature of the call, they immediately know who the caller was. Apparently, the caller and this man have not gotten along for some time and the caller often tries to get the man into trouble. No report is written because the complainant does not want one. We leave with nothing more than an ear-full of complaints from neighborhood cop-haters.

6:53 p.m.—Felonious Assault

The victim is a woman who says her boyfriend threatened her with a gun during an argument. She says the argument started when she confronted him about money, and a sexually transmitted disease he had passed along to her. The suspect has left by the time I arrive and the caller doesn't know where he went. I complete a report to be forwarded to detectives.

7:23 p.m.—Breaking and Entering Alarm

A check of the residential premises shows it to be secure. The call is cleared within minutes.

7:40 p.m.—Disorderly Juveniles

I arrive at the scene of an elementary school to find four kids in their early teens playing football near the building. A neighbor has caller and complained that the kids are throwing rocks at the school. All four stop and stare as I drive up across the lawn.

"What I do? I didn't do nothing," says one of the kids, in what appears to be a pre-programmed response to the sight of a police officer.

When I ask the kids about throwing rocks at the school, they say they were throwing rocks, but just to see if they could reach the roof. They agree to stop the rock throwing and I leave after engaging the kids in a short conversation about police work, at their prompting.

8:13 p.m.—911 Hang-up Call

The residents at the home where I am dispatched say everything is okay. The man and woman who live here are extremely drunk, as they have been on my previous stops here. Both say they had an argument, but they worked things out. Both will undoubtedly get drunk again and call the police in the near future.

9:35 p.m.—Family Trouble

Several calls for a family trouble at a residence lead to my response to an Eastside residence. Everyone involved has departed prior to our arrival and I am informed the police are no longer needed.

Sunday, September 29

3:20 p.m.—911 Hang-up Call

An older woman answers the door. There are several children running around the house. When I inform her of the 911 call placed from her house, she insists I am wrong. I suggest one of the children may have called by mistake. She says that's impossible and starts to engage me in an argument. I cut her off, saying if everything is okay, I'll let her tend to her house full of children. She continues to debate even as I walk away.

4:03 p.m.—Shots Fired

A neighbor reporting shots fired from a sport utility vehicle draws several officers to the area. Fortunately, nobody has been shot. We check the area for about 15 minutes, but the suspect vehicle is never located. Considering the neighborhood where the call originated, the shots being fired is no doubt gang-related.

5:40 p.m.—Vehicle Pursuit

Several undercover officers in unmarked police cars, as well as a Michigan State Police marked patrol car, engage in a drug-related vehicle chase on the city's North side. I respond to assist, but the suspect vehicle has crashed into a tree and the suspect is taken into custody about 30 seconds before my arrival. I clear the call quickly to resume patrol duties.

6:13 p.m.—Breaking and Entering

The man I meet at a dance hall is in his fifties, although he looks much older. His business has been broken into, possibly by former employees and the man lost more than $1,000 worth of belongings. I enter the hall under a plastic window-well cover that serves as an awning over the front door. Inside the building, a thick musty smell fills the room, which is coated with dust. Christmas icicle lights dangle above a dance floor that is worn and checkered with broken tiles. A makeshift DJ both stands sentinel across the room from a wall covered with cheap mirror tiles. The man says he rents the hall out for parties and he barely makes enough money to get by. He is obviously hurt that some employees have betrayed him.

I gather information for the report while standing in a back storage room which doubles as the man's home. He says he sometimes lives at the hall. In the corner, a messed up bed is pushed against a wall. A microwave oven sits on the other side of the room and the man hits the "Off" switch while we talk, halting his dinner from cooking. I give him a case number and tell him he can use it for an insurance claim. He says, however, that he has no insurance on the building. He says he is not even sure why he is making the police report. He says he just wanted someone to know what happened.

7:49 p.m.—Family Trouble

A neighbor called and says a man and woman are arguing in the front yard of a house next door to her. I arrive to find everything quiet. Most of the streetlights have been broken out and the neighborhood is dark.

I knock and the woman who answers the door is crying hysterically. She tells me to leave her alone. I go inside anyway to make sure she is not injured. She says her boyfriend is gone and she will be fine. Along with the other officer who has since arrived, we check the house to make sure the boyfriend is not there and we find he has indeed departed. The woman says she was not assaulted and, again, asks us to leave. Before walking out, I tell her to call if she needs us back. "I'm already in enough trouble because you're here now," she yells, as she orders us again to leave. At her insistence we depart, leaving her to whatever private hell she is hiding from the world.

8:10 p.m.—Family Trouble

The house where we respond on the city's North side is in a new subdivision filled with well-kept, ranch-style homes. I spot the house immediately without even looking at the numbers. The garage door is collapsed. The unhappy ex-girlfriend of a man now staying at this home came over and rammed the garage door in a fit of rage. The other officer at the scene takes information for the report as I survey the damage and request that a sergeant responds to the scene to take photographs of the damaged property. I leave shortly thereafter as the other officer says he will handle the report.

9:46 p.m.—911 Call for Police

Central Dispatch advises the caller asked for the police, but would not say why. I am advised the man also sounds intoxicated. When I arrive, a man staggers down the gravel driveway toward me. He is extremely drunk. He starts babbling and refuses to say why he wants the police. He tries to shake my hand a couple of times, but I refuse. Through his slurs, he says he is okay. He just wanted to talk. Annoyed with the man, I ask if he needs help. He says he does not, and I leave as he tries to shake my hand again. As I walk back to my patrol car, a neighbor says the man gets drunk all the time and acts foolish. Just another day in his life it would appear.

Monday, September 30

3:12 p.m.—Hit-and-Run Accident

The accident occurred during the night while the victim's car was parked on the street. With no information available about a possible suspect vehicle, I am left without leads to investigate. The corresponding reports eat up more than an hour of my day.

4:35 p.m.—Family Trouble

A young woman calls the police during a dispute with her 78-year-old father. The two are arguing over ownership of items in a house where they both have been staying. Through the woman's non-stop yelling, it takes 15 minutes to convince her there is nothing the police can do for her. The matter is not criminal in nature and will have to be sorted out in civil court, if she wishes to pursue the matter that far. She is unhappy with this information and we leave the scene with her still yelling at the other responding officer and myself.

5:30 p.m.—Larceny

A young boy in his pre-teens tells me how another kid took $5 from him in the parking lot of a local convenience store. I remember this boy from a previous call when he had his earring stolen in the parking lot of a different store.

While I listen to him describe the suspect, a steady stream of ragged, depressed-looking people make their way in and out of the store behind him. Most of them exit the store having purchased nothing but a 40-ounce bottle of beer. All of them appear to live well below the poverty line, yet what money they do have goes toward alcohol. Turning my attention back toward the young boy, I finish writing down the description of a suspect I will eventually never locate.

7:50 p.m.—Breaking and Entering of Vehicles

The call from Central Dispatch advises of two males breaking into cars at a local auto repair shop. As luck would have it, four officers, including myself, are within blocks of the business. We arrive at the scene within a minute and catch both suspects after a brief foot chase through the neighborhood. After the pair is in custody, a co-worker says he just arrested one of the kids a week ago for committing the same crime about six blocks from here. Both are lodged at the Saginaw County Juvenile Detention Center.

Tuesday, October 1

3:15 p.m.—Injury Accident

The injuries are minor when I arrive at scene, but that doesn't stop the persons involved from yelling at each other over who is to blame. A short time later, the family of one driver arrives at the scene. They re-ignite problems by starting the who-is-at-fault debate all over again. After nearly an hour everyone finally leaves and I continue completing the accident report.

4:04 p.m.—Injury Accident

After clearing the previous scene, I stop at a West-side convenience store for a soda. While inside the store, Central Dispatch advises of an injury accident with a car on fire only four blocks from my location. I arrive quickly, as do several other officers. A citizen has already put out the flames with a fire extinguisher. Several other motorists are helping the drivers. The scene remains chaotic for a while. An ambulance arrives to treat the injured. A fire truck pulls on scene. Two officers begin re-routing traffic off of the four-lane road onto side streets to ease congestion and give everyone more space to work. Due to a lack of available tow trucks, we are unable to clear the wrecked cars from the street for nearly half an hour. Calls begin to backup elsewhere in the city because three officers remain tied up for nearly an hour at this scene.

5:45 p.m.—Fight

A report of 10 males fighting in the street draws me to a North-side neighborhood, which sits atop an expressway embankment. When I arrive, only one man remains. His shirt is torn and he clearly has been fighting. He tells me the police are not needed and he took care of the problem himself. Sometimes that is a quicker solution than calling the cops.

6:10 p.m.—Domestic Assault

The woman who called to report the assault says her ex-boyfriend burned her with a curling iron during an argument. She has a fresh burn mark to back up her story. The suspect is supposed to be hiding inside a house across the street. When we go to speak with him, family members tell the primary officer the man ran out the back door when we pulled up. A search of the house confirms their story. The victim now says she doesn't want to prosecute him anyway. She just called so someone would know what happened. A felonious assault report is written in case the victim changes her mind about prosecution, or later accuses the officers of failing to help her.

7:26 p.m.—Neighbor Trouble

The dispute involves an argument between neighbors over use of a driveway on an abandoned lot between two houses. The argument is so trivial it is ridiculous. I advise the caller he'll have to settle the matter in court since neither party can prove ownership of the property the driveway rests upon.

8:05 p.m.—Disorderly Adult

The suspect is a regular on disorderly calls. With several physical deformities, he isn't hard to pick out of a crowd. Tonight he is given a trespass warning at a low-income housing facility. He will later return and other officers will be sent back to deal with him again.

9:46 p.m.—Disorderly Adult

The man we get a complaint against is inside a West-side bar. The bar manager wants him removed because he is trying to fight with people. He is very intoxicated and he rambles on, making no sense when he speaks. He keeps his fists clenched the entire time I am talking with him, so I keep enough distance to react to an attack. When we finally convince the man he has to leave, he tries to shake hands. For safety reasons, I refuse the handshake and he again clenches his fists. His girlfriend, however, escorts him to a car before he gets into further trouble. As he staggers to the vehicle, the man drunkenly mumbles how he hates the police.

10:00 p.m.—Suspicious Situation

Two officers are sent to an Eastside automotive plant, along with medical personnel, for an unknown nature call. It could be anything from an assault to a fatal accident. When we arrive and are escorted through the cavernous building, we find it is nothing more than a worker who is experiencing chest pains. Since the call is not police related, we depart, leaving medical personnel to do their job.

Wednesday, October 2

3:10 p.m.—Guard Prisoner

My first assignment out of the gate is guarding a subject involved in a recent homicide. The young male is sitting in an interrogation room, where he has been for the better part of the afternoon, waiting for detectives to interview him. I stand guard outside the room and we don't speak a word for the few hours I am there. Out on the street there are 27 calls for service awaiting the officers checking in for their shift.

7:10 p.m.—Disorderly Person with a Weapon

A resident living about a mile from police headquarters says someone is driving past her house, wielding a handgun. When we arrive to check the neighborhood, the armed subject is nowhere to be found.

7:25 p.m.—Family Trouble

I am the first officer to arrive at a house on the city's Eastside for a report of a family trouble. The call was first received by Central Dispatch at 12:57 p.m. No one answers the door when I knock. It has been more than six hours since the original call and I am sure the problem is long-since over.

7:40 p.m.—Animal Complaint

A loose dog that bit a child on the arm is the focus of the complaint. The dog has been re-secured by the owner by the time I arrive. Due to the fact there was a bite, however, I must write a report to be forwarded to animal control.

10:00 p.m.—Assault

The call involves an assault between an ex-boyfriend and girlfriend who are in their early teens. After speaking with the young man, I follow two other officers to the girl's house to hear her version of the altercation. She is young and dressed in skin-tight clothes. Her parents are understandably angry about the assault. The two teens have fought before, we are told. Tonight, despite being far under the legal drinking age, both were also consuming alcohol. The parents aren't the least bit concerned about this, however. They are more caught up in placing blame for the situation than accepting their share of responsibility for their child's actions.

As the two other officers try to reason with the girl's parents, I look across the street to a green, two-story house. The memory book in my mind flips to a page more than seven years ago. It was a hot early summer day when I was called to the home for what would be my first on-the-job experience with a dead person.

The elderly woman who lived at that home hadn't been seen for days and her mailman called after the mailbox had overflowed. By the time a supervisor and myself finally gained entry into the home, the smell of death was strong and foul.

The elderly woman had passed away of natural causes several days prior while sitting in the living room

"She's coming apart like chicken off the bone," I recall one of the paramedics saying, as he struggled to get the old woman's carcass onto a stretcher. Just hearing those words caused me to nearly vomit that day. Re-thinking the words tonight, my attention snaps back to the call at hand. As I listen to the parents complain about their daughter's plight, my mind again flips back to the picture of a dead old lady peeling apart in the hands of two EMTs as they make jokes to get themselves through the situation. I depart the call and end my night with the vision of the dead old lady still in my mind.

Friday, October 4

3:10 p.m.—Family Trouble

The woman who answers the door to a rear downstairs apartment has been crying. She is also shaking and looks like she hasn't slept in years. She says she and her husband had been arguing, but everything is okay now and the police are not needed. When I ask to speak to her husband, she lets me inside. I find the man sitting in a den, watching television. He barely acknowledges my presence, but does rudely say that I am not needed. The woman reassures me everything is okay.

I depart the apartment and as I walk back to my patrol car, a neighbor asks if everything is all right. I tell her everything is fine. She says disturbances at that apartment are not uncommon. She also says the woman has a drug problem and has been out on a three-day binge, which is probably what caused the fight.

3:37 p.m.—Vehicle Accident

A three-car accident, caused by wet pavement and careless driving, keeps me tied up for nearly and hour and a half completing the appropriate paperwork.

4:47 p.m.—Family Trouble

The dispute is a typical one between a mother and her teenage daughter. The daughter wants to run her own life. Mom disagrees. To mom's disappointment, there is little I can do since the daughter refuses to talk to me. As far as I'm concerned, it's mom's problem to deal with anyway. Not knowing how the girl was raised, I have little hope of connecting with her and helping to iron out deep-seeded family problems.

5:40 p.m.—Breaking and Entering Alarm

A storm swoops suddenly through the area, heavy winds bringing down several trees and causing numerous residential burglar alarms to flood into Central Dispatch. This alarm was undoubtedly caused by the storm. Still, I get soaked checking the premises just to make sure it is secure. The call takes only about five minutes to clear. My uniform does not dry out for hours.

6:10 p.m.—Breaking and Entering Alarm

Checking another weather-triggered alarm, I find the premises—a medical office building—to be secure. Many of the alarms are cleared up quickly and the continuous rain keeps the streets quiet for the balance of my shift.

Monday, October 7

3:15 p.m.—Check the Well Being

A police agency in Indiana requests our department's assistance locating a missing person from their jurisdiction. When I arrive at the venue, a rickety, yellow two-story house, a knock on the door brings an unfriendly: "Who is it!" I tell the woman who I am looking for when I finally convince her to open the door. She says the missing person is staying with her, but she is not there right now. "I'll have her call her people," she says, shutting the door before I can respond.

3:35 p.m.—Abandoned Vehicle

A vehicle abandoned blocking a city sidewalk prompts a call to Central Dispatch. Because it is impeding use of the sidewalk, I waive the usual 48-hour notice for abandoned vehicles and impound it on the spot.

4:55 p.m.—Drug Activity

Checking a call holding for drug activity on a North-side street corner, I find the corner deserted and I advise Central Dispatch to cancel the call.

5:40 p.m.—Parking Violations

Two vehicles parked across the sidewalk are the focus of a neighbor's complaint. The neighborhood, a once-proud area of large, beautiful homes, several of which were once owned by many of the city's 1800s-era lumber barons, is now nothing more than an array of abandoned structures, mixed in with a few occupied dwellings. Many of the homes are boarded up. Some sit open to squatters and drug users. Driveways and sidewalks, trailing off into a grassy abyss, point the way to the vacant lots where houses used to stand. Why someone would complain about vehicles parked over the sidewalk amidst this setting is beyond me. The sidewalks are cracked and overgrown with weeds, making them nearly impassable, not that there is anyone around to walk on them. I issue two parking tickets and continue on my way.

5:46 p.m. - Disorderly Adult

A school principal calls Central Dispatch to report an older man who chased several children home from an after-school program. When I arrive, I get a description of the man and begin to search the neighborhood for him. There are no other officers available to help, so I cover a dozen or so city blocks by myself. I am unable to locate the man, but I place the suspect's description in the roll-call folder so future shifts will be aware of the incident.

Tuesday, October 8

3:20 p.m.—Breaking and Entering Report

The victim is a man in his twenties. I make my way through the maze of broken down lawnmowers that litter the front porch and he invites me inside to see where someone has broken in. Immediately, I am nearly overwhelmed by the stench of old grease coming from the kitchen. Unfortunately, the kitchen is also the point of entry so we head directly to that room, where the smell is unbearable. After checking out the broken window, we walk back through the living room. Through an open bedroom door, I notice a piece of plywood fashioned into a makeshift closet door. Cockroaches skitter here and there. It is the picture of poverty. I draw the man outside as quickly as possible to gather more information about the crime. Within minutes, I depart to write the report. I am itching all the way to police headquarters.

4:20 p.m.—Juvenile Arrest

A local halfway house for children calls to turn in a teenage girl staying there. Workers have discovered she has a court-imposed pick-up order, which has been issued for her apprehension. When I arrive and place her into handcuffs, she offers no resistance. Another officer shows up moments later and we transport the girl to the juvenile detention facility.

5:40 p.m.—Civil Dispute

A dispute between a landlord and tenant brings me to a two-story, Eastside home. After listening to both parties bicker, I inform them the dispute is civil in nature and I cannot help. Neither is happy as each expected the police to take their side. I leave, having made enemies of both parties.

6:05 p.m.—Disorderly Juveniles

I locate some neighborhood kids who have been throwing rocks at an abandoned house. When I tell them to leave, they depart without argument.

6:20 p.m.—Disorderly Juveniles

Two households are at odds with each other as a child from each home has thrown a rock through the other's window. Adults at both houses refuse to hold their own child responsible, even though they both caused damage to the other's property. It's hard enough reasoning with kids about these matters, but when the adults cannot see the problem, the battle is all but lost. I leave having accomplished nothing more than wasting my time.

7:48 p.m.—Retail Fraud

Several undercover security officers summon the police to a drug store on the city's Southeast side. Several suspected shoplifters have been inside the store, removing electronic security tags from high-priced liquor bottles. The security manager says the suspects have left the store, but he knows they will be back for the merchandise they have set up to steal. He asks us to wait in back of the store for an hour or so. I explain we are too busy and cannot wait for the thieves to return. When the bad guys come back, I tell him, he'll have to take his chances dialing 911 again. He will most likely not get a quick response, but there is little else I can advise him to do.

8:12 p.m.—Disorderly Adult

A local rescue mission calls for police assistance removing a client from the property. The disorderly female has broken several rules of the facility. I arrive to find the woman sitting in her room. When I advise her that staff wants her to leave, she says she has no where else to go. After several telephone calls, we find another shelter that will take her for the night. After that, she will be on her own. She packs her belongings and I give her a ride to the other facility. Considering her attitude, she may not last the night here either.

10:05 p.m.—Breaking and Entering Alarm

I respond a little more carefully than usual to this alarm at an Eastside food store. The neighborhood is quite rough and this store has been robbed more than once. A check of the building finds it to be secure, however, and my night ends with this call.

Wednesday, October 9

It is a sunny, mild autumn afternoon as I pack equipment into my patrol vehicle for what seems like the millionth time of my career. The day starts out as mundane as every other day. Within hours, however, I will respond to a call for service which will make this day stand out like none I have experienced. The grizzly discoveries of the approaching hours will lead me to yet again question my faith in mankind.

3:10 p.m.—911 Hang-up Call

Speaking to a middle-aged couple on the front porch of their home, I am told there is no problem and the police are not needed. There is nothing in their demeanor to make me think there is a problem. Without argument, I clear the call.

3:40 p.m.—Disorderly Adult

I am only two blocks from the venue when a call goes over the radio for a disorderly white female sitting at the bus stop, drinking alcohol. When I pull up, I recognize the woman as a troublemaker in the West-side business district. She spots me and slides an open bottle of vodka toward the man sitting next to her. He gives her a what-the-hell-are-you-doing look and slides farther down the bench.

When I bring the woman to my patrol car, she immediately protests, saying she isn't doing anything wrong. As I write out a citation for consuming alcohol in public, she complains that she just paid her last ticket and she can't afford another one. The woman is in her thirties. She is an alcoholic and a prostitute. Her face is greasy and covered with bumps. She is missing several teeth. I have thought for years now that she is only a few steps from death's door. Today, more than ever, she looks like she won't live another six months. I give her the citation and send her on her way.

3:50 p.m.—Malicious Destruction of Property

A relationship gone sour results in a woman cutting up her ex-boyfriend's cloths with a pair of scissors and dumping them on the front porch of his home. At the man's request, I write a report for him so he can seek criminal charges through the county prosecutor's office.

4:45 p.m. - Disorderly Adult

A business near the police station calls to report a disorderly, drunken man refusing to leave the venue. When I arrive, the man is walking away, about a block from the business. He immediately becomes defensive when I stop to identify him. He takes a fighting stance as I approach, but relaxes a bit when a second officer arrives. The man reluctantly shows me his identifications as he bitches about police harassment.

When I ask what was the problem at the store he just left, the man says he thought the clerk gave him incorrect change for the bag of pork skins he is now eating. He has no warrants and I give his identification back. As I do this he squares up again as if he wants to fight. I do the same, expecting him to charge me. I can literally see him weighing in his drunken mind the odds of winning the fight. He backs down again and turns to leave, mumbling obscenities as he walks away. The odds apparently were not to his liking.

5:00 p.m.—Disorderly Adult

A woman calls for police assistance because a neighbor took a photograph of her home. The neighbor says it is for a lawsuit she is filing against the woman. The caller is not happy to hear her neighbor has broken no laws. She threatens to take retaliatory photos of the other woman's home. The thought of the two women outside dueling away with cameras is enough to bring a smile to my face as I drive away.

7:20 p.m.—Suspicious Situation

Workers from a social services agency have called for police assistance trying to locate a 25-year-old man, suffering from cerebral palsy. He is supposed to be living with his mother at a home on the city's Eastside, but relatives are complaining that they have not seen the man in a year or more. I am not originally dispatched to the call, but I take it in place of another officer, as I am not far from the venue. I would soon regret this decision.

When I arrive, another officer is already talking to social workers. They say the missing man's mother told them the man has been staying with relatives in the next county. The caseworkers, however, say they've checked with the relatives and they have not seen the man. When we explain this to the mother, she says the relatives are lying. She gives us permission to search her residence to look for her son. This would prove to be a nearly impossible task.

The apartment the woman lives in is located in a three-story brick building that has been sub-divided into apartments. The structure, which is more than 100 years old, looks to be well over 4,000 square feet in size. The home is in terrible disrepair. There is no electricity or running water. The mother of the missing man is the only resident in the building as everyone else has moved out. We have summoned a sergeant to the scene and he accompanies a female officer and myself up to the house. Darkness is setting in and it is getting colder as we walk up a set of stairs onto a large brick porch. Written in white lettering across a window near the front door, a message there makes an ominous proclamation: *Prepare ye the way of the Lord.*

In the downstairs entryway, the smell of mold, dirt and urine combine, sending out a nasty stench. We make our way upstairs, passing several locked and blockaded doors that we are told lead to apartments no longer being rented. In the apartment of the building's last remaining resident, a few candles illuminate the living room, exposing cockroaches, which skitter here and there. We find no sign of the missing man in the apartment.

Next door is another apartment the woman says she uses for storage. We enter and find it stuffed with appliances, boxes, clothes and garbage. I set off for what looks to be a bedroom. There are a few garbage bags full of clothes in a closet. In the corner of the room, boxes and small appliances are piled neatly about four feet high on top of a makeshift bed.

"That's all my brother's stuff," the woman says. "He stores it here 'cause he ain't got room at his house. Put it back neat when you're done."

Checking through the pile, I find nothing unusual. The woman suddenly breaks open the three garbage bags, which had been sitting in the closet. "You want to check these?" she says, dumping the clothes on the floor. An overwhelming, suffocating smell of old urine immediately fills the room. I retreat to the smelly kitchen, trading one bad stench for another.

We locate no sign of the missing man and move downstairs, where we find a stairway leading to the basement. The sergeant at the scene tells us he is going outside to radio for a police dog to assist in the search. The female officer and I decide the basement is the next logical place to search.

We descend the staircase halfway before being slowed by piles of junk covering the bottom half dozen steps. It takes some effort to scale the obstacles, but we manage to literally climb into the basement, where we are greeted with a three-foot-high layer of junk covering almost every square foot of this level. Wheel rims, lawn mowers, television sets, stereos and boxes and bags of every size and shape stuff yard after yard of the indoor junk pile. There are several doors within reach, and there appear to be several more beyond the vastness of junk, but they are unattainable.

As the other officer and myself look at each other in disbelief, no words are necessary. In the corner is a window, but it is barred from the outside. I push open one of the doors that is within reach and find the adjacent room also filled nearly to the ceiling with broken and discarded items. My flashlight begins to dim. I had meant to recharge it yesterday. The scene is straight out of a horror movie—checking the dark basement of an old home for a body. My skin begins to crawl.

At this point, for some reason, the word "Fire" pops into my mind. I become aware that if a fire were to break out in this house right now, we would be trapped like rats. There is no way out, save for the cluttered staircase that brought us here. Something is definitely wrong within the walls of this home and a fire would be a great way to cover up the mystery. Several relatives of the missing man have gathered outside and anyone of them could be involved in the man's disappearance. My partner takes very little convincing when I suggest we retreat from the basement and wait for the arrival of the K-9 unit.

The fresh air outside is a welcome change and we are both relieved to get out of the house. The missing man's mother is sitting alone in the dark on the front lawn. When I walk over and sit down next to her, she is obviously nervous. We begin to talk about her son and where he could be, but she avoids any eye contact.

After about 10 minutes, the woman begins to cry and I sense she wants to tell me something. Finally, I ask her directly if her son is dead. The answer is a somber "Yes." She says her son has been dead for about a month, but someone in her family said they would harm the woman if she told the police. The woman says her son was not murdered; he died of natural causes. She says, however, she does not know where her son's body is located. I know I am not getting the whole truth, but I stop the conversation there. With this new information, the sergeant at scene tells me to take the woman to police headquarters. Two detectives are summoned, as the situation has now grown much more serious. We are still awaiting a K-9 unit to continue the search.

At police headquarters, I sit with the woman as she sips a bottle of cola I bought for her. She says she hasn't slept in days. She cries for a while and then falls asleep with her head on a desk.

About an hour after our arrival at police headquarters, a K-9 officer asks to speak with me in the hallway. He tells me of his search of the house and asks if I had checked a bedroom in the second apartment upstairs. I told him I had, but found nothing, although I was driven out of the room by the smell of three garbage bags full of urine-soaked clothes that were dumped on the floor by the missing man's mother.

Had I continued to dig through one more layer of junk on the bed in the corner, I would have found what the officer and his dog uncovered. Lying directly on top of the bed, covered by neatly stacked items, was the outline of a small man, turned sideways in the fetal position, embedded in a thick layer of concrete. Scattered around the cement-encased cadaver were the remnants of hundreds of long-since-dead maggots, which had presumably made a meal of the deceased man's flesh.

The officer relating the story is visibly upset by his findings. They are awaiting specialists to crack open the concrete tomb because it will have to be done carefully, he says. I thank him for passing along the information and I return to the room where I had left a woman sleeping with her head on a desk. God only knows what kind of dreams she is having.

Later that night, detectives arrive to interview the dead man's mother. I leave the woman in their care and call my wife, telling her not to wait up for me. I then sit down to begin writing the gruesome details of the case. I would later hear that the man's death went unreported so family members could continue cashing his government assistance checks.

By 1:30 a.m., I am on my way home, happy to be starting a vacation soon. Sitting alone watching television, four bottles of beer fail to clear my mind of this day's events. Sleep does not come easy this night.

Saturday, October 19

3:10 p.m.—Family Trouble

A drunken man arguing with the 16-year-old daughter of his girlfriend leads to a 10-minute refereeing match by another officer and myself. The intoxicated man finally decides to leave with a friend, solving our problem, at least for the time being.

3:35 p.m.—Hit-and-Run Accident

A string of six auto accidents within about 20 minutes keeps the entire shift playing catch-up for hours. By the time I arrive at the scene of a hit and run, the driver of one vehicle has long since fled the scene on foot. A car he had driven over a traffic sign and then onto a fire hydrant sits half-mangled, obstructing traffic. Due to the barrage of accidents, it takes a half an hour for a tow truck to arrive. The entire call keeps me out of service for nearly an hour and a half.

5:25 p.m.—Suspicious Situation

A female caller says there are strange noises coming from an abandoned house next to her home. When I arrive simultaneously with another officer, we find the abandoned house easily accessible to the public. A large front porch gives way to a smashed out picture window in the front. In the back of the structure, the rear door is wide open.

Prostitutes and drug users often prowl within these abandoned buildings, so we enter with guns drawn. The main floor is a maze of garbage, broken furniture and animal droppings. Broken glass litters every room, accompanied by empty liquor bottles and soiled condoms. We locate nobody inside the house, however, and clear the call within 10 minutes of our arrival.

5:55 p.m.—Fight with Weapons

An anonymous report of a knife fight near a street corner on the city's Eastside draws three patrol cars to the area. The combatants are never located.

8:30 p.m.—Family Trouble

The venue is a multi-story apartment building in the downtown area. The once-proud structure is now home to low-income housing units. The building is infested with drugs and plagued by violence. A security guard lets another officer and me into the building and summons an elevator, using a special credit-card-style key. The rickety elevator arrives to take us to the sixth floor. The ride upward is uncomfortable as the elevator jerks at every floor, seemingly struggling to complete just one more trip before it dies.

Finally, reaching our floor, we are told by the caller that the police are no longer needed. Within a minute, I am back on the same elevator, hoping it's got six more floors worth of life left.

9:40 p.m.—Malicious Destruction of Property

The venue is an Eastside convenience store, pasted with signs delivering the news of the cheapest beer of the day. The store also cashes checks and accepts welfare coupons, carries cellular phones and pagers: One-stop shopping. The store manager says he caught a regular customer shoplifting some booze. He told the man to put the bottles back and he would not call the cops. The man returned the items to the shelf, but kicked out the glass in the store's front door before leaving. I finish the report quickly enough to end my shift on time.

Sunday, October 20

3:02 p.m.—Family Trouble

The caller is a man in his sixties. He and his wife sit quietly as their forty-something son rants and raves about being mistreated by his parents. The son is recently out of prison and on parole. He has a distinct dislike for the police and his anger immediately turns toward me as I listen to his father tell me he wants his son to leave his home.

"Oh, man, that's right, listen to him, cop! Believe him," the son screams, exposing a mouth with few teeth, including none in the front.

The father says he doesn't want his son arrested. Just get him out of the house, he pleads.

"Man, call the cops on me. Fuck you. I'll do my eight years," the son yells, referring to the balance of the prison sentence he must serve if he violates conditions of his release.

When I tell him he is getting closer to going back to prison every time he opens his mouth, he quiets somewhat. He then begins to gather some clothing. He is leaving, he says. Near the back door, as the man prepares to leave his parent's home, his mother asks that he not return.

"You can suck his dick," the convict yells in a final display of disrespect as he points toward his father. With that he leaves, having avoided a return trip to jail today. With his temper, however, the man's freedom will surely be short-lived.

4:55 p.m.—Family Trouble

The man who called is fuming when we arrive. He is standing at the kitchen table in the house, which belongs to his daughter's boyfriend. The boyfriend, a soft-spoken man in his twenties, stands a few feet away, clad in a bathrobe and slippers. The caller says his daughter lives here with her boyfriend. He wants his daughter to leave and come back home because the boyfriend is mistreating her. His daughter is an adult, however, and doesn't want to leave. There is nothing I can do, I say, drawing a smirk of approval from the boyfriend.

"Yeah, you a real asshole now that the police here," the father yells, knowing he has lost the battle. "You ain't nothing but a faggot."

With that the man storms out the back door, still cussing under his breath. The homeowner thanks us and we clear the call. The irate man's daughter remains at the home.

5:20 p.m.—Family Trouble

A headache sets in as I walk into my third consecutive family trouble call. There is a teenage boy sitting in the living room, getting his hair braided by a girl of the same age. The boy's sister (and guardian) is standing in the kitchen when I walk in. She immediately barks orders to me.

"Just take him! Take him outta here for a couple of hours!" she yells at me, as if I'm a babysitter for hire.

"Would you like me to take him to my house for a while so he can play with my kid?" I reply with as much sarcasm as I can muster. The response draws a dirty look, but she gets the point.

Talking to the teen, I learn his sister is mad because he was arguing with other family members. The whole thing seems to have gotten overblown. The teen says he's going to a friend's house and there will be no more arguing. The sister says that's fine. I leave, getting neither a "good-bye" nor a "thanks for coming."

8:34 p.m.—Disorderly Person

A feud between the caller and another now-departed woman leads to threats to "shoot up" the caller's house. At the caller's request, I write a brief report, documenting the threats.

9:45 p.m.—Shots Fired

A woman calling on a cellular telephone says she is being followed by another car that is shooting at her. Several patrol cars respond to the area. The caller, however, keeps giving Central Dispatch conflicting information about her location. The proverbial wild goose chase lasts for nearly 10 minutes until the caller finally hangs up. Neither the suspect nor the victim vehicle is located in the several neighborhoods where the caller said she was being chased and shot at.

10:10 p.m.—Weapons Call

The previous caller is back on the line now. She says the vehicle that was shooting at her is parked at a local convenience store, getting ready to leave. She says the two women in the car are armed with handguns.

Two patrol cars arrive at the store as the suspect vehicle is leaving. They wait for the car to get away from the store and the numerous pedestrians in the area before conducting a felony stop. Several other officers, including two from the Saginaw County Sheriff Department and one from the Michigan State Police, arrive within minutes to help. In total, eight officers assist with what is later learned to be a false call. There are no guns in the vehicle and there is no indication there ever were. The women in the car say the caller doesn't like them and has been trying to get them into trouble. Looking over the scene, the waste of manpower caused by one person's dislike of another is ridiculous.

Monday, October 21

3:17 p.m.—Traffic Accident

A distracted motorist causes a minor accident in a residential neighborhood on the city's Eastside. Both drivers are patiently waiting when I arrive and neither is mad at the other, which seems to be a rarity these days.

5:05 p.m.—Shots Fired

When I arrive at the house where we have received a report of shots fired in the area I am waved down by a man in his early thirties. He tells me his wife is inside the residence smoking crack cocaine. He has knocked repeatedly, but she keeps telling him to go away. The man says they have only been married for a month and he has discovered she has a bad drug problem. At the man's request, I knock several times to try and lure the woman from inside the drug den, but she refuses to come out. The shots fired call was probably made by the crackheads inside the house in an attempt to get me to shoe away the woman's bothersome husband. There is nothing more I can do for the man, except wish him luck, which he finds of little consolation.

5:33 p.m.—Panic Alarm

Several people walk away upon sight of the two patrol cars pulling up in front of the house. An older man identifies himself as the owner of the home and he says the alarm was set off on accident. We verify he is indeed the homeowner. Several other people in the backyard give us blank, cold stares as we talk to the man. Their reaction to the other officer and me is sad, yet not unexpected. Many people we deal with cannot hide their dislike of the police, even when we are there to help them, answering an alarm at their home.

6:46 p.m.—Family Trouble

The venue is a well-kept brick, two-story home on the city's Eastside. The Hispanic family I encounter inside is embroiled in a heated argument involving a 19-year-old daughter. As they argue, I try to decipher what is causing the problem. I interject several times to try and calm them and find out why they are yelling. This leads several family members to start speaking Spanish so I cannot understand them.

The daughter who is at the center of the controversy asks if I can take her and her son to a local shelter. She wants to get away from her family. I oblige and make the arrangements via police radio with the assistance of the desk officer. The girl takes at least 20 minutes to pack her belongings, but it seems like an hour as intermittent arguments break out in both English and Spanish as she gathers her things. Finally, we depart and I drop her and her child at a local shelter where they can stay until she sorts out her problems. The entire call takes well over an hour but, thankfully, it is the last call of my night.

Tuesday, October 22

5:07 p.m.—Attempted Suicide

We are dispatched to a residence where a mother has overdosed on pills. I have just gotten out of a late afternoon court case and this is my first call of the day. So far, it has been very busy. So busy, in fact, that the ambulance has already taken the woman to a local hospital by the time the police arrive at her house.

I find three crying, hysterical children inside the home. Their father informs me the victim has already left the scene. I respond to a local hospital to talk with the woman. She is cooperative with hospital staff and I am advised they need no paperwork from me on the matter because the woman in now voluntarily seeking help for her depression and suicidal actions.

5:43 p.m. - Family Trouble

The victim says his girlfriend pulled a gun on him. The woman has since departed the scene. I am the second officer on scene so I simply stand by while the primary officer gathers information for a police report.

7:27 p.m.—Dead Body

I am summoned to the scene of a dead body. The death appears to be of natural causes, but the police are called to make sure there is nothing suspicious about the situation. Medical staff is preparing to depart the scene when I arrive. They brief me on the circumstances. It appears to be a natural death, despite the victim having no major known medical problems. Inside the small, tastefully decorated two-bedroom house, a semi-hysterical woman sits on a bed beside her husband, who still lies on his side in a sleeping position.

"No. He's going to wake up. Come on. Wake up," she says with a shaky voice, patting her deceased husband lightly on the shoulder. "Why did you leave me?"

I wait for the woman to leave the bedroom and I offer my condolences. She looks for a lighter for her cigarette as we talk. She says the previous night she went to sleep and her husband was still watching television. Unknowingly, this would be the last time she saw him alive. Early in the morning she got up, prepared for work and departed like she always does, leaving quietly so not to wake the man, who was still lying in bed. When she came home later in the day, she found him deceased, lying in bed the same way she left him.

Per departmental policy, I have summoned a sergeant to the scene. He has the responsibility of assessing the scene and briefing a detective supervisor on the situation. Eventually, he also contacts the medical examiner.

It doesn't take long for family and friends to arrive, as news of the man's demise spreads quickly. Within half an hour, there are 20 or so people packed into the small home. Some are concerned relatives. Others are simply there gawking at the sight of fresh death. The centerpiece of the crowd is the widow's elderly mother, who has a calming effect on her distraught daughter. She speaks with the even tone of experience. She is clearly annoyed at all the people coming in and out of the house.

"In a minute, I am gonna put everybody outta here," she says just loudly enough to be heard.

Upon hearing the older woman, some people take the hint and leave. Others ignore her not-so-discrete words. Others still just stare coldly at my sergeant and myself. We are the only white people in the room, and this in itself is an obvious annoyance to some people here.

In the middle of the confusion I stand trying to be as compassionate as possible, while not intruding on the family's private grief. This effort is hampered extensively by my uniform, my skins color, and the occasional chatter from the police radio strapped to my utility belt. The medical examiner eventually arrives, completes his work and calls for an ambulance to transport the man to the morgue. Before the ambulance arrives, the widow spends a few final moments with her husband, saying goodbye in the bedroom they have shared for years.

Wednesday, October 23

3:20 p.m.—Armed Robbery

It's a mild, sunny day and my first call is for an armed robbery, which occurred outside a pager and cellular telephone store. Years ago, the building housed a dentist's office, but neighborhood decay finds the brown brick building now adorned with gaudy neon signs proclaiming the latest deals in communication devices.

I meet the victim inside and he appears to be shaken. He says he just got paid and came to the store to pick up a cellular phone. As he walked from behind the building a gunman approached and stole several hundred dollars from the victim. I find it ironic that the man was robbed just after cashing his paycheck, but he insists he does not know the suspect. Assisting officers are unable to locate the suspect. The report is forwarded to the detective bureau for follow-up investigation.

3:35 p.m.—Hold-Up Alarm

Employees of a downtown bank advise the first responding officer that the alarm was accidentally tripped. Despite being tied up on the previous call, I assist on the alarm because there is no one else available. I clear quickly to resume investigation of the armed robbery.

4:36 p.m.—Recovered Stolen Vehicle

A female caller informs Central Dispatch she has located her supposedly stolen vehicle. She says there are several men hanging around and she is afraid to approach the car. When we arrive, the car is in the street unoccupied. The caller is no where to be found. Eventually, she calls back and says she had to leave. She says her mother will come and pick up the car. A review of the report shows that the vehicle was reported stolen, but it is actually listed as an Attempt to Locate (ATL) vehicle. This usually means it was traded for drugs and the owner has since come down from their high and wants the police to find their car.

I wait with the car for nearly an hour, but the mother never arrives. Finally, a supervisor and myself agree to leave the car. Too many calls are waiting to be answered. I cannot spend my entire day babysitting a crack addict's recovered vehicle.

5:42 p.m.—Shots Fired

A report of two men shooting at each other outside a neighborhood store draws several officers to the scene. We round up several men standing outside the store. They all bitch and complain and say they weren't doing anything. It takes nearly five minutes for a couple of them to tell us where the shooting was coming from and that there was a vehicle involved. With little help from these not-too-concerned citizens, we are unable to locate the suspects.

6:55 p.m.—Traffic Stop

Having very little down time these days due to a lack of manpower, I rarely initiate traffic stops. However, when a female disregards a train-crossing signal right in front of me, crossing about 20 yards in front of an oncoming train, I pull her over.

The woman is courteous and is dressed in hospital scrubs. She apologizes for the traffic infraction. She says she left her license at home and she is driving her sister's car. A check of the name she provided shows she has a valid license, however, the registered owner of the car has a warrant. I suspect she is actually the owner of the vehicle. When I walk back up to talk with her, I see her work nametag and it reads the same as the vehicle's owner. She smiles sheepishly and admits to the lie. Fifteen minutes later, she is locked up at the county jail for the outstanding warrant with several traffic tickets to take care of as well.

9:55 p.m.—Attempt Suicide

Upon arriving at a small, unfurnished apartment, I locate a man in his late thirties. He has taken about fifty pills during a suicide attempt. He is cold and clammy and turning a bluish hue when I find him. Fortunately, medical personnel arrive at the same time. They quickly transport the man to a local hospital. Another officer at the scene handles the paperwork.

Saturday, October 26

3:10 p.m.—Felonious Assault

The female victim tells me her baby's father, who has since fled the scene, punched her and threatened her with a carpet cutter. She says he is a known drug dealer who recently got out of prison. I wonder why she would have a child with such a person, but I don't bother to ask. The answer would be too confusing or infuriating and it's too early in the shift. Instead, I quietly take information for the report, give her the corresponding case number, and inform her of the follow-up procedure.

4:48 p.m.—Family Trouble with Weapon

The afternoon call volume is surprisingly low and several other officers beat me to the call. I am disregarded before I can make it to the scene.

5:08 p.m.—Fugitive Tip

An anonymous caller tips off Central Dispatch to the possible whereabouts of a man wanted for parole violations. We have been unsuccessfully trying to locate this man for more than a month. The word on the street is that the man is armed and has vowed to kill any cops who try to arrest him. Only two officers are sent to the venue, but at least five more respond due to the potential for a violent outcome.

Within three minutes, we have the house surrounded, but the situation is complicated by the fact there are three apartments within the building. The caller did not specify which apartment the suspect may be in, so we are stuck leaving several officers outside the building as three of us enter to check each apartment.

Two younger men are in the first apartment. They say they don't know the man we are looking for. They are not good liars. After getting permission to search their apartment, we do not locate the suspect. Nor do we locate him in the rest of the building. We either just missed him, the caller was misinformed, or it was a tactic to divert officers to this location for some other reason. Either way, we leave the house empty-handed and are greeted by a throng of curious neighbors, who apparently are undeterred by the sight of cops with guns surrounding a house. A gunfight probably would have resulted in injuries to innocent persons on this day. Ironically, the suspect is apprehended by the midnight shift without incident later that night about a mile from this location.

Monday, October 28

3:05 p.m.—Shots Fired

Several witnesses have called in reports of two cars shooting at each other as they drive through a residential neighborhood. The first officers on scene have located a van abandoned and shot up in the middle of an intersection. Witnesses said several men fled the van after the gunfight.

When I arrive to impound the van so the day shift officers at scene can go home, an inspection of the vehicle shows that it was somebody's lucky day. One bullet hole had penetrated the rear hatchback door of the van, ripped through the back seat and into the headrest of the front passenger seat, where amazingly it lodged in the seat without going through. One of the men that fled the scene had been sitting in that seat when the shot was fired. I don't think he'll ever get that lucky again.

After impounding the van, I am called back to the area twice more by neighbors who have since discovered bullet holes in their houses from the shootout. The call eats up the first few hours of my shift.

6:30 p.m.—Breaking and Entering Alarm

Arriving at a small house on the city's Eastside, we find someone had tried to gain entry through a bedroom window, but the thieves were scared off by the home's burglar alarm. The neighborhood is a checkerboard of abandoned houses and vacant lots, with the exception of a few well-kept homes, including the house where I now stand. When the homeowner—a young woman in her twenties—arrives, she is hysterical. Judging from the neighborhood, the woman shouldn't be surprised. She clearly has more than most people on this block, which makes her nothing more than a target in this poverty filled neighborhood.

7:10 p.m.—Breaking and Entering Report

Several small children—two clad only in diapers - scurry around the house as a woman relates how someone kicked in her front door. It's hard to hear the woman over the screaming of her kids, yet she does nothing to quiet them. Within 10 minutes of my arrival, I leave for the relative quiet of the police station to write her report. Cold weather has cut down the calls holding to only one or two an hour. I receive no more calls for service during my shift.

Tuesday, October 29

3:15 p.m.—Breaking and Entering Alarm

Checking the premises with another officer, I find the residence is secure.

3:33 p.m.—Breaking and Entering Alarm

My second consecutive call of this nature also turns out to be a false alarm.

3:55 p.m.—Breaking and Entering Report

When I arrive at a weathered, two-story home on the city's Northeast side, a younger, stocky man greets me in the front yard. He identifies himself as the nephew of the recently deceased homeowner. He says his uncle passed away during the weekend. Word must have spread quickly through the neighborhood because scavengers have already broken into the dead man's home to steal what he has left behind. While I take down information for the case report, the nephew carts leftover valuables to his car. He says he will take these things to his house until relatives can decide how to dispose of the man's estate.

5:00 p.m.—Disorderly Juveniles

Two different motorists report young kids throwing rocks at passing cars near a busy intersection. I check the area for about 10 minutes, but I cannot locate the youths.

6:50 p.m.—Disorderly Adult

Two other officers beat me to the call and I am disregarded after they find the subject in questions has left the scene.

7:30 p.m.—Sexual Assault

A woman in her twenties reports being sexually assaulted by two men in an Eastside residential neighborhood. While we often receive false reports of this nature, this one appears to be legitimate. Two officers are initially dispatched, but we later call for a sergeant and a K-9 officer to assist in tracking the suspects. Two hours of investigation lead to nothing, however, as we are unable to locate the assailants. Hopefully, the detective assigned to the case will have better luck.

Nearly three hours after being dispatched to the sexual assault call, I end my night, loading my police equipment into my personal vehicle, which is in the parking lot across the street from the police station. As I do this, I hear a man screaming from an upstairs window of a Victorian-style home located across a side street from the parking lot

"I know what you did in the warehouse!" the man screams, yelling in the direction of the police parking lot. "No man lives forever!"

I know the man well, having dealt with him on many occasions. He appears to be mentally ill and often accuses officers of being out to get him. The man has been quiet recently. I have not heard him nor been dispatched to a call at his house for months. The veiled threats he yells tonight, however, will continue for the next three days. His screaming seems a fitting end to my day.

Wednesday, October 30

3:25 p.m.—Stolen Vehicle

The caller says his vehicle was stolen from the parking lot of an auto repair shop near downtown Saginaw. He is relieved when I tell him the county's auto theft team has already recovered the car, which they found abandoned in the road over the weekend. I make arrangements for the man to contact an auto theft detective the next day so he can get his car back.

4:35 p.m.—Malicious Destruction of Property

Construction crews have been working for more than a month now, pulling up abandoned railroad tracks, which run the width of Eastside Saginaw, through some of the roughest and most depressed areas in the city. Today someone shot out the back window of one of the construction vehicles. The site foreman is not the least bit rattled by the incident, even though one of his workers had been sitting in the vehicle moments before the incident. It's a cost of doing business in this part of town, he says. There are no suspects and the amount of damage probably is lower than the insurance deductible it will cost to replace the window. Still, I write the report at the request of the foreman.

5:57 p.m.—Disorderly Juveniles

For the second straight day, I respond to a report of kids throwing rocks at passing cars in an Eastside neighborhood. Again, I am unable to find the culprits, who probably live in the area and have ducked into a house.

7:14 p.m.—Family Trouble

The suspect—a drunken man in his forties—is gone when I arrive. The female caller relates details of an assault as she picks up pieces of a broken table from the dining room floor. She says the man is her baby's father and he came over intoxicated and assaulted her. The domestic assault report I file will be forwarded to an investigator in the morning.

Moments after leaving the woman's house, I am sent back again when Central Dispatch receives two 911-hang up calls from the residence. When I re-contact the woman, she laughs and says the 911 calls were an accident.

9:59 p.m.—Shots Fired

An anonymous resident calls in a report of shots being fired from a dark-colored van. The area is quiet when I arrive. There are no vehicles speeding away from the scene and nobody shot in the street. I clear the area and call it a night.

Saturday, November 2

Checking into service on this chilly November day, several other officers and myself are again greeted by the psychotic screaming of the man in the old house across the street from the police parking lot. He is yelling about some sort of police conspiracy again, but I don't stop to listen for long. You can never be sure when someone like this is going to snap, and rifles aren't hard to come by these days.

4:50 p.m.—Disorderly Adult

Driving past a now-vacant downtown department store, I notice a man in his forties standing on the sidewalk, drinking his lunch from a brown paper bag. When I pull up, he sets the bag at his feet. The answer to my question is obvious, but I ask it anyway.

"You know it's illegal to drink beer on a public sidewalk, don't you?" I ask the man.

"Yeah, I know, but I didn't think you would stop," he says. "I can't drink at work so I had to drink out here before I go to work. They would get mad if I drank at work."

"Where do you work?" I ask.

"Downtown at the Democratic Headquarters. I pass out literature for the election," says the man. "I just bought one can 'cause if I buy a forty or a six pack, I'll get too drunk - that's a lot of beer."

The man's honesty is refreshing. I check him for warrants and he has none. I don't issue him a ticket and let him leave with a warning.

5:00 p.m.—Disorderly Adult

The venue is an adult foster care home. One of the clients feels the staff has been mistreating him so he calls the police. After about fifteen minutes of mediation, the first responding officer clears up the matter and we are on our way.

5:59 p.m.—Family Trouble

The call involves another mother-child dispute that is best handled by the family, but now somehow involves the police. The call is a waste of our time and I tell the caller such. There is nothing we can do for them and they will have to work out the problem themselves.

6:20 p.m.—Disorderly Adult

The venue again is a group home, but it is a different one from where I was dispatched previously today. We arrive to find a client standing on the front porch. He says the woman on staff won't let him inside. When we knock, a woman comes to the door, surprised to see us. She says she did not hear the male client knocking and instructs him to come inside. He heads inside, slightly embarrassed, and walks away. The staff worker closes the door without so much as a thank you. For a brief moment I am the highest paid doorman in the city.

6:41 p.m.—Disorderly Adult

When I pull up in front of a downtown low-income housing high rise, the man who walks out to greet me is all-too-familiar. His most distinct characteristic is not his lazy eye or his physical deformities, but his lousy attitude toward the police. Today is no different as he walks to the street to tell me some people threatened to assault him. He is drinking a 40-ounce bottle of beer as he walks up. A security guard is following the man and tells me the man is trespassing and has been warned to stay off the property.

After taking the caller's beer away, I check him for weapons prior to putting him into my patrol car. He protests slightly, but really gets steamed when I tell him he is going to jail for trespassing. We have had numerous complainants about the man from security staff at this building the past few weeks, and I refuse to spend the rest of my night getting called back to chase him away.

I write the man several tickets, including one for consuming alcohol in public. As I write out the citations on the hood of my car, a woman pulls up asking for directions. I begin to point her to her destination when two juveniles ride up on bikes to see what is going on. They match the description of two suspects in an unarmed robbery from a few hours earlier so I instruct them to go to my car and put their hands on the hood. They do so and are taken into custody by the other officer at scene.

Meanwhile, the woman who asked for directions is becoming unnerved by all the activity. She hurries on her way. I am unsure if she listened to the end of my directions.

Back at my patrol car, I have one juvenile suspect sit on the sidewalk and I call for a sergeant to assist. The second juvenile is already in the other patrol car. When I bring the disorderly drunk out of my car to secure him in handcuffs, he directs his anger at the security guard standing nearby.

"I should kick that fat, punk bitch's ass!" he screams. I tell him I should remove the handcuffs and let the security guard have at him. Now he turns his anger toward me.

"Man you are always fuckin' with me. You remember me! Remember me?" the man says. "I'll see you again on the street, motherfucker!"

A sergeant has now arrived. He identifies the two juveniles as the suspects from the earlier robbery. They and their bikes are transported to police headquarters and both are later lodged at the juvenile detention facility. Meanwhile, I take the disorderly drunk to the county jail. With three tickets and an impending night in jail to look forward to, he bitches during the entire ride. At least the corner we have just left will be quiet for a while.

Sunday, November 3

3:25 p.m.—Family Trouble with Weapon

The caller says her former boyfriend is threatening her. She says the man just got out of prison. She also says he has a knife. The fact that there is a weapon draws a quick response and officers are at the scene within minutes. The story changes by the time we arrive, however. The female caller says the man has left and she does not need the police. After verifying everything is ok, we clear the scene.

3:42 p.m.—Officer Needs Assistance

An officer from a neighboring township has become involved in a vehicle pursuit while trying to arrest suspects in a larceny. The car chase takes him through several neighborhoods and a construction zone on the city's Eastside.

By the time I catch up to the officer, he has the suspect vehicle stopped and is holding the driver at gunpoint. Two suspects have fled the vehicle on foot, leaving only the driver inside the small pickup truck. He refuses to show both of his hands and I physically remove the man from the truck while the other officer provides cover in case the man has a weapon. After a brief struggle, we get the man handcuffed. In the back of the pickup are numerous items supposedly stolen from a store outside the city; the shopping cart used in the alleged larceny sits tipped over on its side in the truck bed.

Within minutes at least six other patrol cars arrive. The two suspects that fled on foot are also captured. All the suspects are turned over to an officer from the jurisdiction where the crime occurred. A large crowd gathers to watch as we identify the suspects and impound the truck. Surprisingly, they cause no problems for officers at the scene. They are more interested in making fun of the suspects for getting caught. Talking to another officer, he says at least two of the suspects appear to be under the influence of cocaine. I clear the call, resuming patrol duties after nearly an hour assisting at the scene.

5:50 p.m.—Panic Alarm

A residential panic alarm turns out to be the result of someone who doesn't know how to operate the keypad properly. The homeowner apologizes for wasting our time. The call is cleared within 10 minutes of the reported alarm.

5:58 p.m.—Family Trouble

The upper apartment we are sent to is small and dirty. A boyfriend and girlfriend are having a very vocal argument when we enter. Two other roommates sit watching television, obviously tired of the noise.

Both combatants continue to yell at each other as we interview each. Both admit to getting physical with the other during their fight and both go to jail for domestic assault. Neither of them are happy with the resolution to the problem.

7:30 p.m.—Family Trouble

A girl says her baby's father punched her and then assaulted a male friend who tried to intervene. The suspect ran off on foot when he heard the police being called. We never locate the suspect. The victim gives details of the assault to the other officer at scene, who writes a domestic assault complaint for her.

Tuesday, November 5

It's Election Day and many people at the police department are nervous. Today, city voters will be asked to approve a property tax hike to help fund, among other things, police and fire services for the city of Saginaw. If the issue is defeated, it will surely mean further layoffs and cutbacks. If it passes, we may even hire some new officers for the first time since 1999. Some people I sit with through roll call on this day, and rely on for my very safety at work, will not be here a year from now if the results are negative. Their anxiety today is so obvious it is nearly measurable.

3:18 p.m.—Suspicious Person

Checking a large park on the city's South side for a suspicious male, we are unable to locate him. He appeared to have been soliciting for sex. He is undoubtedly with a customer even as we search for him.

4:00 p.m.—Breaking and Entering Report

A small club on the city's Eastside was the target of a break-in. The thieves did not get much by the way of cash. Still, I get the necessary information from a manager who has waited hours for my arrival. I also seize a cash drawer from the cash register. It is later tagged into evidence in hopes that detectives can get fingerprints from it.

5:32 p.m.—Breaking and Entering Alarm

Checking the building, I am met by an employee who says she set off the alarm by accident.

5:50 p.m.—Suspicious Person

Several neighbors have reported a stocky man with a military-style haircut walking back and forth in their neighborhood. When I arrive, I find the man immediately. He is wandering down the sidewalk. When I instruct him to come to me, he does so without hesitation and allows me to pat him down for weapons.

I get the man's identification and ask him to sit in my car while I check him for warrants. He complies. I have already told him the nature of the call. Finally, he tells me why he is there. He is trying to find his mother's car, which he says he traded for crack cocaine after an all-night drug binge. He says his mother will kill him if she finds out, especially since he has been off drugs for some time and was on his way to living a clean life. The man refuses my offer to report the car as an ATL vehicle. He says he would rather find it himself. I release him after confirming he is not wanted.

The following day, I would meet the man's mother by chance as she is standing at the police department front desk, waiting to report her car stolen. When I tell of this encounter with her son, she is heart-broken. By luck, her car is located within two days. The car has minimal damage. The damage to a woman who has lost her son to the grips of crack cocaine, however, is far more extensive.

9:10 p.m. - Runaway

The call is hours old by the time I am dispatched. When I arrive, the runaway has already returned home. The caller and her family, however, offer their encouragement for a positive outcome on the election results. They say they voted for the tax increase because they know we need more police officers and firemen. Their offer of moral support is the highlight of my day.

Unfortunately, by 3 a.m. the results are in and the proposed tax increase fails miserably. A police department that had 165 officers when I was hired in 1994 will mostly likely have 100 or less within 18 months. When I hear these results I decide I will soon sell my house and move my family from the city I have called home for nearly 10 years. I sleep less than two hours the entire night.

Wednesday, November 6

The mood in roll call is depressing at best as everyone talks of the previous day's tax defeat. A couple of people talk about what other police departments are accepting applications. A young officer sitting behind me ponders how he will make the mortgage payments on his new home. He and his wife are also expecting their first child. He is at the bottom of the seniority list and likely be the first relieved of duty.

It strikes me again that the nation-wide affection for policemen and firefighters following the September 11 terrorist attacks was just a passing fad. For a short while, it was fashionable to thank those public servants for their daily sacrifices. That time has clearly passed.

For the third straight year, some of my co-workers will be sent to the unemployment lines, further compromising the safety of those still serving. Twice during those three years, voters in the city of Saginaw have turned down tax requests to keep the city safer by keeping these people employed. Today, a city council member even tells the local newspaper part of the reason the tax vote failed is because people don't trust the police. My feelings after reading that particular comment fall somewhere between hurt, betrayal, and total disgust.

During my police academy training in the summer of 1994, classes were taught by a variety of persons, including many long-time, and some retired, police officers.

The bitterness of those current and former officers often crept into their teachings. There was a common viewpoint among them that police work is a wonderful occupation. But it is also frustrating work that is seldom appreciated by the general public. I used to chalk up this point of view to the character flaws of each individual. After nearly nine years on the job, I now know they were right.

On the side of my refrigerator, held up by magnets of various shapes and sizes, a piece of paper -yellowed by passing years - keeps its place next to hockey schedules and report cards. It is a letter to the editor of a local newspaper, written by a former Saginaw police officer. It was written in response to comments made by a staff member at Saginaw City Hall. The comments, in essence, said the city's police officers are lazy and unwilling to work hard. The police officer's rebuttal letter reads as follows:

> *This regards the comments of...the information officer for the city of Saginaw, regarding police conduct.*
>
> *When was the last time (this person) was shot at, kicked, punched, spit on, slapped, had racial slurs hurled at him, or had someone try to stab him?*
>
> *When did he ever pull a drowned toddler out of the water of a swimming pool, tell someone that a loved one had killed himself, or try to comfort a child or adult at the scene of an accident or homicide or felonious assault?*
>
> *When did he ever deal with the aftermath of child abuse, try to deal with a non-responsive parent about their delinquent child who "wouldn't do something like that," or referee family trouble calls over everything from "my eggs weren't done right" to "I caught him (or her) sleeping with someone else?"*
>
> *When did he ever arrest a husband or wife for domestic assault, and the moment he put the handcuffs on the offender, the spouse asked, "When can I get him (or her) out?" And when did he ever come back days later, only to find the same two together and fighting again?*
>
> *When did he ever stand in 100-degree heat or sub-zero cold, guarding the hoses of our brave firefighters battling a fire, only to have a citizen argue with him about why they can't drive down the street or why they can't get any closer to the fire?*
>
> *When did he ever dodge a skidding car on the ice-over freeway bridge as the car slammed into the other six that were already piled up on the bridge?*
>
> *When did he ever climb through a broken window at a breaking-and-entering in progress, not knowing whether the suspects were still inside or whether they were armed?*
>
> *When did he ever confront armed suspects from a shooting or a robbery, and disarm and arrest them without getting too rough?*

When did he ever try to comfort a fellow officer, a partner for years, who was injured on duty? When did he ever go to that officer's house to take a spouse to the hospital?

(This person) said Saginaw police officers don't want to do anything beyond the status quo, and they don't want to work hard. Well, the above list of incidents is the police officers' status quo. Believe me, officers must work hard just to survive the work day, stay sane and return home to their spouses and kids.

The above list is the police officers' lot in life. We chose this profession to do what is right and protect the citizens of this city. And what do we get in return from a City Hall minion? A slap in the face.

Oh well, just add it to the above list. The police officers will come to work and do our jobs, no matter how difficult, despite our "resistance to change," our "lack of accountability" and our "unwillingness to work hard."

I'm sure (this person) works very hard at his job, and I'm glad to know he never has to answer a gun call. That's my job.

After nearly thirty years of service, Officer James Robinson retired, several years after writing this letter. As I pack my gear into my patrol car to start another day, I think of his words and how true they are. It's no wonder the rate of divorce, alcoholism and suicide is higher for police officers than most other professions. These are my thoughts as I leave to serve the public one more day.

4:06 p.m.—Family Trouble

The woman caller sits in the middle of her living room and tells me how her roommate assaulted her. Since the two live together, the assault is domestic in nature and will be assigned to a detective for follow up. The victim doesn't know where the suspect went so no arrest is made. The report and a domestic violence incident sheet take me about an hour to complete.

6:00 p.m.—Prisoner Transport

Another officer requests assistance transporting four teens to the juvenile detention facility. The four were caught breaking into a home. I load the two handcuffed males into my car, while the other officer puts their female counterparts into his patrol vehicle.

The ride to the juvenile center takes about 15 minutes. I talk with the two teens in my back seat, who seem to be decent kids, despite running afoul of the law today. They ask me to change the radio to a station that plays rap music, which I do. The music doesn't appeal to me, but it keeps them happy for the last five minutes of their freedom on this day.

7:41 p.m.—Drug Activity

I respond to a report of a vehicle in the area that was traded for crack cocaine the previous day. Supposedly there are drug dealers inside the car. The vehicle, however, is no where to be found when I arrive.

8:15 p.m.—Abandoned Vehicle

Speaking to the caller, he says some former tenants left behind a broken down vehicle in the driveway. I tag the vehicle for future removal. An otherwise slow night ends with this call.

Thursday, November 7

3:25 p.m.—Disorderly Juveniles

The female caller lives in a prominent area of the city, a several-blocks-long boulevard lined with beautiful houses. She says several kids from her son's school have been following him home and harassing him. She is quite angry and says her son is upset about the matter. When she calls her son outside to talk to us, however, he is smirking. He is obviously not upset. I am assisting on the call so I let the primary officer do all the talking. After dealing with the caller for about 10 minutes, we leave, having only wasted our time.

4:01 p.m.—911 Hang-up Call

Nobody answers the door at the residence where we are dispatched for a 911 call. We try each door of the home, but it is secure. Central Dispatch says they are now getting no answer when calling back to the home. With no further leads we clear the call.

4:29 p.m.—Suicidal Person

The venue is an adult foster care home. The owner of the home says a client just left and said she is going to kill herself. She has caused problems before, the owner says. She also likes to fight with the police.

I check the neighborhood and locate the woman a block from the home. She walks away when I ask to speak with her. I follow her for a short distance and she tells me she is going to kill someone and then kill herself. Her suicidal and homicidal threats leave me with no alternative but to take her into custody.

The other officer at scene and myself end up physically restraining the woman as she tries to bite through her own wrists. We have already called for an ambulance and I ask Central Dispatch to have them hurry as the woman is fighting now. She spits in my face once and tries to kick me in the groin. We handcuff her and keep her restrained on the ground until an ambulance arrives. She fights with ambulance personnel upon their arrival as well, but eventually we get her to a hospital.

The emergency room nurse assigned to our room isn't excited about her new patient. However, the suicidal woman has calmed somewhat and is much easier to deal with now. We complete a mental petition and stand by for several hours waiting for a mental health worker to arrive. Eventually we depart the hospital and go to police headquarters to complete a report of the incident. This call ties up the majority of my night and is my last call for service.

Friday, November 8

3:44 p.m.—911 Hang-up Call

The call from a residence has been holding for nearly half an hour. Central Dispatch hasn't sent anyone here yet because there is nobody to provide me with backup. There are 10 other calls also holding by the time I am finally dispatched. Those calls will have to wait. When I arrive at the South side residence, a woman runs from across the street to my patrol car, screaming.

"They're shooting down there at Morris and Jefferson (streets)!" she exclaims. "There's two boys running down the street shooting at each other! You better go get them!"

I advise Central Dispatch and tell them to send two more officers to investigate the shooting, but there is nobody available. I have been approaching the house from where the 911 call originated as I try to report the shots being fired. I turn my attention now to where it should be—on the problem at hand. Had there been someone inside *this* house with a gun, the distraction could have cost my life. Fortunately, this call turns out to be just a family trouble, which we mediate for about five minutes before moving on to the report of shots fired.

3:55 p.m.—Shots Fired

Several neighbors confirm there were two teens shooting at each other as they chased one another down the street. We have arrived far too late to do anything about it, however. The two are long gone. Apparently they had poor aim also. Neither appears to have been shot. We continue to check the area for some time, but we never locate the suspects.

4:45 p.m.—Breaking and Entering Alarm

Downshifting to a less dramatic call for service, I respond to a residential burglar alarm. The residence appears to be secure and the call is cleared quickly.

5:15 p.m.—911 Hang-up Call

Arriving at the same time as another officer, we check the house, but find nobody home. A neighbor says the people at the house just left, but they appeared to be okay. With nothing further to go on, we clear.

6:03 p.m.—Breaking and Entering

The first responding officer disregards me from the call as it turns out to be just a report.

6:05 p.m.—Family Trouble

A complaint of two brothers arguing draws us to a call at a residence not far from downtown. When I arrive, one brother is noticeably drunk and he is clearly the problem. Several relatives ask that we stand by until the sober brother can pack some things and leave.

While waiting, I talk to the intoxicated brother. He is too drunk to be rationale. He is even too drunk to be civil, which leads to he and I having words. At one point standing on the front porch, he clenches his fist as if he is going to swing. Knowing he is too drunk to land a good punch, I stand ready to block his fist, but the punch never comes. He takes a couple steps back and ignores me until the other officer and myself leave. The drunken man is standing on the porch—drinking yet another beer - when I pull away behind the car of the relative who just left the residence.

It's has gotten considerably colder since the sun went down, which quiets the streets for the rest of the night. I receive no more dispatch calls for the remainder of my shift.

Tuesday, November 12

3:15 p.m.—Guard Prisoner

The prisoner I am sent to guard is a man in his twenties. He was arrested earlier in the day for domestic assault and during a scuffle with officers his forehead was cut open. He has been waiting to get stitches before being taken to the county jail. The day shift officer accompanying the man is going off shift so another officer and myself take over.

The man we are guarding is surprisingly nice. He keeps the conversation going, telling us how he came home from work to find his wife "fucking the crack man from down the street." He thought his wife had gotten over her drug problem, but recently she has been losing weight and money has been coming up missing. Today, he decided to do a surprise inspection and found his suspicions are accurate. When he found his wife in action with another man, he says he lost control.

"I kicked that motherfucker in the ass all the way down the stairs and out of the house," he says, referring to the man who was trading drugs for sexual favors with his wife. "He kept saying 'man, I didn't do nothing. I didn't do nothing.' I should have killed that motherfucker."

Eventually, he turned his anger on his wife, mildly assaulting her. "Man, I didn't even punch her or nothing. Then that cop came in and, it was like, whoom! He tackled me and I hit my head on the table."

The prisoner recounts the day's events like someone telling a story around a campfire. He is not mad, just recalling the story. We talk about marriage, infidelity and the power of drugs. He says his wife has several children, one of which is also his. He says he would like to get custody of all of her children and take them away from their rotten home atmosphere. We talk for nearly two hours before a doctor finally has the time to stitch the man. Not once does he display animosity toward us for his situation. After giving the man a soda before leaving the hospital, we drop him at the county jail and wish him good luck with the problems he is facing.

6:11 p.m.—Breaking and Entering Alarm

The alarm is originating from an Eastside gift shop. It goes off nearly every week. Once again, it is found to be a false alarm.

6:38 p.m.—Abandoned Vehicle

Today the call volume is low enough that I have time to impound an abandoned vehicle. It has been tagged and awaiting removal for about a week.

8:01 p.m.—Attempt Suicide

A woman unhappy with a relationship in which she is involved tells us she took several pills and wants to die. Medical personnel pull on scene shortly after we arrive and take the woman to a local hospital. At the hospital, we complete a petition for hospitalization, which orders mental health treatment for the woman based on her suicidal statements. Mental health workers arrive within a couple of hours and we clear the hospital with time for lunch before checking out of service.

Thursday, November 14

3:22 p.m.—Breaking and Entering Report

The venue is a shelter for abused and homeless women. The victim is a woman in her fifties, who is on the run from her husband of many years. She says her husband abused her to the point that she moved into her own apartment a while back. Eventually, she came to this shelter, seeking safety after her husband continued causing problems. Now she has learned through her old neighbors that her husband broke into her apartment.

After gathering the woman's information, I ask for another officer to go to the woman's apartment with her. She wants to see what her husband might have taken during this break-in, but she is too scared to go alone. When we get to her apartment, there is nobody there and a few items are missing. The woman packs a few belongings and leaves everything else behind, saying she will never return.

6:29 p.m.—Assault

A caller reports a man and a woman struggling inside a van behind a party store on the city's West side. When we arrive some 10 minutes later, the van is abandoned halfway in the street. As we check over the vehicle, a female returns to the scene. She says the van belongs to her. She and her estranged husband and their kids were in the vehicle, she says, when her husband began attacking her for no reason. She says he fled the scene on foot after one of the kids jumped out of the van to call the police. We check the area, but are unable to locate the man. A domestic assault report is filed and will be forwarded to a detective in the morning.

10:35 p.m.—Shots Fired

As I am unloading my patrol car for the night, a few other officers and myself hear several shots fired from relatively close proximity. At first none of us even react. Hearing gunshots in Saginaw is not that unusual. Then a dispatcher comes across the police radio, saying she is getting a report of a man firing a handgun outside a bar a few blocks from downtown. Several of us head to the venue and there are at least six patrol cars at the bar within a minute.

Outside, a couple of people describe a man who just fled after firing nine or 10 shots from a semi-automatic pistol. They believe he just had an argument with someone inside the bar, but nobody was shot, they say. When we enter the bar, guns drawn, there are a dozen or so people inside. Several look at us as if we are from another planet. Another man steps forward and attempts to make us leave. "There ain't nothin' goin' on here," he says. "Ya'll can go."

We push past the man and go inside. Everyone is acting strange and I feel like I am playing one of those shoot-the-bad-guys video games: Look out for the guy with the gun because he's somewhere in this room. Don't shoot the innocent bar patrons, however, or you'll lose 10 points.

Some people just stare at us and say nothing. Some will not make eye contact at all, looking instead at their drinks. One man is on the pay phone in the corner. I am surveying the room, waiting for someone to jump out and start firing at us, but luckily, no one does. Several officers and I fan out and walk through the bar.

"Awe, man, you better tell them what happened!" one guy protests to an older man, who has identified himself as the bar owner.

The owner shoots an evil stare at the patron. "Ain't nothin' goin' on in here. He left. Ain't nobody here," the owner says to another officer, who has asked the owner what happened.

Meanwhile, I check the bathrooms, which are empty. Another officer, who has been here on previous calls, tells me there is a door to the basement right behind the bar. The owner turns and protests when we head for this door. We tell him to stay out of the way and he does.

The basement is damp and unpleasant. There are several hiding places, but no one is hiding. I find another door leading to an adjacent downstairs barbershop. This business also has an entrance from the outside, but it is secure. A blue neon light near the barber chair illuminates the area, offering an easy view of the entire room. Satisfied that nobody is hiding inside the basement or the barbershop, we head back up to the bar, where other officers have finished checking for the gunman. As it turns out, the first people we spoke to outside the building weren't lying. The gunman had fled prior to our arrival. The only other people not lying were those who said nothing. I leave the scene and call it a night.

Friday, November 15

4:04 p.m.—Malicious Destruction of Property

The woman who called says a teenage boy threw a rock through the double-paned front window of her home. She says the boy used to date her daughter, but she put a stop to that when she learned he is a drug dealer. The boy became upset today when the victim refused him entrance into her home. The damage he caused before leaving the scene is no more than $200, which I document with a report at the woman's request.

7:17 p.m.—Family Trouble

The caller is a middle-aged woman, who is having trouble with her two foster care children, both of whom are teenage girls. She says the two have threatened to stab her.

I locate the girls in their basement bedroom. They are both foul-mouthed and disrespectful. Both deny making threats to the victim. An intake officer at the county's juvenile detention facility refuses permission to lodge the two on domestic assault charges, so we are forced to leave them at the venue. A domestic assault report is written, however, based on the victim's statements. The victim says she'll call back tonight if she has more problems with the two. In the morning, she says she will call the girls' case worker and make arrangements for them to be placed in a different foster care home. This is last call of one of my slowest workdays in recent memory.

Tuesday, November 19

3:07 p.m.—Court Appearance

The day begins with a nearly two-hour-long court appearance, shorting road patrol efforts by one officer from the start of the shift. The felony case I appear for is eventually waived to circuit court and I will most likely have to come back on another day.

5:40 p.m.—Disorderly Person

Two other officers beat me to the call and take into custody a disorderly woman who has walked away from her mental health treatment facility.

6:15 p.m.—Suspicious Vehicle

I am unable to locate a suspicious vehicle, which was reportedly drivingly slowly through the downtown area. From the description, the vehicle's driver was most likely looking for a prostitute. He has probably found one and moved on.

6:35 p.m.—Family Trouble

Several calls come in to Central Dispatch describing a family trouble. Each subsequent call says the problem is getting worse. The final caller says there now are weapons involved. The story changes when we arrive, however. Now everyone says it was no big deal and the people involved have left. They don't want the police anymore.

8:10 p.m.—Civil Stand-By

The shift commander has requested two officers accompany a man to his home. The man's girlfriend kicked him out last week and he wants to come back and retrieve his clothing. We are there to make sure there is no trouble. The girlfriend, however, isn't there and the house is locked up tight. We advise the man to call back another day and we'll try again.

9:37 p.m.—Runaway Report

The woman who called had been concerned about her teenage son. She said she had heard her son was caught in a stolen vehicle earlier in the day. The son has since returned home and mom tells me everything is all right.

Wednesday, November 20

3:35 p.m.—Vehicle Accident

The accident occurred only fifteen minutes prior to my arrival, but traffic is backed up enough that I request another officer to direct cars around the scene while I wait for tow trucks to arrive. No one was injured, but there is heavy damage to both vehicles. The at-fault driver is upset with me and he tries to blame the accident on the other driver. He is found at fault regardless. I clear the scene after about a half an hour.

5:10 p.m.—Prisoner Transport

Another officer and myself drive South to the town of Birch Run to pick up a prisoner. An officer from a police department in Genesee County has arrested a woman on a Saginaw Police Department arrest warrant. To save time, we meet halfway, in this town best known for its outlet shopping mall.

The officer we meet forewarns us that the woman we are taking custody of smells badly. We are not overly concerned until about five minutes into the drive back to Saginaw when the woman's stench becomes overwhelming. Her smell, which can best be described as a mixture of sweat, urine and corn chips, has taken over the car. We roll down the windows to let in some fresh air. The drive to the county jail does not go nearly fast enough. At the jail, we turn the woman over to some equally unhappy intake officers.

8:40 p.m.—Assault Report

The call comes from emergency room staff at an Eastside hospital. Following hospital procedure, they report that an assault victim has come in for treatment. When I arrive to talk to the woman, she says she does not wish to file assault charges against the suspect. She says the suspect simply got the best of her during a fight and she does not want police involvement. I respect her for her honesty, but mostly for the fact she accepts responsibility for her actions. She is polite and thanks me for coming to check on her.

Thursday, November 21

Roll call starts with the news that the night before officers on the midnight shift were shot at while checking an apartment complex for a felonious assault suspect. The information is disheartening, but useful. The apartment complex where the incident occurred is the scene of numerous calls for service, but this is the first time in my career I've heard of the police being shot at there.

3:20 p.m.—Vehicle Accident

It is snowy and wet as the shift starts. Predictably, several car accidents are awaiting officers calling into service. The accident I am sent to is a simple one where one vehicle slid into another due to the snowy pavement. Nobody is hurt and the scene is cleared within about 25 minutes.

4:16 p.m.—Family Trouble/Assault

The caller says his girlfriend assaulted him. He is calling from a pay phone and says he is bleeding, but doesn't want an ambulance. He says he is returning to the scene and we are to meet him there. When we arrive we find the call to be a hoax. There is no victim. The woman we encounter at the venue says the caller was her ex-boyfriend, who is constantly trying to get her into trouble. The entire call proves to be nothing but a waste of time.

4:40 p.m.—Motorist Assist

A vehicle stalled in traffic draws me to a busy downtown intersection. The vehicle's owner says his car just quit. He has already called for a wrecker. Due to the traffic volume, I stand by until the tow truck arrives, to make sure the man's car does not get struck.

5:22 p.m.—Disorderly Adult

The disorderly person we are called to deal with has departed by the time we arrive.

6:00 p.m.—Breaking and Entering Alarm

The alarm is at a bank on the city's Eastside. Due to the poor weather conditions, my backup officer, who is coming from the other side of town, never arrives. I check the building alone and, fortunately, it is a false alarm.

6:40 p.m.—Disorderly Adult

The convenience store where a disorderly person is reported is a haven for drug activity and gunplay. I find it ironic that the store's owner is concerned about a man begging for money in his parking lot. I would think this would be the least of his concerns. In any case, the man is gone when I arrive.

7:20 p.m.—Motorist Assist

I am dispatched to assist the driver of a vehicle, which has broken down on Interstate 675. I stand by with the woman until a tow truck arrives, feeling very vulnerable to the cars whizzing past at more than 70 miles per hour on the slick expressway. The vehicle is removed, none too soon, after the tow truck arrives.

Friday, November 22

3:24 p.m.—Drug Activity

Investigating a report of drug activity in front of a neighborhood convenience store, we arrive to find none of the described dealers at the store.

3:37 p.m.—Prisoner Transport

I am sent to assist another officer at an East-side hospital, where he is guarding a suspect in a felonious assault case. The suspect is a young man. He was wounded in an altercation, where he and another man allegedly exchanged gunfire. The suspect is being treated and puts on the predictable tough guy face in front of the police. When a nurse eventually comes in with his discharge paperwork, she is also carrying a syringe and needle. Suddenly, the teen grows concerned, asking the nurse several questions - the most humorous of which is "Will this hurt?" This tough gun-toting teen, wounded in a supposed shootout with another man on the mean streets of Saginaw, is afraid of needles. The scene brings a smile to my face.

8:12 p.m.—Breaking and Entering Alarm

The house where we are sent is found to be secure when I check the premises with a back-up officer. This is my last call of a fairly uneventful shift.

Tuesday, November 26

3:15 p.m.—Drug Activity

The area where we are dispatched is overrun with drug dealers. The crack peddlers run like cockroaches when they see the approaching police cars. They make it quickly inside their house, never straying too far from the safety of a rickety, two-story structure on the corner, which they call home.

This cat-and-mouse game is repeated on this street corner several times a day. Every now and then we catch one of the bad guys. Most often, however, we are unable to respond quickly enough or with enough stealth to make an arrest. With the number of other calls holding today, this simple drive by is about all the police can offer.

3:30 p.m.—Drug Activity

The venue is a party store only about four blocks from our previous call. There is never a shortage of drugs around here either. By the time we arrive, the dealers have moved on and the parking lot in front of the store is empty. I am certain officers will be called back for the same problem before my shift is over.

4:25 p.m.—Attempt Suicide

The victim says she is depressed and took some pills because she wants to die. She is talking to me as medical personnel arrive to treat her. The pills the woman has taken are dietary supplements and pose no threat to her health. Since she is making suicidal threats, however, she is taken to a local hospital for psychological evaluation.

5:29 p.m.—Fight

I am dispatched to a fight call at the same drug infested street corner where my day began. Several cars respond as many of the dopers in this neighborhood carry guns and they would not hesitate to take a shot at a cop under the right circumstances. All our precautions are for nothing. The fight has ended and everyone has disbursed by the time we arrive.

6:31 p.m.—911 Hang-up Call

The call to Central Dispatch turns out to be a family trouble. Two other officers arrive prior to myself and I clear the call.

8:14 p.m.—Abandoned Vehicle

For an unknown reason, someone has left a new truck abandoned, parked in front of a local party store. A check of the vehicle shows it is not wanted or stolen. I tag the vehicle for future removal at the store manager's request.

9:55 p.m.—Officer Needs Assistance

An officer who just pulled a traffic stop calls for assistance as the driver he pulled over jumps from the car and flees on foot. At least six officers respond and the foot chase covers several blocks. After a few moments the suspect is finally taken into custody. As he sits handcuffed on the ground, the man begins whining.

"Can I blow my nose, please? I gotta blow my nose," he says. "Man, can we loosen these 'cuffs?"

It's funny how the guys running from the police are quick to ask for favors after putting an officer's life in danger during a foot chase or vehicle pursuit. He is walked to a patrol car, still handcuffed with snot running down his face.

Wednesday, November 27

3:29 p.m.—Breaking and Entering Report

The woman who called said someone broke into her house while she was out today. She says they didn't take anything. They just opened up her windows and turned the thermostat up. The woman appears to have mental problems. She requests I write a report for the incident. I oblige, as she would only make a complaint against me if I refuse the report. I waste nearly an hour on this call.

3:40 p.m.—Breaking and Entering Alarm

The home where I am sent is a modest, three-bedroom house. Checking the perimeter, I find all doors and windows are secure.

5:01 p.m.—Officer Needs Help

An officer calls out that he is checking several subjects for drugs in front of an Eastside party store. The store is well known for drug activity and gunplay. Within seconds, several empty microphone clicks come over the police radio and I know instinctively he needs help.

I am two blocks into a lights-and-sirens response when Central Dispatch tries in vein to draw a response from the officer, asking him if he is okay. Within seconds, Central Dispatch then says they are receiving reports from neighbors near the store that an officer is being assaulted. The officer himself then comes over the air, screaming for help.

I am the third car to arrive and I have to fight through a group of on-lookers, who are blocking the entrance to the store. Just inside the doorway officers are trying to get the suspect handcuffed. Several people begin yelling about police brutality and tell us to let the man go. Nobody offers assistance. It takes more than a minute to finally get the man handcuffed as he resists the entire time. When we bring him outside to a patrol car, the crowd has grown and everyone has something to say.

"Look at all you cops!" yells one woman. "You don't stop no one from getting shot, but a cop gets hit an ya'll come out!"

"Man, we should riot up in this motherfucker!" yells a male voice, maintaining his anonymity from the safety of a large group across the street.

These same people who complain about the drugs and gunfire that daily tear their neighborhood apart now stand in force and bitch about officers looking out for the safety of one of their own. The officer who was assaulted was in a struggle for his life in front of a crowd of people for several minutes before help arrived. Nobody - not one single person—came to his aid. Too often the sad reality of law enforcement is when an officer needs help, the only people that come forward to offer assistance are other officers.

6:31 p.m.—Breaking and Entering Alarm

The house I check is an older, three-story structure. It is vacant, but it's not a house I would consider abandoned yet. It is still very much salvageable if someone takes the time to restore it within the next year or two. There are no signs of entry.

As I walk back to my patrol car, I look at the house next door. The dark, brick structure sits ominously silhouetted against the backdrop of a cold November sky. It was only a few months ago that I was sent to this house to look for a missing, physically handicapped man. We eventually located that poor soul, entombed in cement inside the house. I wonder now what happened to the dead man's family. I had heard there would be no charges filed against anyone relating to the man's death and his unusual disposal. I shake my head, remembering that night's events. My thoughts are soon disrupted, however, as Central Dispatch sends me another call. There seems no time to ponder the past. The present, in the form of a years-long, never-ending stream of calls for service, moves on day after day after day.

6:39 p.m.—Breaking and Entering Alarm

This alarm is on the far North end of the city. It also turns out to be false, as there are no signs of entry into the house.

6:40 p.m.—Assault Report

The victim is awaiting treatment at a local hospital. He was assaulted earlier in the day and is just now seeking treatment. He wants no assistance from the police, but I write the report anyway in case there is a need for prosecution at a later time.

Friday, November 29

3:10 p.m.—Traffic Stop

The woman I pull over just ran a red light right in front of me while I was sitting at the same intersection. When I approach the car, I am expecting the usual excuses and bad attitude. To my surprise the woman is pleasant and admits she ran the red light. She is even somewhat embarrassed. Thankful for her honesty, I give her a verbal warning and send her on her way.

3:15 p.m.—Abandoned Vehicle

The call is for a vehicle that has been abandoned on the roadway for a week. The car's windows are broken out and it is in terrible shape. Looking around the neighborhood, there are burned out and abandoned houses everywhere. The car itself fits right in. I am surprised anyone even bothered to complain.

3:26 p.m.—Disorderly Adult

A worker at an adult foster care home calls and reports a client is being disorderly. When I arrive, the client is already talking to medical personnel, who have been summoned to the scene. They inform me the police are not needed and I clear the call.

4:28 p.m.—Attempt Breaking and Entering

The venue is a new home in an older neighborhood. The home was just built within the past year and the owners moved in only last month. Already someone has tried to break into the home by smashing out a bedroom window. New things don't last long in this neighborhood.

I write a report for the homeowner and I am able to recover some evidence at the scene, which I secure at the police station. The evidence will be checked for fingerprints. The chances of gaining good prints are slim, but I request assistance from the department's identification bureau anyway.

5:32 p.m.—Domestic Assault

I am summoned, with another officer, to a local hospital for a domestic assault. When we arrive on the correct floor, security personnel advise us of the situation, which involves a patient and a female visitor.

The woman says she came to see her boyfriend and he assaulted her in the hospital room. For medical reasons the man cannot leave the hospital. I take information for a domestic assault complaint at the woman's request. She says they have a long history of domestic violence. I wonder why they are still together, but I don't ask. The answer would only make me mad. After I get the necessary information, the woman is escorted from the hospital by security staff and I return to police headquarters to write the report.

9:25 p.m. - Shooting

I respond, lights-and-sirens, about three miles to the scene, only to find this is a prank call. The other officers at the scene clear after checking the area for about 10 minutes. I clear the area as well.

9:35 p.m.—Gun Call

An anonymous caller gives a description of a vehicle driving through the neighborhood, the occupants pointing guns out the window. I check the area along with several other officers, but we are unable to find the suspects.

Tuesday, December 3

3:50 p.m.—Domestic Assault

The house where I am dispatched is very familiar to me. A middle-aged man approaches me outside when I arrive. His clothing is dirty. His body is thin, his skin weathered and his thoughts are scattered when he speaks. Years of heavy drinking and drug abuse have taken a hefty toll.

The man is cursing and half-drunk and begins yelling about his wife. I have fought with the man before, having taken him to jail several times, though I doubt he remembers me as anything more than a blue uniform—one of many he has dealt with over the years. There are no available patrol officers to provide backup, so a plainclothes detective volunteers to assist on the call. I leave the man in the care of the detective and I go inside to talk to the man's wife.

Nobody answers the door when I knock, so I enter the house to make sure the woman is okay. She is sitting inside the living room with her daughter, amidst countless empty, 40-ounce beer bottles. The house smells like a bar at closing time. The woman has been drinking, but she is still coherent. Eventually, she tells me her husband had threatened her with a butcher knife during an argument. Talking to the daughter and another family friend who was here during the assault, there is more than enough evidence to arrest the man.

Outside, the detective is talking calmly to the suspect, who is seated in the back seat of my patrol car, crying. When I inform the man he is being arrested, the tears turn to rage and he spews a string of expletives, which are directed at me. Soon we are off to the county jail, but not without an uninterrupted verbal tirade from the back seat of my car.

"Fuck you, you blue-eyed motherfucker," he screams. "I'm gonna die, but I ain't going alone, motherfucker…I'm going to war. I'm going to Iraq."

Past experience has shown me it's easier to ignore prisoners in this situation and I do not speak to the man. He is not thinking clearly. My silence only infuriates him.

"You go ahead and go back and fuck her 'cause she ain't going to jail," he says. "Yeah, I know you been fuckin' my wife, motherfucker. You been fuckin' her all along."

Thankfully, the ride to jail is a short one. The man turns up the volume once inside the jail to impress the other inmates who are watching. When a deputy removes the man's handcuffs, he clenches his fists and looks like he wants to throw a punch at me, but I've seen this from him before and it's all for show. Soon he is locked up and he's someone else's problem.

5:30 p.m.—Fraud Report

The report involved a woman who says her home health care worker stole her identification and opened a telephone account in the woman's name. The report is pretty basic and I get it completed within about half an hour. It is forwarded to the detective bureau to determine if follow-up investigation is needed.

7:40 p.m.—Range Training

The call volume tonight is exceptionally slow and I am summoned to the police shooting range for monthly handgun qualifications. The training involves shooting from various positions under timed conditions in normal and low-light situations. The training lasts nearly an hour and it is my last activity of the day.

Wednesday, December 11

3:22 p.m.—Illegal Dumping

I am dispatched to an abandoned rental house for an illegal dumping complaint. The landlord is already at the house when I arrive, cleaning up piles of scrap wood which someone has left in the back yard of his rental unit. He demands a report be made, even though I tell him there isn't much to be done about the incident because there is no indication of who dumped the items. While I gather his information for a useless and time-consuming report, I look around at the neighboring houses. Only one is well kept. The rest are dilapidated and near the end of their usefulness. Trash litters the landscape. The junk dumped in the yard of this man's rental house fits right in.

4:33 p.m.—Missing Child

I respond, along with five other officers, to a report of a missing child. The search lasts about 20 minutes and covers a couple square miles. The child is eventually located at a relative's house and the search is called off.

5:04 p.m.—Breaking and Entering Alarm

The house where I am sent is secure when I respond to check the residential alarm.

6:18 p.m.—Audible Alarm

A resident has called Central Dispatch to report an audible alarm coming from somewhere in the neighborhood. Checking the area, I find nothing. The alarm has since stopped and I never locate the origin. The day ends quietly and I am given no more calls the remainder of my shift.

Thursday, December 12

3:25 p.m.—Drug Activity

The complainant is an older woman, who appears to be in her late sixties. Ten steps from her front door sits one of the busiest drug-infested street corners in the city. The woman calls constantly about the neighborhood thugs and drug peddlers. More often than not, the police arrive too late. However, she is an understanding lady. She seldom complains about the police department's lack of staffing and inadequate response time.

Today, as usual, the bad guys are gone before I arrive. This day, however, the call ends in a different way. After I apologize for not arriving sooner, the woman tells me she is moving. She has finally had enough. She has relatives on the West side of the state. Soon she will sell the house she has lived in since the 1960s and she will leave Saginaw forever.

Auto plants and good-paying jobs lured people to this once-thriving Northeast Saginaw neighborhood. The last of these plants stands sentinel two blocks from the woman's house, and as we talk it looms in the background like an aged and tired relative; an old familiar face, much like the neighborhood which surrounds it. The plant and this neighborhood have grown old together, much like an elderly married couple might. Each appears now to be at the twilight of their lives, as the clock continues to count down the moments until their demise.

The woman tells me how beautiful the neighborhood was when she moved in some forty years ago. She beams as she recalls the good times. Her smile dims, however, as she talks about the racial strife of the sixties and seventies, as well as quick departure of the auto industry and in turn, many residents of this once booming section of town. As she looks out across the street at the vacant field, which used to sprout houses instead of weeds, the woman seems near tears, if for only a split second. She quickly gathers herself and grasps my right hand with both of hers.

"You're my angel," she says, repeating a phrase I have heard from her often. "You police are my angels."

She tells me to be safe and turns to walk away. I wish her the best and watch her, maybe for the last time, as she walks slowly up her front steps. While I am happy the woman is finally making her way from this neighborhood, it saddens me to see yet another person give up on a city which so many have already turned their back on.

4:05 p.m.—Prostitute

The description of a prostitute given by a passing motorist matches that of a woman we deal with regularly. Not long ago, the woman actually jumped into the backseat of an unmarked police car and offered oral sex to two plainclothes detectives, who were scouring a neighborhood looking for a suspect in another crime. Today, however, she appears to have found a legitimate customer, as she is nowhere to be seen when I arrive.

5:10 p.m.—Stolen Vehicle

An employee at an auto parts store makes the mistake of warming up his car before leaving work. Within minutes, the car is stolen by an unknown suspect. I take the report and the information is given out to other officers via Central Dispatch. Weeks later I am subpoenaed to court to testify against the man who is eventually caught in the stolen vehicle.

7:57 p.m.—Disorderly Adult

A store clerk calls to report a disorderly male refusing to leave the premises. The man, however, flees the scene when the clerk calls for the police. He is gone when we arrive.

Friday, December 13

4:42 p.m.—Assault

A court case has kept me tied up for nearly the first two hours of the shift. When I finally get checked into service, an assault in progress is immediately waiting. The fight is over when I pull on scene, but the victim remains and gives me information for a report so she can seek charges against the suspect through the county prosecutor's office.

6:01 p.m.—Breaking and Entering

I arrive on scene, along with two other officers, within minutes of the call. Checking the address, however, we can find no sign of entry into the home. It is only then that Central Dispatch advises us the caller gave an incorrect address. The other officers and myself are a full two blocks from where the crime is occurring. By the time we arrive at the real venue, the suspect has entered a residence and left, via a bedroom window, carrying a television set. The suspect is not located. The minutes we spent checking an incorrect address prove to be crucial.

8:00 p.m.—Shots Fired

Officers working an overtime assignment at a high school boys' basketball game call for assistance as there are gunshots fired between two groups in the school's parking lot. The scene is brought under control before I arrive and I am disregarded.

9:07 p.m.—911 Hang-up Call

Upon checking the house where we are dispatched, the resident advises everything is alright. Someone inside the home has dialed 911 by mistake.

9:14 p.m.—Family Trouble

The woman who called is furious. Her husband is drunk and playing music on the stereo. After speaking to both parties, it is clear the man is drunk and playing music. When we inform the woman it is not illegal for the man to be doing either in his own home, she immediately turns her fury toward us and tells us to leave if we're not going to help her. I gladly oblige and leave with the other responding officer.

Saturday, December 14

3:10 p.m.—Family Trouble

The venue is a large two-story house on a private court of about 10 houses. The dispute involves two sisters - one of whom lives on the court - and their views on how one sister is raising her children. I help resolve the problem after about 10 minutes and stand by as one of the sisters packs her children into her car.

This sibling relationship isn't the only thing broken in this neighborhood. Looking around at the houses on this tiny court, it is obvious this was once a nice neighborhood. Now most of the two-story structures are in some state of disrepair. Paint peels off many of the homes. A loose gutter hangs from one. An abandoned car partially blocks the already crowded drive leading past the homes. My sightseeing is interrupted by the sound of one of the sisters starting her car. I follow the woman's vehicle out to the main street, leaving this quiet block to continue its slow death.

3:51 p.m.—Prisoner Pick-up

I am dispatched along with another officer to neighboring Buena Vista Township where that jurisdiction's police department has arrested a man on a domestic assault case, which recently occurred in the city. The officers from Buena Vista Township turn the suspect over to me. The suspect is stocky man of medium height. He is clearly pissed off. I expect a fight, or at least a verbal altercation from him, but he offers none. The man is agitated, but keeps most of his anger inside, making the ride to jail a surprisingly quiet one.

7:25 p.m.—911 Hang-up Call

When a woman finally answers the front door, she is nervous, but says everything is okay. Through a window the other responding officer has seen the woman's boyfriend duck into the bathroom prior to her opening the door.

We ask to come inside to make sure everything is all right and the woman grudgingly agrees. When I ask why her boyfriend is hiding in the bathroom, she offers only a blank stare. After several knocks on the bathroom door, the man finally comes out. He protests when I check him for weapons, but I continue anyway. The woman is clearly nervous, but she refuses to say there is a problem. She says several times everything is fine and asks us to leave. The man says he doesn't need us there either. With no cooperation and no alternatives, we leave the house and let the woman go back to whatever problem she is facing.

7:42 p.m.—Hit-and-Run Accident

The accident involves a visitor from one house striking the car of a neighbor when he backed out of a driveway. Only the victim's car remains at scene. The suspect left after the accident, possibly not even knowing he hit the other car. The report takes an hour to complete and it is my final call of a fairly slow evening.

Thursday, December 19

The day starts off with more talk of impending layoffs as Saginaw reportedly is facing at least a $3.5 million budget shortage for the upcoming fiscal year. Rumors run rampant all day about future staffing levels within the department, one of which is that the city will be down to 85 police officers within two years. That unimaginable number would put my department at nearly half of its 1999 authorized strength.

3:15 p.m.—Supplemental Reports

I am sent to police headquarters immediately after checking into service to correct three reports from earlier in the year. An audit of all case reports for the year found these three to be among many that contain no narrative, describing the case details. Fortunately, they are all simple cases such as warrant arrests, and there was no follow-up investigation required on any of them. Clearing up the mess, however, takes more than an hour of my shift.

6:00 p.m.—Drug Activity

Returning to a party store where the police are called several times per day to clear the lot of drug dealing thugs, I find no one matching the suspect descriptions given. The call is cleared quickly.

6:33 p.m.—Breaking and Entering Alarm

The alarm is an hour old and, fortunately, is a false alarm. I find the house to be secure upon checking the residence.

6:58 p.m.—Drug Activity

Checking a local apartment complex for a report of drugs being dealt from a specific vehicle, we locate the vehicle, but it is unoccupied. We watch the vehicle from a distance for a brief period, but nobody approaches it. The cold weather assists in keeping the rest of the evening quiet.

Friday, December 20

1515 hrs—Desk Duty

While it is not my scheduled day to work the desk I am ordered to cover desk officer duties for three hours due to an emergency involving the regularly scheduled desk person.

During desk duty I field the usual telephone calls from citizens wanting assistance or advice, the most absurd of which involved a woman calling from another state. She says she answered an E-Mail solicitation to purchase cheap cellular telephones from a man in Saginaw. The caller says she sent the man a check for $395 and she was surprised when he never sent her the telephones. He now will not answer her telephone calls and he has given her a phony address.

When the woman asks what she should do, I want to tell her bluntly not to be that stupid again, but that will only get me into trouble. I inform her that with our current investigative staffing levels, there is probably nothing we can do without being able to identify the suspect. I check the suspect's name several different ways, but there is no record of him. She is not happy to hear that she is basically out of luck. I do, however, refer the woman to the Michigan State Police, who may have a more specialized internet fraud unit.

4:31 p.m.—Felonious Assault

A blood soaked man walks into the front lobby of police headquarters, claiming his girlfriend just assaulted him with a straightening iron. After calling for an ambulance, I find another officer to answer telephones and the desk radio and I go to the lobby to gather information for the report.

The victim says his girlfriend accused him of cheating and an argument ensued. He says she then grabbed a straightening iron - he says black people use this to straighten their hair - and struck him in the head several times with it. The ambulance arrives shortly thereafter. He is treated at the police department and refuses to go to the hospital. I write the case report. After not being able to locate the suspect, I forward the case to the detective bureau for further investigation.

7:02 p.m. - Assault

Security personnel from a downtown, low-income housing development call for assistance as one of their officers has been assaulted.

When I arrive, the suspect, who is a resident of the building, is still outside with two security officers. The suspect is somewhat mentally incapacitated. He is also obviously drunk. He continues to beg for cigarettes from the security staff as I gather details of the assault, which appears to have been very minor. With the help of the security officer, we finally get the man to go back to his apartment. I write an assault report for one officer, as he needs documentation of the incident. The report will never see the inside of a courtroom and is a waste of half an hour.

Michael S. East

Saturday, December 21

3:30 p.m.—Drug Activity

The corner where I am dispatched to investigate drug activity lies in the heart of what remains of Northeast Saginaw's once sprawling housing projects. There is a biting, cold December wind whipping through the streets and the area is deserted. I clear the call within five minutes of being dispatched.

3:39 p.m.—Breaking and Entering Alarm

The residential burglar alarm turns out to be a false alarm and the homeowner advises me everything is okay.

7:56 p.m.—Suspicious Vehicle

An anonymous resident in this nearly all-black neighborhood calls in to report a suspicious vehicle driving slowly through the area. The vehicle's occupants are white, the caller advises. That means they are probably looking for a crack cocaine salesman to get their weekend party rolling. One person's suspicious vehicle is another person's sales opportunity, I think to myself. However, the car is gone when I arrive, probably having already completed the deal and fled the area.

9:25 p.m.—Assist with Traffic Stop

Another officer reports a vehicle he is trying to pull over is slow to stop. I arrive to assist within about a minute, but the situation is under control. The driver is cooperating. The officer who initiated the traffic stop advises he just let the same driver go with a warning for speeding less than a month ago. I stand by while he completes a speeding citation and sends the driver on his way.

9:39 p.m.—Family Trouble

The call revolves around a couple fighting over where their infant child should spend the night. The couple found out today the child has ringworm and one of the parents doesn't want their other children exposed to the infant. Naturally, they called the police to help with the decision. Not being members of the family, the other responding officer and myself decline to help with the decision. We leave the young parents to figure out, on their own, where the child should stay.

10:00 p.m.—Felony Traffic Stop

An officer calls out he is following a vehicle matching the description of a subject wanted in connection with a brutal double-homicide which occurred in Saginaw a few days ago. The man is presumed armed and the officer doesn't take any chances, waiting for several other officers to assist before he pulls the vehicle over.

The car takes a few blocks to stop after the officer activates his overhead lights. Pulling up about 50 feet from the vehicle in an adjacent parking lot, I take cover quickly, expecting shots to be fired as soon as the vehicle comes to a halt. The car is boxed in by police cars now and nearly a dozen officers have concealed themselves behind police cars, trees and buildings, shotguns and handguns at the ready. Still, several civilians come walking down the street, some right into the line of fire, to get a better look at the action.

As the onlookers clear out when yelled at, the original officer gives commands for the driver, and later the passenger, to exit the vehicle and walk backwards, hands raised, toward other awaiting officers. Both men clumsily comply and are taken into custody without incident. Neither turns out to be the man we are looking for. Both have been drinking and are clearly shaken by the incident. I clear the scene and head back toward the police station as my shift is about to end.

Tuesday, December 24

It's Christmas Eve and we are at minimum staffing because the city is too cash strapped to pay expensive holiday wages. The roll-call talk revolves around a still-outstanding homicide suspect, who has apparently made statements that he will kill any cop who tries to arrest him. Several citizens have called in various sightings of the man over the previous few days and many have said he is heavily armed. With that information we hit the roads.

3:31 p.m.—Warrant Arrest

I am dispatched to a home to check for a subject who has warrants for his arrest. There is nobody at the home, or at least no one is answering the door, when we arrive.

3:38 p.m.—Drug Activity

The usual call, from the usual party store about the usual guys selling drugs, who are, as usual, not there when the police arrive.

3:41 p.m.—Panic Alarm

The homeowner advises me he set off a residential panic alarm by mistake. He apologizes for the inconvenience and we part with a "happy holidays."

3:58 p.m.—Breaking and Entering Alarm

En route to the call, I stop for a red light in downtown. In front of me passes a man, woman, and, presumably, their two children, who appear to be in their early teens. All four glare at me as they cross the street, the adults with deep, hateful scowls. I guess when you dislike the police, it's too much to muster a smile or a wave, even on Christmas Eve.

The first responding officer disregards me from the call before I arrive at scene.

4:20 p.m.—Family Trouble

The caller originally said she needed the police because her niece stole a ring, which belongs to her. She has since retrieved the ring and says she no longer wishes for our assistance.

4:37 p.m.—Audible Alarm

The call is for an audible alarm somewhere in a North-side Saginaw neighborhood. I check the area, but I am unable to locate the alarm.

4:38 p.m.—Suspicious Person

While I check for the previous alarm, Central Dispatch airs a call for a suspicious person, possibly selling drugs nearby. I am unable to locate this person either, as they may well have moved back indoors at the sight of a patrol car in the area.

4:48 p.m.—911 Hang-up Call

A teenage girl stands in the door, staring blankly at me as I approach the house. She is sucking on a candy cane and continues her blank stare when I tell her of the 911 call from her house.

"Is everything okay?" I ask.

She pulls the candy cane from her lips and responds with a mumbled "Yeah, ain't nobody call you."

Another young girl walks to the door. "I was dialing numbers," she says, in a half-hearted attempt to explain the 911 call. Both state they are okay and there is no need for the police.

5:39 p.m.—Family Trouble

The man who called is frustrated, but courteous. His wife is sitting in a chair in the living room when I arrive, being treated by medical personnel for a cut to her hand. She is drunk and, quite probably, high on other drugs. She continually yells at her husband while I talk to him.

He says they are in the process of getting a divorce because of her drug and alcohol abuse. Tonight, the woman came home intoxicated and he didn't want to let her in, so he kept the door locked. Eventually, she broke a window and made entry into the home, cutting her hand in the process. Neither is claiming to have been assaulted and I tell the man I cannot make either of the two leave their own home. He says he understands, although he would like her to leave.

The woman sits, refusing medical treatment and taunts her husband about the fact the police can't make her leave their home. She appears too drunk to feel the pain in her hand and she tells the fire rescue staff to leave her alone. She may feel the physical pain of the cut tomorrow, but she looks to be too far gone to feel any emotional pain, or shame, for that matter. I leave the man, telling him to call back if things get out of hand later on.

7:52 p.m.—Attempt Suicide

A call from a family member directs us to a residence where a man has told relatives, via veiled threats over the telephone, that he plans to kill himself. There is no response at the residence and we wait about 10 minutes for a relative with a key to the house to arrive and let us inside. Once in the house, we find the man is not home. To my knowledge the man is not located that evening.

8:36 p.m.—911 Hang-up Call

My second 911 call of the day turns out to be nothing more than some kids playing on the telephone.

9:44 p.m.—Family Trouble

An argument has turned quite heated between a mother and daughter over the daughter being two hours late coming home. The daughter is cocky and defiant. Mom is also strong-willed and the two continue to yell for nearly 15 minutes after our arrival. The girl finally agrees to go for the night to a facility which houses troubled youths. Another officer gives the girl a ride to the facility and mom follows, going along to sign her daughter in.

Eight hours and twelve calls after it started my Christmas Eve shift comes to an end. I leave to spend time with my own family, thankful that I have so much more than many of the people I have seen this evening.

Wednesday, December 25

Christmas Day brings a bit of a change, if only for eight hours. Due to a scheduling glitch, I am moved for a day to a patrol district on the city's West side. It is a welcome change, if only for the different scenery.

4:18 p.m.—Verify the Return of a Runaway

A juvenile runaway has returned home and the child's mother calls to have the missing person report cancelled. After verifying that the child has indeed returned, I write a quick supplemental report and cancel the juvenile as missing in the statewide computer system.

5:15 p.m.—Assist Desk Officer

The desk officer requests assistance, as several arrest warrants need to be taken to the county jail. Other police departments in Saginaw County have arrested the subjects of the warrants. Jail personnel need the actual warrants in hand before the individuals can post bond and be released.

5:10 p.m.—Breaking and Entering Alarm

Nobody is at the home and it appears to be secure when we check the residence.

6:31 p.m.—Officer Needs Assistance

An officer requests assistance in the Southwest area of the city. A suspect involved in a stolen vehicle case has just fled from the officer and run into a residence. I respond in emergency mode, but the two-mile drive takes way too long as slippery roads hamper my progress. Several officers are checking inside the residence when I finally arrive. After a few minutes, we locate the suspect hiding in the attic. He surrenders without a fight and I clear the call shortly thereafter.

9:21 p.m.—Traffic Stop

At the start of the shift, day shift officers advised they had collected numerous toys from local businesses and they asked that we distribute them throughout the day to needy families. Having forgotten about the assignment for most of the day, I turn my attention toward this task as there are no calls coming in and the radio has gone fairly quiet.

After about 10 minutes, I spot a woman driving an older, somewhat weathered car. There are two young girls in the car as well. When I pull in behind her and initiate a traffic stop, she pulls into a driveway. One of the young girls is crying when I approach the woman's window and I suddenly think this may not be a good idea. After telling the woman she is not in any trouble, I explain that I have a trunk full of toys and ask if she can help me put them to use. She looks confused, but follows me to my patrol car.

As I open the trunk, I think she is still half expecting that I will take her to jail. Only when I start piling toys into her arms does the woman smile. I apologize for scaring her daughter. She nods and says "thanks" as she walks back toward her car with the load of toys. Before I pull away, the daughter who had been crying runs up to my patrol car and shakes my hand. She is smiling now. It is the best moment of my day.

10:01 p.m.—Traffic Stop

With less than an hour until the end of the shift, I find a car with a rear light out. The two women in the front seat are not happy about being pulled over. I tell the driver about the taillight and then tell her I have several large teddy bears in my patrol car that I must find a home for within the hour. Two children in the back seat stare at me silently and the woman softens a bit and shows signs of a slight smile. She agrees to accept the bears and I stuff them into the back seat next to the children. We part with a "Merry Christmas" and she says she'll get the taillight fixed as well. With all toys and teddy bears delivered, I call it a night.

Thursday, December 26

4:58 p.m.—Assist Officer with Felony Traffic Stop

In a continuing effort to find and outstanding homicide suspect, an officer requests assistance as he pulls over a vehicle matching the description of one reportedly being driven by the suspect. The stop goes according to plan. Unfortunately, it is not the correct vehicle.

5:55 p.m.—Assist Officer with Felony Traffic Stop

Another vehicle matching the description of the one being driven by a homicide suspect is stopped by an officer. He uses the same precautions as previously. Again, the vehicle turns out not to be the one driven by the man we are trying to locate. For the past week we have been responding to numerous tips about sightings of the suspect, as well as tips about several vehicles he is said to be driving. So far, none of the tips has produced the suspect.

8:13 p.m.—Disorderly Adult

Responding to a call for assistance from the security staff of an Eastside hospital, I manage to get within about four blocks when I am disregarded by another responding officer, who advises the suspect is gone.

9:13 p.m.—Motorist Assist

A motorist stranded on the expressway prompts Central Dispatch to send me to assist the person. I stand by for a few minutes until a tow truck arrives.

9:30 p.m.—Panic Alarm

A woman at the residence where I am dispatched advises she is okay. She simply cannot figure out her home's alarm system.

Friday, December 27

I wake before dawn this morning and report for day shift duty, completing my half of a shift trade with another officer. The city is quiet as the shift begins, which is a welcome change from the hit-the-ground-running pace of my normal afternoon shift.

9:10 a.m.—Parking Complaint

The complaint of an illegally parked car goes unresolved as the car in question is parked in a perfectly legal manner. The caller just didn't like the fact he had to be cautious backing out of his own driveway so he wouldn't hit his neighbor's car.

10:26 a.m.—Family Trouble

The two-story, light-colored house where I am dispatched is nearing the end of its life expectancy. I am sure I will see this home boarded up within the year. Paint peels off the exterior. Gutters hang loosely from the roof. The porch steps are creaky and slanting to one side.

Inside the home, a mother is arguing with her 16-year-old daughter. Several smaller children lay sleeping on the living room floor, oblivious to the argument or the presence of the police. The argument involves the teen not obeying house rules and being disrespectful toward her mother. The mother finally informs her child to leave if she doesn't like the rules.

Sitting atop a banister at the bottom of a worn staircase, the teen screams out: "So I can move? You sayin' I can move!?"

"As long as you don't come knocking back on my motherfuckin' door!" the mother screams. The other children stir somewhat, but remain asleep.

Finally, we advise the woman there is nothing we can do for her. She previously had advised us that her daughter was on probation through the juvenile court. We tell her to contact the child's former probation officer and see if anything can be done through the court about the child's behavior. "I ain't got paper no more," the teenager yells, referring to her probation status. "I've been off paper since December." We leave with the problem still unresolved.

11:35 a.m.—Retail Fraud

A store on the city's Southeast side calls after having taken a 10-year-old into custody for shoplifting some liquor. They have the child locked inside a closet when I arrive. I take the child into custody and, after several attempts, I am able to locate a relative to whom I can release him. The corresponding report and custody forms take more than an hour to complete.

2:45 p.m.—Assist Department of Corrections

Department of Corrections personnel have asked for assistance checking a residence where an escapee is supposedly hiding. I remain outside stationed at a back door, but after about five minutes of checking the residence, I am advised the suspect is not inside.

3:20 p.m.—Injured Person

Central Dispatch puts out a call for a tow truck driver trapped under a truck, which has fallen on top of him. The dispatch message is strikingly similar to a call I received several years prior, where a man had been pinned underneath his sailboat, which had fallen on top of him while he was repairing it. I arrived first on scene on that cold winter day to find the man's lifeless body trapped underneath the weight of a rather sizeable boat, the impact having caused the victim to spit his dentures yards from where his body lay.

Responding today, lights and sirens helping cut a path through a main Westside thoroughfare, I pass the house where earlier in my career I had encountered the man crushed to death underneath his boat. I think of him only for a moment, then focus again on the task at hand, expecting upon arrival to find a similar scene. I arrive with another officer moments ahead of responding medical units. Luckily, the tow truck driver is okay, having suffered only a relatively minor arm injury when the falling truck struck his limb. He is transported to the hospital for treatment and I call it a day shortly thereafter.

Monday, December 30

3:00 p.m.—Court Appearance

My first task after roll call is to appear in court on a stolen automobile case. It is my second appearance on the case and, like the first time I showed up for the pretrial proceedings, the case is adjourned to a later date because one side or the other isn't ready to proceed.

4:41 p.m.—Breaking and Entering Alarm

The alarm is originating from a residence. I am disregarded, however, before I can make my way to the scene.

4:50 p.m.—Drug Activity

A popular South-side street corner is the venue where I am dispatched for drug activity. Arriving simultaneously with the other responding officer, we check the corner and several surrounding blocks to find the streets deserted.

5:10 p.m.—Family Trouble

The man who called is upset because his estranged wife has been coming to their house and removing belongings. We advise him there is little the police can do because there has been no court order regarding division of property. He is not happy with the answer, but he understands. The man says he will call his attorney as soon as possible to expedite the divorce proceedings.

5:36 p.m.—Family Trouble with a Weapon

The call involves a mother and daughter arguing. The original call from Central Dispatch said one of the parties had a knife. However, when we arrive the weapon has been put away and, from what we are told, was never used to assault anyone at the scene.

The mother tells us she pretty much has things under control now. She was upset because her daughter called her "a fat, nasty whore." Mom says things have calmed since the argument started. She says she will call the police back if the situation gets out of hand again. We leave the scene at the mother's request. The late December cold keeps the rest of the night quiet and this is the last call of my night.

Tuesday, December 31

3:36 p.m.—Injury Accident

I volunteer to assist another officer who is sent to an injury accident at a busy intersection. When we arrive at the scene, we find the injuries appear minor. Traffic is disrupted a bit, but it is flowing fairly well and there is no need for me to get involved in traffic control. I clear the call quickly and leave the other officer to the task of writing the accident report.

3:55 p.m.—Larceny Report

The report I am sent to take on the city's Northwest side is a misdemeanor larceny. However, I recognize the venue as an address where a wanted homicide suspect has reportedly been hanging out. I drive by the house once to check things out and see a man fitting the suspect's description entering the house. Pulling around the corner, I request several back-up units as the man is considered armed and has allegedly made threats to shoot police officers.

A detective in an unmarked car arrives within minutes and he sees the suspect get into a vehicle and leave the scene. We follow the man at a distance until other patrol cars can get into the area. Finally, we find a good location to make the traffic stop about a mile from where the man was first spotted. Eventually, we discover this is not the man we are looking for. I release the driver with an apology. He is not upset. In fact, he says he knows the suspect we are looking for, but says he has not seen him recently.

I return shortly thereafter to take the larceny report. The caller is a relative of the suspect wanted in connection with the homicide. She also says she has not seen the man we are looking for. She then tells me how someone stole $40 from her at a local convenience store earlier in the day. I give her a case number for the larceny report and spend about half an hour writing the criminal complaint.

6:20 p.m.—Breaking and Entering Alarm

The residential burglar alarm turns out to be false and I clear the call within about five minutes.

6:30 p.m.—Disorderly Adult

The call is from a rooming house on the city's Eastside. The woman being disorderly is not breaking the law and we inform the complainant there is little we can do for her. The complainant and the disorderly woman trade insults as we try to calm them both. Finally, we bid them both a good evening, as we are unable to settle their differences.

As we leave, the disorderly woman gets in her final words: "You officers have a blessed New Year," she says, the sarcasm so thick it nearly drips from her mouth. I leave without responding, as there is no winning an argument with a woman like her.

6:45 p.m.—Shots Fired

Officers responding to a family trouble call report hearing several shots fired on the next block. When they pull around the corner two men run inside a house and slam the door. I arrive within a minute and there are already several officers surrounding the house. The doors are locked. One officer knocks for several minutes to no avail.

In front of the house one of the men who fled has left a car running in the street. We call for a tow truck to impound the vehicle as it has been left abandoned, blocking the roadway. Only when they realize the car is going to be impounded do people come out of the house. The first person to emerge is a woman, who pretends we just woke her. She acts surprised to see the seven or so patrol cars in front of her home, as if she had no idea we were outside for the past 10 minutes.

We order everyone from the house and two other adult males come out, also feigning surprise. They, however, are not as convincing as their female counterpart. Eventually, one of the men says he was shooting off a rifle in celebration of New Year's Eve. We impound the rifle and inform the man it is illegal to discharge a weapon within the city for obvious safety reasons. He offers no resistance to the gun being impounded, but the woman is confused.

"It ain't illegal to shoot on New Year's Eve, though," she says. "It's a holiday, isn't it?" Incredibly, she is not joking. I walk away without answering, as it would probably be a waste of breath.

This is my last call of the night, and it is my last call of the year.

There is no time to be sentimental about the passing of time, however, as the beginning of another year of death and violence is only hours away. Tomorrow I will return to work and the crime statistics will begin anew. The only difference is the numbers will start again at zero and climb their way toward another sad total 365 days from today.

About the Author

Michael East is a nine-year veteran of the Saginaw Police Department, where he works as a patrol officer, spending every day dealing with the public. Michael has twice been awarded his department's Exceptional Performance Award and has also received a Distinguished Service Award. Additionally, he works as one of the Saginaw Police Department's Field Training Officers, assisting with the training of newly hired police officers. This is Michael's first book about his on-the-job experiences. After graduating from Ferris State University with degrees in Journalism and Advertising, Michael worked for several daily Michigan newspapers prior to entering the field of law enforcement.

Printed in the United States
104192LV00003B/143/A